Michelle,
Though we've never [met?]
that you share his concern [...] [...] [...].
In that way, you are part of this book, and
I thank you for that. I hope we meet
before long.

Ross

Michelle,

Merry Christmas 2004.
You've been an absolute
mainstay, which has
allowed me to devote
time to projects like
this one. Love,

Gaby

Arthur Nortje

POET AND SOUTH AFRICAN
NEW CRITICAL AND CONTEXTUAL ESSAYS

CRAIG MCLUCKIE AND ROSS TYNER

UNISA
PRESS
UNIVERSITY OF SOUTH AFRICA
PRETORIA

Copyright: The University of South Africa and its Press (Unisa) for permission to quote from Dirk Klopper's *Anatomy of dark* and the Special Collections material on Nortje.

© 2004 University of South Africa

First edition, first impression

ISBN 1-86888-259-4

Published by Unisa Press
University of South Africa
PO Box 392, 0003 Pretoria

Printed by the ABC Press, Epping

House editor: Liz Stewart

Cover design and layout: Jörg Ludwig

For
BJ, Liam and Esme
and for
Michèlle McLuckie, Fiona and Max Webber and Callum McLuckie

Contents

Acknowledgements

We extend our grateful appreciation to the following people and institutions, for their contributions to the overall improvement of this volume.

For information related to Nortje's time in Canada: Raymond Leitch (Toronto), Victor Smith (Hope), Olga Reed (Toronto), Brian Warner (Hope), Tama Kawase (Hope), Peter McPhedran and Mrs McPhedran (Hope), John P Norman (Etobicoke), Professor Leon de Kock (*Scrutiny 2*, South Africa), CKGO Radio 1240 (Hope, BC), Hope Cable Television, the staff of the *Hope Standard*, Clifford Mack (Hamilton), and Jo-Ann Hannah (Ottawa), Malcolm Hacksley and Paulette Coetzee (NELM, SA), E J Bevan (Johannesburg Public Library, SA), Lesley Hart (University of Cape Town, SA), V Haddad (South African Library), Daniel Britz (Northwestern University, USA), Louise Ray (School of Oriental and African Studies, London, England), S J Mason (Fraser Valley Regional Library), Christopher Sheppard (Leeds University Library, England), Helene Baumann (Duke University, USA), Roy Fischer (University of Toronto), A J Henley (University of York Library, England), David Blake (Institute of Commonwealth Studies, England), Jac Smith and Holly Smith (Vernon).

Jeanne Boekelheide assisted in the review and compilation of information at the *Hope Standard*; she has maintained an interest in this project since its inception. Jim Hamilton (Vernon, BC) and Dr Allan Markin (Penticton, BC) have maintained an interest in the project and have provided practical assistance. Faith Peyton, Inter-Library Loans, Okanagan University College, has excelled, as she has in the past, in tracking down particularly obscure items. We are also cognisant of the benefits derived from student engagement with specific writers, thus our appreciation of those who actively participated in English 480: South African Literature in the Spring 2002 semester; we are particularly appreciative of the engagement shown by David Helm, Jana Munro and Jennifer Sanders.

And, our thanks to Prof Craig McKenzie, *English in Africa*, for his encouragement and early publication of chapter 8.

John Lent, Ronald Ayling and Ronald McLuckie provided thoughtful readings and insightful commentary to early drafts of the manuscript. David Levey's careful reading permitted us to improve stylistic matters and linguistic accuracy.

Unisa has been a wonderful and professional press with which to work: Sharon Boshoff, the Acquisitions Editor, has shown enthusiasm for this project throughout its genesis.

This volume was conceived two years ago, with the intention that it should have an international flavour and a strong South African critical presence. While Calls for contributors were placed in the *African Literature Association Bulletin* and *Research in African Literatures*, we also undertook a direct e-mail and mail campaign in South Africa. Time and the vicissitudes of life, some happy (births – congratulations Sally Ann) and others not (illness, deaths), led to shifts in nuance, direction and contributors. To those contributors who appear in this volume, our thanks for your work and your patience.

Introduction

Craig McLuckie and Ross Tyner

All I have are his letters from Sept. 1970 to Dec. I'm sure Ray Leitch has told you that he and I went to England and arranged Arthur's burial. I have not been back to England since so presume there is still no marker on the grave. (Mrs Olga Reed. Correspondence to Mr Ross Tyner. 6 August, 1996)

It is our hope that, hand-in-hand with Dirk Klopper's critical reconstruction of Nortje's *oeuvre*, *Anatomy of dark: collected poems of Arthur Nortje*,[1] the present volume will act as a marker for Nortje. Arthur Nortje's place in South African literature is by no means assured, yet the relatively small body of work published during his lifetime, as well as the posthumously published work, has generated substantial critical attention. Because the poet's journals, notebooks, postcards, napkins and letters reflect a desire to capture an idea at the moment it arrives, with greater or lesser sense of order, the poetry sent out by Nortje for publication is the only solid textual evidence we have of where his poetic concerns were concentrated and, hence, the problems we face in formulating his aesthetic.

The contributors to this volume re-affiliate Nortje's work into the South African context. We reassess Nortje's career, biographically, poetically (in terms of theme and structural attributes), pedagogically and bibliographically, in light of the new corpus of work made available in *Anatomy of dark*. Our use of established and emerging scholars is, in part, an attempt to read Nortje's work and its reception through a melding of old and new. For the same reasons, we intertwine the specific, concrete critical explications of single texts with the more abstract, theoretically oriented interpretations.

Dead roots, a posthumous volume, suffers from frequently conflicting and varied methods of textual recuperation and editing by Raymond Leitch, Olga Reed, Dennis Brutus, Arthur Ravenscroft, and others. While Klopper writes that 'in some instances [poems in *Anatomy*] have required fairly extensive editorial reconstruction' (*AD* xxx), his *Anatomy of dark* does have consistency and a holistic approach to the editorial process.

Of the poetry Nortje himself saw through publication, the principal thematic concerns are with South Africa's race classification laws, with love, and with exile, as each impinges upon the poet's consciousness. Extant poetry, particularly from the Canadian period, is among 'his most epic and haunting verse, with a breadth of vision and political understanding that had been lacking before' (Bunn 'Arthur Nortje' 75). 'Native's letter', from this period, dated Toronto, May 1970, is illustrative of Bunn's point:

> Darksome, whoever dies
> In the malaise of my dear land
> Remember me at swim
> The moving waters spilling through my eyes:
> And let no amnesia
> Attack at fire hour:
> For some of us must storm the castles
> Some define the happening. (*AD* 361)

It is clear from his return to Oxford to take up postgraduate studies that Nortje was not literally going to 'storm the castles'. Through his poetry he would 'define the happening', or at least his small portion of it. Most significant is the inclusiveness and announcement contained in his use of the first person plural: his part was to be a microcosm of the whole.

Nortje left South Africa as a student. His poetry reflects the narrative contours of his life. Technically, 'Nortje has a strong poetic feeling for, and an acute perception of, the colors and sounds which contribute greatly to the integration of the hero with his environment' (Alvarez-Pereyre 158). Nortje affirms a sense of belonging to South Africa through history and compares himself to other exiles to define his relation to the country. Yet he 'was never able to commit himself in the sense understood by the political parties and organizations [and] he showed just as much hostility towards an art that isolates the individual from his social context and just as much contempt for intellectual activity which is incapable of opening out on to a life as a whole' (Alvarez-Pereyre 166). Dennis Brutus defines Nortje as 'perhaps the best South African poet of our time ... mostly he preferred the reasoned line: developed statement: was interested in constructing a poem which moved and convinced and delighted' (Brutus 'In Memoriam' 27).

Chapman's substantive review of *Lonely against the light* and *Dead roots* offers exile as the defining theme in Nortje's work, where 'alienation is ultimately not a matter of geography, but of temperament'. (Chapman 'Arthur Nortje: poet of exile' 60). A more thorough engagement with the poet's diction leads Chapman to criticize some of the poetry because it 'contains much that is excessive. He is often too close to his subject, and he lacks the critical sense to eliminate unnecessary epithets, nauseous scatological references and banalities generally. Yet ... his contribution to South African literature [is] an adventurous one' (Chapman 66, 70). Chapman, in his 'Poets and anti-poets', writes that 'Nortje's modernist response to city life [reveals] an imagination receptive to mythic patterns and symbolic images ... [The] movement from the abstract to the concrete is a feature of Nortje's best poetry. [Though, it] is rare ... to find any one poem that is entirely successful' (243, 248). Such criticisms are measured, pointing to the obscure, the uneven, the failed work.

Though critics *en masse* have used Nortje's 'Oxford journal' for biographical insight, Bunn rightly argues that it is 'a highly unstable literary document [of] different generic paradigms, unsure of its audience' (Bunn 'Some alien native land' 34). However, it is precisely this instability and Nortje's successes and failures in aesthetic containment and expression that make his work inviting.

Where modernist concerns have been a part of the overall critical examination of the aesthetic Nortje worked through, recent studies have begun the process of examining the poetry within the rubric of one or another *post* (-structuralism, -colonialism, and so on). Grant Farred, for example, presents an illuminating discussion of Nortje's treatment of women in the poetry that adds a significant new direction to the critical examination of this lost soul: 'a more disconcerting feature of Nortje's poetry [is] a tendency to implicitly, and with a certain lyrical effectiveness, absolve men ... of sexual accountability by shifting responsibility onto the body of coloured women' (61). Indeed, 'through his refusal to indict white men, Nortje situates himself as revisionist patriarchal historian' (63). These new avenues of literary-critical exploration complement the more traditional close readings. Together, used well, there is a robustness that moves beyond the text and its descriptions to a form of agency.

Nortje had 'defined the happening' earlier in his career, when he wrote of Brutus's shooting and arrest, from the vantage of his flight into 'exile':

36 000 feet above the Atlantic
I heard an account of how they had shot
a running man in the stomach. But what isn't told
is how a warder kicked the stitches open
on a little known island prison which used to be
a guano rock in a sea of island blue. (*AD* 196)

The physical and psychic violence visited upon his mentor becomes the subject, 'Autopsy', a self-vivisection. While 'little known island prison' may be seen as a conceit today, that line was a realistic assessment of international awareness at the time.

In our time, Mark Espin's review of *Dead roots* highlights the critical work that lies ahead:

The portrayal of Nortje as a conscience of exile, and more specifically, the condition of social alienation, ignores the context of that alienation and marginalisation and thereby suggests that it was wilful and deliberate, apportioning only a minor part of the motivation to society and its dynamics. (14)

Grant Farred builds off these comments; he attests, 'Nortje's poetry is most salient in the canon of South African literature in those moments when he does not consistently try to overcome the condition of partial affiliation or disaffiliation' (Farred 72).

In this volume, Dirk Klopper himself brings a fine updated sense of the poet's life, arising out of original research undertaken in 2001–2002, in South Africa, Oxford, England and Canada. Klopper sees the life of the psyche, as poetically caught, 'in the ambivalent moment between its self-apprehension and its self-delusion, its narcissistic isolation and its desire for community' (17). Amanda Bloomfield's formalist approach treats Nortje's indebtedness to the Romantics. She illustrates Nortje's 'use of seasons ... to discuss racial issues, his feelings of exile, and his lack of hope in the future' (55). Sarah Nuttall also combines close readings of selected poems, adding a theoretical frame that draws on Merleau-Ponty and Foucault to investigate the 'anatomical and material body ... as a means of elaborating less well traced fields of inquiry' (68). Richard Volk builds on Nuttall's theoretical perspective, playfully, but limits his analysis to a delineation of the uses and effect of expectoration: one result is its ability to undermine 'hierarchical constructions of class' (98). Kwadwo Osei-Nyame Jnr makes use of Fanon in his interrogation of the poetry, concluding that, for Nortje, 'a counter-discourse of "Black" Nationalism nevertheless remained ... a viable ideology' (109). Poet Tanure Ojaide provides a general formalist overview of Nortje's initial stylistic conservativism, weaknesses and late innovation. Kelly Hewson and Aubrey McPhail's anecdotal chapter recounts their empirical experiments with the poetry, reading and a multi-cultural classroom. It emphasizes the need for careful contextualization – geographic, historical, political – and thus underscores the decision to vary the approaches in this volume, as well as to add the appendices. Craig McLuckie and Ross Tyner extend their earlier work on Nortje in Canada to illuminate the lived context (political, social, personal) of his life there, in first person anecdotes and remembrances. Annie Gagiano comprehensively investigates the theme of exile in the poetry, in its standard, theoretical and psychological aspects. She reminds us just how significant South Africa is to Nortje's mental health. Her work, decisively, brings the poet home.

The intent of this volume of essays is to offer a complementary, multi-voiced response to Nortje rather than a univocal and exclusive assessment.

That is, we have attempted to elicit, through the contributions, Nortje's complex, developing and contradictory voice. The diversity of response has, we think, mediated Said's cautionary note on exile and definition:

> No one today is purely *one* thing. Labels like Indian, or woman, or Muslim, [or *kleurling*], or American are not more than starting-points, which if followed into actual experience for only a moment are quickly left behind ... It is more rewarding – and more difficult – to think concretely and sympathetically, contrapuntally, about others than only about 'us'. (Said 336)

It is for the foregoing reason that we have entitled this volume of essays *Arthur Nortje, poet and South African*. The competing tensions within the man are, as we will see, those bound up in the aesthetic deployment of a specific landscape, within a specific historical moment; what essence there is remains bound by his poetic personae.

Note

1   *Anatomy of Dark: collected poems of Arthur Nortje,* ed Dirk Klopper (Pretoria: Unisa, 2000). All subsequent references to this edition, in this book, will be noted *AD*.

Works cited

Alvarez-Pereyre, Jacques. 'Arthur Nortje' in his *The poetry of commitment in South Africa.* Trans Clive Wake. London: Heinemann, 1984:153–169.

Brutus, Dennis. 'Protest against apartheid: Alan Paton, Nadine Gordimer, Athol Fugard, Alfred Hutchinson and Arthur Nortje', in *Protest and conflict in African literature.* Eds Cosmos Pieterse and Donald Munro. London: Heinemann; New York: Africana, 1969:93–100.

Brutus, Dennis. 'In memoriam: Arthur Nortje,' *Research in African Literatures* 2 (1971):26–27.

Brutus, Dennis. 'Poetry of suffering: the black experience', *Ba Shiru* (Madison, wis) 4.2 (1973):1–10.

Bunn, David. 'Arthur Nortje', *Dictionary of Literary Biography* volume 125:170–177.

Bunn, David. 'Some alien native land: Arthur Nortje, literary history and the body in exile', *World Literature Today* 70.1 (Winter 1996):33–44.

Chapman, M J F. 'Arthur Nortje: poet of exile', *English in Africa* 6.1 (1979):60–71.

Chapman, M J F. '5: Poets and anti-poets' in his *South African poetry: a modern perspective*. Johannesburg: Ad Donker, 1984:243–253.

Dameron, Charles. 'Arthur Nortje: craftsman for his muse', in *Aspects of South African literature*. Ed Christopher Heywood. London: Heinemann; New York: Africana, 1976:155–162.

Espin, Mark. 'A book that changed me', *Southern African Review of Books* (May/June 1993).

Farred, Grant. '2. The poetics of partial affiliation: Arthur Nortje and the pain of origin' in Farred's *Midfielder's moment: coloured literature and culture in contemporary South Africa*. Boulder, Colo: Westview, 2000:55–80.

McLuckie, Craig and Ross Tyner. ' 'The raw and the cooked': Arthur Kenneth Nortje, Canada, and an annotated bibliography', *English in Africa* 26.2 (October 1999):1–54.

Nortje, Arthur. *Dead roots*. [Eds Dennis Brutus et al] London: Heinemann, 1973.

Owomoyela, Oyekan. *A history of twentieth century African literatures*. Lincoln: University of Nebraska Press, 1993:131–132.

Said, Edward W. 'Movements and migrations' in his *Culture and imperialism*. New York: Knopf, 1993.

Chapter 1: Arthur Nortje: a life story

Dirk Klopper

Arthur Nortje died shortly before his twenty-eighth birthday in a rented apartment in Oxford. He had been out for the night and had consumed a large number of beers. For him, this was not exceptional. On arriving back at the apartment block, he had a lengthy and apparently sober conversation with a fellow lodger, recounting the evening's exploits, and then went to bed. In the privacy of his room, alone with his own thoughts and feelings, he ingested twenty-five barbiturates, leaving a few blue-and-white capsules scattered on his bedside table, alongside a draft copy of 'Wayward ego', the last poem he had written, possibly the very night he took the fateful dosage. He slipped into a coma, threw up, and suffocated on his own vomit. Nortje's death took friends and family by surprise. He had spent five years abroad, studying at Oxford University and teaching in Canada. Despite periods of despondency, his career as academic and vocation as poet seemed secure. His tutors and pupils spoke appreciatively of his intellectual abilities, and the poetry he left behind was beginning to ensure his reputation as one of the most engaging poets of his generation, a writer of lyrical self-disclosure and psychodynamic insight. Notwithstanding his achievements, it is clear, however, that he was in crisis in the months leading up to his death. Ten months earlier, he had taken sick leave on account of a nervous disorder. Thereafter, his health seemed to improve. Nevertheless, his late poetry speaks of a loss of purpose and meaning which, even if recoverable, would likely prove inadequate, for 'what is lost and found again/seldom is as beautiful',[1] he says.

This chapter reconstructs Nortje's life story from published material,[2] unpublished studies,[3] archival documents,[4] interviews with former acquaintances,[5] and the poetry itself. Although the poetry is introspective, dealing with states of mind and feelings, and offers an imaginative reconstruction of experience, it does register Nortje's external historical and social contexts, the conditions of possibility of the life and the work. Because these conditions are shared by others, the poetry gives voice not only to Nortje's experience but also to the experience of those who had similarly suffered deprivation, repression, alienation, exile, and despair, those 'broken guerrillas, gaunt and cautious' who fled South Africa to seek refuge in London, those 'dark princes, burnt and offered/to the four winds, to the salt-eyed seas' who were '[t]o their earth / unreturnable' (AD 195). Nortje certainly regarded himself as a mouthpiece of his generation, saying 'I speak this from experience, speak from me' (AD 372). The story that this chapter reconstitutes from the circumstances of the life, from reminiscences by acquaintances, and from poetic representation, is significant, therefore, both for its own sake and for the insight it might give into the historical moment in which Nortje lived. Nortje's story, Athol Fugard was to observe, is the story of his times (Interview with Athol Fugard, 7 October 1979, Unisa). This is not to say that the story is representative in an abstract or formulaic manner. On the contrary, it is deeply personal, embodied in the complex and inimitable life of the individual. Nevertheless, from the discernible circumstances that surround, impinge upon, and ultimately constitute the life and work of the poet, from the lines of force that traverse these psychic and textual spaces, it may be possible to posit a general pattern, a structural dynamic.

Nortje's life story begins in Oudtshoorn, a dusty town on the fringe of the sprawling Karoo, where he was born on 16 December 1942. His mother, Cecilia Nortje, was a coloured woman and employed as a domestic worker. His father was a young Jewish businessman, whose name was withheld, even from Nortje. Presumably the mother wanted to avoid a scandal. Only in Nortje's late adolescence was he informed that his father was Jewish, and therefore white. He had always assumed that both parents were coloured. Given the context of South Africa's racial policies, the news of his mixed racial parentage would, conceivably, have had a decisive impact. Various apartheid laws had been promulgated during his youth, the purpose of which was to keep the European, African, Indian, and coloured communities separate, particularly the white and non-white communities. By the time that he was told his father was white, a legislative and psychological barrier had been erected between white and black. The Prohibition of Mixed Marriages Act (1949) prohibited marriage across the colour line, the Immorality Amendment Act (1950) prohibited extramarital sex across the colour line, the Group Areas Act (1950) prohibited mixed residential areas, and the Reservation of Separate Amenities Act (1953) prohibited mixed recreational facilities. The implication, which Nortje was to explore subsequently in his poetry, is that, in his very person, he represented a transgression, an illegality, a 'stamp/of birth, of blackness, criminality' (AD 372).

Nortje's racial heritage has both material and symbolic significance. The coloured population of South Africa constitutes a heterogeneous group comprising individuals of mixed ancestry. A significant number are Malaysian, but many are the offspring of sexual relations across the colour line between white settlers and individuals from other population groups. Accordingly, the coloured population constitutes a group of persons who do not fall within the other seemingly homogeneous categories. In terms of social position, the coloured population has historically been positioned between the European and African populations. Neither white nor black, coloureds were regarded as brown people. Generally, they spoke Afrikaans. Although coloureds suffered discriminatory legislation, they were also relatively privileged. In the Cape, their traditional home, they were granted preferential treatment over Africans in terms of educational opportunities and employment prospects. Moreover, they had representation in parliament until 1956, when, with the promulgation of the Separate Representation of Voters Act, they were struck off the common voters' roll. Thereafter, categorised as non-European, and increasingly denied access to decent housing, schools, and jobs, coloureds began to identify themselves as part of the larger black resistance movement against white oppression. These social contradictions emerge in Nortje's poetry where he describes himself as situated between 'the wire and the wall' of South African cultural politics, a 'dogsbody half-breed' (*AD* 345).

The sense of a dual or indeterminate identity contributes to the distinctiveness of Nortje's poetry. Not only was Nortje schooled in English, he actively assimilated the English literary tradition, making its symbolic universe his own, using its conventions and value systems to explore and articulate his deepest intimations of selfhood. Nevertheless, he was also acutely aware of his social interpellation as a person of colour, and, more obscurely, of his illegitimacy in the absence of the biological father and of the legitimating symbolic father. In both a familial and a social sense, the father had disowned him. Much of his writing career as poet would be devoted to exploring issues of identity and belonging from a position of division, displacement, disaffiliation, and loss. His poetry would create a context in which he could explore the anomalies of being. 'Origins', he would say, 'are dim in time, colossally / locked in the terrible mountain, buried in sea-slime, / or vaporized, being volatile' (*AD* 217).

Cecilia Nortje's family, who were middle-class tradespeople and lesser professionals, and were closely involved in the local church parishes of Oudtshoorn's coloured community, were dismayed by her illegitimate pregnancy. Under pressure, in particular, from her older brother Andrew, she was persuaded to leave her hometown and take up residence with her Aunt Piedt in Port Elizabeth. Nortje was three months old at the time and would spend the rest of his childhood in this coastal city, a large but not major centre of economic and cultural activity situated in the Eastern Cape. The Eastern Cape was prominent in the nineteenth century as home of the British settlers, with its border region serving as a buffer between the European farmers and neighbouring Xhosa tribes. As the original site of the European and African encounter in South Africa, the Eastern Cape, as a frontier zone, continues to play a significant role in the cultural memory. Symbolically, Nortje was to inhabit this border, this liminal space, all his life.

Nortje was christened at the St Philips Anglican Church, in Central, Port Elizabeth, and later enrolled in two successive Anglican mission schools, the lower primary school St James, in Sidwell, and the senior primary school St Marks, in North End. A teacher from these early years, James Davidson, would remain a mentor for many years to come, and would help fund Nortje's subsequent studies. St Philips Church became the focal point of Nortje's religious life and also, subsequently, through the Christian Youth Club, of his social life. Here coloured youths would meet over weekends and play indoor sport, stage plays, and hold meetings. Thus, in spite of Nortje's Afrikaans-speaking background, Anglicanism, and, more generally, English liberal-humanist values, dominated his early education. Although liberal-humanism was not in open opposition to South Africa's ruling apartheid ideology, thereby compromising itself in the eyes of political activists, it did provide a humane conception of the nature and value of the individual.

Cecilia Nortje lived with her Aunt Piedt at 7 Stent Road, Dowerville, for almost ten years, during which time she was employed as a domestic worker in the white suburbs of Port Elizabeth. The eldest Piedt daughter was married to Jonkers, and Arthur spent time with both families, alternating between the two households while his mother was at work. Several other families originally from Oudtshoorn lived in the area, including John and Margaret Rousseau, who resided at 24 Stent Road. Cecilia and Margaret had been at school together and were good friends. John and Margaret helped Cecilia to settle in and were named as Nortje's godparents at his christening. The Rousseau family comprised six children, at least two of whom had left home by this time. Nortje became firm friends with the son Mervyn, who was four years his senior. He was also greatly influenced by the older sister Carrie, who was the political activist of the family. Later, Nortje was to stay with the brother Louis in Cape Town. The Rousseau family was culturally active, with music, art and literature forming an important focus of learning and pleasure.

Nortje was soon absorbed into the Rousseau household, becoming an integral part of the family. As he grew up and the demands of schooling increased, he would study at the Rousseau house in the afternoons, eventually spending his weekends at the house as well. The reason that Nortje gravitated towards the Rousseau household is attributable partly to the fact that the Piedt home accommodated a large family that included married children, and was therefore crowded, and partly to the affectionate and stimulating environment of the Rousseau household. After Cecilia married Max Potgieter in 1950 and gave birth to their child Susan in 1952, the family had no option but to leave the Piedt homestead. Max turned out to be an unreliable provider, and the Potgieter family was forced to move frequently from one impoverished dwelling to another, with the result that Nortje drew even closer to the Rousseau family. Throughout his senior primary school and secondary school years, the Rousseau home provided a measure of security lacking in Nortje's own home.

If Nortje's ambivalent position as coloured might be construed as an important factor in his psychic organisation, so might his dislocated family life. Certainly, the poetry was later to invoke a sense of homelessness, a restlessness that leaves the heart 'hollowed with the boots passing through' (*AD* 171). The nomadism of childhood and later exile of adulthood are not, of course, identical, but there is a continuity, a general pattern of behaviour. In attempting to understand this pattern, it would be too simplistic to say that a disruptive childhood caused an inability in adulthood to settle down in one place. Similarly, whatever emotional vulnerability Nortje may have suffered later, it would be simplistic to say that this stems from emotional deficiency during childhood. There is no evidence that Cecilia neglected Nortje. She was poor, her husband was thriftless, and work was scarce. She was forced to spend a lot of time away from home. By all accounts, she was good-natured, kind, and religious, perhaps even affectionate. Nevertheless, it is true that Nortje later claimed to have long been estranged from his family (letter to James Davidson, 4 November 1963, Unisa). In other words, he felt he had been emotionally deprived in respect of family bonds. It is therefore legitimate to look for evidence of an inability to sustain intimate relationships in adulthood, on grounds that this might also constitute a pattern of behaviour. As an adult, Nortje was to have many friends, for he was sociable and engaged with a wide range of people, but he seems never to have developed a longstanding intimate relationship with any one person. Certainly, this is true of his relationships with women. Even his relationships with men, however, tended to end, or were suspended, in acrimonious quarrel.[6] Given Nortje's early death, it is risky to posit adult behaviour patterns. Nevertheless, it is evident that for all his personable qualities, his enthusiasm and sociability, he was difficult to get along with, and antagonised people as well as endeared himself to them. He was to say later, with painful honesty, that 'There are no people I can closely know' (*AD* 106).

As legislation passed by the National Party began to take effect in the 1950s, popular resistance among the black communities increased, culminating in the adoption of the Freedom Charter by the Congress of the People in June 1955. Supported by a range of opposition movements under the leadership of the African National Congress (ANC), the Charter called for a representative government of all the people of South Africa. Political meetings became a feature of life in the black townships, with Port Elizabeth a particularly vibrant centre of oppositional activity. Radicals in the coloured community tended to support the Unity Movement, a grouping with strong Trotskyite leanings that followed a policy of boycott of all racist institutions. Carrie Rousseau was active in organising meetings, which Nortje often attended. Other meetings of a less radical nature also took place, organised by groups such as the Christian Youth Club run by St Philips Church. At these meetings, Nortje participated energetically in the discussions, asking probing and discomforting questions. He was unafraid to speak his mind, and did so intelligently and articulately, with sharp and sometimes caustic wit. Yet he would also, at social gatherings with friends, often sit quietly observant, only afterwards delivering devastating mimicries of those present, accompanied by astute analyses of character. The qualities of passionate involvement and analytical detachment characterize these social interactions as much as they were to characterize his poetry.

Nortje entered Patterson High School, Schauderville, in 1957, where he made an impression as a conscientious student who excelled at languages. Nortje's English teacher and form master in his Standard 8 (Grade 10) year was the South African poet Dennis Brutus, who recognized and nurtured Arthur's poetic talent, and was later editor of one of the posthumous editions of Arthur's poetry. Educated at the universities of Fort Hare and the Witwatersrand, Brutus taught at Patterson High School for 14 years, and is remembered as being a creative if eccentric teacher. Aside from his academic responsibilities towards his pupils, Brutus sought to educate them politically about the injustices of apartheid. He would take the pupils to places such as the beach, the art gallery, symphony concerts, and book-shops, encouraging them to read widely and think incisively. Class discussions were wide-ranging, often in response to current events and places visited. Nortje subsequently paid tribute to Brutus in his poetry, saying that 'Thus – sensitive precise / he stood with folded arms in a classroom/ ... with deep inside his lyric brooding, / the flame-soft bitterness of love' (*AD* 196).

Brutus spoke highly of Arthur, claiming that he was perhaps one of the best poets to have come out of South Africa. Describing their relationship, Brutus says that they 'were more than teacher and pupil', they were 'friends, and in many ways almost colleagues', as they 'did things together'. He refers to Nortje as 'a brilliant all-round student', and says that Nortje started writing poetry as a schoolboy, winning top prize in a school poetry-writing competition. Nortje was highly motivated, he says, and 'did extensive study on poetry outside school hours'. Brutus stresses Nortje's impoverished circumstances, referring to Nortje having grown up in the 'ghetto' and having been intimately acquainted with its 'seedy aspects' (Dennis Brutus lecture, NELM). These remarks underscore the discrepancy between school and home, between Nortje's academic pursuits and his deprivation in the township where he was 'reared in rags' and instructed in 'the violence of the mud' (*AD* 376). School was not so much an extension of the home environment as a denial of it. At home, when Nortje wanted to study, he would block his ears with cotton wool, symbolically shutting out the world of noisy poverty. This division between school and home can be construed as a split that operates at several levels, between the cultural and the domestic, between the wealth of intellectual life and the diminished life of the body, between the ideal and the actual. It underscores the divided and indeterminate subject positions occupied by Nortje in respect of the social formation as well as of the poetry.

Nortje began consciously to adopt a literary life style when he was at high school. He attended readings and discussions organized by Brutus. In his final year of high school, he befriended the librarian Rachel Gregory, who used to invite young people to literary gatherings at her house, where she would play recordings of poetry for their literary entertainment. Here Nortje was introduced to Athol Fugard, whom he would meet again later. The year 1960 witnessed the mass mobilization of the black population against the passbook system. Organized by the newly created Pan African Congress, the disobedience campaign turned violent on 31 March 1960 when police opened fire on unarmed demonstrators in Sharpeville, killing 69 and injuring 180. This event galvanized the political struggle in South Africa into a new, more militant phase with the formation of Umkhonto we Sizwe (Spear of the Nation), military wing of the ANC. The state responded with ferocious oppression, banishing and imprisoning activists. By 1965, two hundred political trials had led to the incarceration of 1 300 individuals for an average of seven years each. With the leadership of the black resistance movements in confinement, and its infrastructure smashed, the struggle would be conducted for several decades from outside South Africa's borders. Nortje began seriously to write and distribute his poetry at this time. The early poems evince a clear awareness of the political turmoil engulfing the country, and anticipate a future reversal for the white state, invoking a 'sun-scorched vengeance' (*AD* 4). At the end of the year Nortje matriculated with a first grade pass.

The bleak, wind-swept townships of Port Elizabeth had been Nortje's home for eighteen years. Shuttling between small brick-and-plaster houses and corrugated iron shacks, from embattled schoolyard to the stout piety of the church, he grew into adulthood. As a young boy, he rolled his bicycle wheel, festooned with crinkle paper and guided by a stick, on streets alternately muddy and dusty, furrowed and buckled by rain and sun. Heading towards his teens, he sold newspapers in the neighbouring industrial areas during the evening traffic, collected empty wine bottles for refund at liquor stores, and tried to avoid bruising encounters with aggressive street gangs. As a young adolescent, he attended beach picnics on great sweeps of sand pounded by the Indian Ocean, preferring to stay on land and attend to the meat on the open fire rather than venture into the water. He found friendship in the company of the Rousseau siblings, and was treated as one of the family. At school and at cultural meetings he showed glimmers of the passionate intellectuality that would eventually find expression in the poetry.

Nortje was awarded various bursaries to continue his studies after school, the largest being a bursary from the Department of Education. He would have liked to have enrolled at the University of Cape Town, which was highly regarded academically, or even the University of Fort Hare, near Alice in the Transkei, where many African leaders such as Nelson Mandela, Govan Mbeki, and Robert Sobukwe had been educated. However, the Extension of the University Education Act of 1959 had led to the establishment of racially based universities and colleges. Not only were non-white students prevented from enrolling at the nominally white universities such as the University of Cape

Town, non-white students themselves were assigned to ethnic universities for Africans, coloureds, and Indians. Thus Nortje was forced to enrol at the newly invested University College of the Western Cape (UCWC) in Bellville, Cape Town. During Nortje's time, UCWC offered courses run by the University of South Africa. Later UCWC was to become an independent institution, the University of the Western Cape.

The resources at UCWC, including the library, were rudimentary. During orientation week, students were addressed in the Dutch Reformed Mission Church in Bellville by the white rector Dr Meiring. In his address to the students Meiring tried to justify the establishment of the university, saying that the students should be grateful for the government's 'kindness' in following the logic of separate development, and that they should be 'happy' to have their own institution. He concluded by assuring students that he had the interests of the coloured people at heart (interview with Ambrose George, 9 September 2001). Students protested against the paternalism and hypocrisy of the institution, and refused to constitute a Student Representative Council, believing that such a council would confer political legitimacy on an institution that was founded on the execrable principles of apartheid. Radical students went as far as wanting to blow up the university. Although Nortje was not militant, he identified with the struggle against apartheid and its institutions, and is said to have adopted the role of an impassioned observer rather than an activist. His individuality precluded active participation and his critical mind often placed him at odds with students whose participation was wholehearted and uncritical. Nortje's primary objection to UCWC seemed to be, however, that it was an inferior academic institution. Along with other students, he referred to it contemptuously as Bush College. Nevertheless, he was to work hard at his degree.

The lecturers at the university were recruited largely from the nearby University of Stellenbosch, and classes were conducted in Afrikaans. Nortje enrolled for a BA degree and majored in English and Psychology. He was taught Philosophy I by the coloured writer Adam Small, whom some students regarded as a collaborator for aligning himself with the university. His English lecturer, Professor Stopforth, was impressed by Nortje and invited him to his house in Stellenbosch. He wanted Nortje to speak to his daughter, who was studying at the University of Stellenbosch and not doing very well, hoping that some of Nortje's 'magic would rub off on her' (Hendricks 35). Aside from his involvement in English literature, Nortje was also absorbed in his other major, Psychology. The poems he was to write would later reveal an uncanny ability in deploying apt metaphors of psychic processes, particularly the psyche seen in the ambivalent moment between its self-apprehension and its self-delusion, its narcissistic isolation and its desire for community. Irony becomes a favoured device in conveying the disjunction between separation and togetherness, as in the lines where Nortje says, 'Empty houses are the grief beginnings / to those who've wanted to be reconciled' (*AD* 122).

On his arrival in Cape Town in 1961, Nortje stayed with Louis Rousseau at 63 Rust Street, Crawford, and later with James Davidson in Wynberg, before the latter's departure for Canada. Louis taught art at the nearby Alexander Sinton Primary School and led a sociable life, with friends constantly dropping by for a few drinks, some music, and lively conversation. Many artists and musicians frequented these 'convivials', including Abdullah Ibrahim (then known as Dollar Brand). They would listen to such jazz legends as Duke Ellington, Count Basie, Gerry Mulligan, and Miles Davis, and busy themselves at playing chess, shuffling cards and quaffing copious quantities of sweet Lieberstein wine. Louis played the clarinet and saxophone, and Raymond Leitch, another frequent visitor and later a good friend of Nortje's, played the piano. Sidney Gardener, a fisherman, played the guitar. Jamming sessions would continue late into the night. At a time that the ANC and other opposition groups were persecuted and banned, driven underground and into exile, politics was a constant topic of conversation, and gave rise to lengthy and animated discussions. Many personal acquaintances were harassed by the police, detained and imprisoned, and several intellectuals and professionals chose to leave the country. These were uncertain times of fear, desperation and helplessness, a time, as Nortje puts it, of 'mute fury' (*AD* 22).

In his second year of study, Nortje took up residence with Mr and Mrs Albertyn, a childless couple, at 2 18th Avenue, Elsies River, where he shared rooms with Neville Johnson and Desiré Slater, fellow students from Port Elizabeth. Nortje developed a pattern of intensive study during the week and unbridled socialising over weekends, a pattern he was to follow throughout the remainder of his life. In giving expression to these divergent desires, he was in fact leading two lives, the life of the sober-minded and conscientious academic and the life of the dissipated libertine. During the week he chose to work in the library, surrounded by books, and read widely. Existentialism proved to be an important intellectual influence, particularly the writings of Jean Paul Sartre. Nortje also read some Marx, but not with as much enthusiasm. Without rejecting socio-economic explanations, he nevertheless sought a correspondence between the social and the personal, the external and the internal. The poets he admired most were Hopkins, Yeats, Eliot, Auden, and Plath. He was in the habit of quoting poetry in company when he wished to make a point or simply to impress, and particularly enjoyed quoting from Eliot's *The wasteland* and *Four quartets*. Some saw this as an affectation; others were taken with his wide reading and extensive knowledge of literature. This trait, at once annoying and endearing, suggests above all that Nortje fully inhabited the world of literature. It took possession of him and became a mode of self-expression, a way of being in the world, securing his role as a 'timeserver to the muse' (*AD* 380).

Nortje's assumption of his poetic vocation, in a self-conscious, sustained, and focused manner, dates back to 1962, and is evidenced by two events. The first is his commencement of a writer's notepad in July 1962 (Notepad A,

Unisa), in which he began to develop ideas for poems and to script rough drafts from which fair copies were later transcribed. The notepad was discontinued in September 1962 and another was started in January 1963 to July 1963 (Notepad B, Unisa). Aside from their function as workbooks for the poetry, the notepads also contain comments about Arthur's poetic practice, as well as observations about other poets. In addition, they serve as record of Nortje's experiences, often communicated in a stream-of-consciousness manner. The notepads reveal a poet in the making, sharpening his skills of observation, clarifying his expression, experimenting with the rhythmic, aural, and semantic ranges of language, disciplining his feelings, and trying to find a way of relating social and political events to his own authentic experience. The second event is Nortje having been awarded third prize for poems entered in a literary competition run by the Mbari Writers' Club at Ibadan University, and sponsored by the Congress for Cultural Freedom based in Paris. Brutus won second prize in the competition, but returned it because the competition was for *non-white* Africans, which he regarded as a racist designation. The poems for which Nortje won the award were published in *Black Orpheus* the following year. During this period, Nortje also published poems in *Adelphi*.

In his third year of study Nortje took up residence with Mr and Mrs Halford at 140 Kromboom Road, Crawford, not far from Louis Rousseau, whom he again visited regularly. During this period Nortje began actively to seek the company of writers and other literary personalities. In Port Elizabeth he had known Dennis Brutus and had made the acquaintance of Athol Fugard. In Cape Town he met Cosmo Pieterse, Richard Rive, and Jonty Driver. A letter written to Raymond Leitch indicates his resolve to embrace the poetic life as he conceived it:

> I know personally (because I *feel* it) that I have poetic talent ... I want to extend tendrils in various directions. All of us, after all, would like to avoid rigidity and partisanship, particularly those of us trying to interpret the tensions and foibles of a society as motley, stupid, brilliant, disparate as this one ... The more I think about it, the more I consider that the miserable world needs every living and deceased man or woman who has something poetic to contribute ... something from the spirit.

The letter goes on to yoke together poetic ambition and psychic change, indicating important transformations occurring in his life. Nortje recognizes that his assumed vocation as poet will involve changes to self, perhaps even the sacrifice of self as it had been constituted in former relationships. He talks about the dissolution of his relationship with his girlfriend Sybil Grimsell, with whom he had been erratically involved for several years, and about his estrangement from his mother (letter to Raymond Leitch, 4 November 1963, Unisa). In order to become a poet, he felt a need to break with these relationships in order to enter into a new kind of relationship with the world.

At the end of 1963 Nortje graduated from UCWC with a BA degree in English and Psychology. A graduation photograph shows him dressed in academic cap and gown, holding his degree scroll in both hands, looking at the camera lens from behind inscrutable, black-frame, dark glasses. The academic pose does not quite accord with the shades. There is a doubling of persona here, the academic and the maverick, the public self and the hidden self. An acquaintance from this time, Rita Rousseau, who became Louis Rousseau's second wife in 1963, says that Nortje wanted to be cool, wanted to be a chum, one of the boys. She says, though, that he could not quite pull it off. He was too separate, too detached, too much beyond his contemporaries, too critical and self-aware, somehow alone even in the midst of the drinking and partying. He wanted to belong, she says, but did not quite fit in. He tried too hard (interview with Rita Rousseau, 27 June 2001). Nortje's frame of mind during this period in his life is conveyed in a letter to James Davidson: 'I should tell you that I am spending my weekends more dangerously than ever, roistering and sowing chaos. Much disgust and/or embarrassment of friends and relatives: but even the attempt to make forgetting a more intense and lasting stupor is wearing thin at the edges' (letter to James Davidson, 15 March 1964, Unisa). If, as Rita maintains, Nortje tried hard to be a credible weekend rebel, drinking, boasting, and womanizing, his behaviour tended towards excess. He courted rejection from the very people to whom he turned for approval. Most obviously, the act of 'forgetting' refers to the political situation, but it may also refer to an attempt at the forgetting, or anaesthetization, of self. As Nortje himself recognized, self-assertion is merely the obverse of self-effacement. 'Wherever I stand there slants shadow' (*AD* 79), he says.

Nortje returned to UCWC the following year to enrol for a University Education Diploma. He continued to live with the Halford family, where he had been sharing a room with Tyrone Yong. Yong introduced Nortje to the Cornelius family, who lived close by, a few houses from Louis Rousseau. Nortje developed a friendship with the son Brian and an attachment with the daughter, Joan. After completing school at the end of 1963, Joan took up a job as a typist, and helped Nortje produce fair copies of his poems. To others, Nortje's relationship with Joan appeared to have been a friendship rather than a romantic attachment. Joan herself was unaware that Nortje had fallen in love with her. As far as the parents were concerned, Nortje was just another disreputable youth lounging around, making a nuisance of himself. Given the discrepancy between Nortje's private invocation of the image of the beloved in the poetry and the public conduct of the relationship, it would seem that the relationship flourished in Nortje's mind rather than in actuality. By this time Nortje's relationship with Sybil Grimsell had ended. She expected more commitment than Nortje was willing to give and her religiosity irritated him. For the rest, he had engaged in fleeting sexual liaisons, as he would continue to do. Joan immigrated to Toronto, Canada, in the course of 1964, where she received training as a physiotherapist. In the years to come, Nortje wrote many love poems inspired by her. Nevertheless, it was her absence, not her physical proximity, that stimulated his poetic imagination. The poems are essentially about the fragility and provisional nature of love as offering a meagre hope of wholeness. Nortje suggests tentatively, 'My frail scope is to hope for this, / that love may knit the fragments and shreds together' (*AD* 155). This simultaneous desire for integration and despair at its realization would become a characteristic attitude in the poetry. In this respect, the love poetry is as much about identity formation as it is about relationship.

Cape Town had witnessed the making of a poet and an academic. It had also paved the way to a life of excess. It was in Cape Town, the 'mother city', that Nortje had begun to chart his ambitions and map his desires. He acquired intimate knowledge of the city, from Elsies River to Crawford, from Athlone to District Six. During his time there, 'Bush College' had relocated from the Goedehoop Primary School premises where it had initially been housed to the new campus that would become the home of the University of the Western Cape. Here the university would acquire a reputation in years to come as an institution at the cutting edge of radical, democratic change in South Africa. Nortje had not only immersed himself in English literary culture within the confines of the academy, but had also taken this culture out onto the streets. He could be found in the Athlone Hotel lounge, or the living rooms and kitchens of literary-minded friends, quoting poetry and discussing ideas. He might be seen on the rocky beach at Kalk Bay, at bus stops and railway stations, walking down wine-drenched alleys, partying in a back room, absorbing impressions and linking these with inner stirrings and compulsions as material for his own poems. Nortje had discovered jazz music and sex, had smoked and drunk, and had renounced these pleasures only to take them up again more determinedly than before. He had drifted away from his earlier Christian beliefs and had assumed a sceptical stance towards issues of faith. He had also met Raymond Leitch, who, like James Davidson, Dennis Brutus and Louis Rousseau, would stand in for the absent father, a friend but also a guide, someone to identify with, and someone who was in a position to provide intellectual, emotional, and financial support.

When Nortje graduated at the end of 1964, the Dean of the Faculty of Education offered qualified praise, saying 'Mr Nortje was one of our three most outstanding student teachers of 1964. Somewhat of an individualist, he never hesitated in expressing his views' (testimonial, Unisa). Having spent four years in Cape Town, Nortje returned to Port Elizabeth at the beginning of 1965 to take up a teaching post at South End High School. At first, he moved in with the Rousseau family, but subsequently moved out as he came into conflict with the older sister Joan. He resumed his friendship with Dennis Brutus, who, in the early to mid 1960s, had been banned, imprisoned on Robben Island, and then released. He also resumed his acquaintance with Athol Fugard, visiting him at his house and showing him poems he had written. Nortje had been toying with the idea of emigrating for some time. Several acquaintances had already left the country. After the Rivonia Trial of 1964, which had led to the imprisonment of most of the ANC leadership, including Govan Mbeki and Nelson Mandela, the prospect of a peaceful political settlement in South Africa seemed remote. In the course of 1965, Nortje applied for and was awarded a scholarship for study at Jesus College, Oxford University, thus realizing his dream not only of leaving South Africa but also of getting an education at a prestigious academic institution. The scholarship was sponsored jointly by the undergraduates of Jesus College and the National Union of South African Students, and was intended for a deserving candidate from the underprivileged black community of South Africa.

Nortje's relationship with the black community from which he had been selected for this opportunity was ambivalent. He had been reared in destitution but was ashamed of this fact and often went to some lengths to hide his impoverished upbringing. Moreover, although he had lived amongst Africans in Kortsen, Port Elizabeth, and identified with the African-led black liberation struggle, he saw himself as culturally different from Africans. In a letter to Raymond Leitch, he expresses this difference in a way that indicates his cultural identification with the European settlers and his distancing from what he calls, condescendingly, the '"primitive" races': 'Sometimes I think the Indians, Negroes and other "primitive" races are some of the most unlucky human beings, "civilized" late and horribly "corrupt", as they say ... [S]ee how we pervert our brothers and our sisters ... We teach them hygiene but we don't stop there. When they are clean in body and soul we sell them ... deodorants and detergents and cancer' (letter to Raymond Leitch, 14 November 1963, Unisa). There is some irony in the fact that Nortje had acquired a scholarship based on a status with which he felt uneasy. He was not African, he was coloured. He was black but he was not black. Being coloured meant being of mixed race. He was confused, and had begun to indicate that rather than resolve questions of origin he wished to escape his origins. The previous year he had written to James Davidson, saying 'If I could leave now for another place and another time, I would ... I want to be submerged among strangers' (letter to James Davidson, 15 March 1964, Unisa). In a sense, he wanted to take on the life of strangers and become a stranger to himself. In the poetry, blackness registers this ambivalence, signifying both alienation and solidarity. Nortje invokes the recovery of a communal history in terms that suggest an estrangement, speaking of 'Our souls, condemned to their ancestral black' (*AD* 41).

Nortje arrived at Jesus College in October 1965, and enrolled for a BA degree in English. Because he already had a qualification in English, he was granted senior status and required to complete the degree over two years rather than the mandatory three years. He had entered England as a student and was granted a twelve-month visa, which was subsequently extended for a further eight months to 31 July 1967. On arrival, Nortje immediately applied for citizenship, and was given to the end of 1970 to register his application, following an uninterrupted residence of five years. This confirms Nortje's stated intentions in letters to James Davidson written in late 1964 and early 1965 that he had resolved to leave South Africa and settle overseas. The reasons for his decision were twofold. In the first place, the repressive atmosphere in South Africa had become intolerable, with banning, imprisonment and exile creating a sense of paranoia and despair in the black communities. Secondly, Nortje felt that his intellectual and literary aspirations were being stifled in South Africa, and that he would have to go elsewhere to foster his talents. He saw himself as having being 'shackled' for his 'sharpness' (*AD* 189), and looked forward to going where he might 'earn more purpose than this narrow world / affords its children' (*AD* 139). At the time of writing to Davidson, his intention had been to seek refuge in Canada, and in conversations with friends he continued to speak of possible emigration to Canada. It may be that when registering his intention to apply for citizenship in the United Kingdom, Nortje was keeping all his options open. He would find, however, that there was no place he would ever call home. In a sense, he wanted to keep on travelling as a form of avoidance. Writing to James Davidson a few years earlier, he had said,

> Nothing is permanent but change. If one could go on travelling, the change ought to be painless. Unfortunately, the bus or train or boat or aircraft or what have you must stop somewhere, and that is when the sober realization comes that now it is you alone up against the world: there is no longer air or water or a cosy window between the two of you. (Letter to James Davidson, 15 March 1964, Unisa)

Jesus College was endowed by Queen Elizabeth in 1571, and her life-size sixteenth-century portrait hangs above the high table in the wood-panelled Hall. It is a moderate-sized college with strong Welsh links, less eminent than many other colleges, and possibly not as formal and pompous. Nevertheless, it adhered to the customs and ceremonies prevalent in all the colleges at the time, including formal dinners and membership of arcane fraternities such as the Elizabethan Society. Like all the older colleges, Jesus College, with its common-rooms, vaulted chapel, green quads, and narrow staircases, is steeped in the sense of antiquity and in the traditions associated with Oxford University. The city of Oxford itself projects such antiquity and tradition in its solid stone buildings, solemn graduation processions, low-ceilinged pubs, distinguished museums, stacked libraries, and numerous bookshops. The contrast between the city's air of sedate studiousness and earnest round of academic activity and the dereliction and bleak misery of Port Elizabeth's townships could not have been greater. As if to affirm his arrival in a place of readers and writers, such as he regarded himself, Nortje began immediately to keep a journal in which he reminisced about South Africa, recorded his experiences at Oxford, developed his thoughts about literature and his responses to films, and into which he transcribed fair copies of his poems.

Students at Jesus College tended to affiliate to one of two groups: the traditionalists, who were students from private schools and affluent homes, and the rebels, who were students who had achieved a place at Oxford University by virtue of the relatively new system of entrance examinations. The latter group regarded itself, to some degree, as alienated from, and in revolt against, the elite culture of Oxford University. Nortje did not affiliate to either group at Jesus College, but maintained a cordial relationship with both. His dedication to his studies and the esteem with which he regarded Oxford University as a centre of learning and culture meant that he was, to a certain extent, in sympathy with the establishment group. Nevertheless, he could identify with the nonconformist energy and defiant spirit of the rebel group, and enjoyed its lively social activities. This duality extended to his interpersonal relations. Nortje gave the impression of being at once engaged and detached, passionate and analytical, serious and cheery. He was intimate in his manner but also capable of rigorous self-scrutiny and relentless intellectuality. Always a good conversationalist, no matter the company, he was liable to switch roles and register, assuming different subject positions at different times. This simultaneity of a rational, analytical response and an emotional, subjective response is increasingly evident in the poetry, which brings together thought and sentiment, intellectual distance and intense feeling. The conflicts and contradictions in Nortje's life, his straddling of many ways of being, and his range of experience emerge in the poetry as a complex, at times fractured, perspective on life. The quality of being partly inside and partly outside, being in-between, on the margins, is evident where he describes himself as having 'leaned in on half-doors, wryly regardant, / observing events, reactions, atmospheres – / and resigning myself to the pen's cool guidance' (*AD* 179).

During his residence in England Nortje re-established links with Jonty Driver, whom he had originally met in Cape Town, and with Winston Nagan, whom he had known from Port Elizabeth and who had played an instrumental role in the success of his application for the Jesus College scholarship. Both Driver and Nagan had left South Africa and were studying at Oxford University. He also visited London frequently, staying in Chelsea with Barbara Kaplan, a former partner of Dennis Brutus, and in Croydon with Albert and Martha Smith, people he had known in Port Elizabeth. Later, he fell out with the Smith family, and ceased to visit them. In London he met Maggie Lennox through mutual friends. Nortje's relationship with Maggie replicated, in an odd, displaced way, his relationship with Joan Cornelius. Both women typed his poetry, both provided a romantic attachment of an oblique kind, and both served as muse for subsequent poetry. Nortje had maintained contact with Joan, and in a letter from England openly declared his love for her, receiving, in return, a surprised and cautious response (Journal 52, Unisa). Nortje also briefly met up with Raymond Leitch, who was immigrating to Canada, and with Athol Fugard, who was staging a play in London. In Oxford, he socialized with David Bartlett, Pete Jones, Ian Macdonald, and Phil Garner, among others.

These were the heady, adventurous years of the mid-1960s. Nortje revelled in the liberating atmosphere of the times, which included experimentation with drugs. He writes about taking hashish and LSD, and at least one poem intimates the use of a euphoric drug taken intravenously. At times the poetry is alive with a sense of newness, renewal, a sense of promise. Other times, the poetry records mental anguish, bordering on paranoia. There are poems of wonder at the multiplicity of sensory existence, poems that pay loving attention to the varieties of weather and mood, the nuances of romantic liaisons, and the quiet but resonant pleasures of the intellectual life. There are also poems in which the state of mind appears almost hallucinatory in its apprehension of disembodied desolation, the dark mood mutating into a kind of sardonic cheerfulness. Always, in the background, like an unconscious thought, there is Africa, the past, shadowed in the interstices of conscious awareness. Nortje celebrates his release from an oppressive and racist regime, saying 'I have fled with my wounds' (*AD* 153), but also regrets his having come to England, confessing 'I am sorry I spilled across your borders' (*AD* 177).

On the face of it, Nortje was having a great time. He drank English beer and partied, joined the unofficial College cricket team and travelled to various towns to play informal matches, and delighted in art films at the Scala and cultural programmes on television. He was invited by a College friend David Robert to spend a weekend at his home in Wales, and was invited by his tutor John Burrow to dinner at his home in the village of Eynsham, six miles west of Oxford. He worked long hours in the Bodleian Library and in the Radcliff Camera Library, and became a member of the Oxford Union. In other words, he generally presented an assured exterior to the world. His letters tended to be full of bluff bonhomie and facetious observations on Oxford manners. Whatever psychic struggle he might have experienced was endured in private and found utterance only in the poetry. Nortje attempted, through poetic expression, to control painful experience, giving shape and distance to raw emotion by formalising it. As such, the poetry might be seen to function in one of two ways. Either it is a defensive formation, repeating and ritualizing psychic conflict without integrating it into normative psychic functioning, or it is a form of therapeutic self-disclosure in which conflict is verbalized and satisfactorily resolved. In all likelihood, the poetry performs both functions simultaneously. It accesses and knits into the fabric of consciousness ideas and experiences that would otherwise not reach consciousness, but it also displaces these experiences through the figurations of metaphor and the constraints of metre. Nortje incorporates concerns around the therapeutic function of poetry into his writings. While he affirms the therapeutic possibilities of poetry, he also fears its depletion of self. He claims, on the one hand, that 'Out of poignance of longing the poem / reveals its healing purpose' (*AD* 154); on the other hand, he says that 'I couldn't afford another poem / in terms of ... breakage through the surface' (*AD* 256). This ambiguity is best captured where Nortje writes: 'Spreadeagled in the blue gore on the page / or tightening the words to pearls of sweat / that the busy brain fosters from a latent life, / shock is the stilling therapy for the poet' (*AD* 347).

The literary education Nortje received at Oxford University focused on the great tradition, from the sixteenth to the nineteenth centuries. He received formal tuition on such writers as Chaucer, Shakespeare, Milton, Fielding, Wordsworth, Keats, Austen and Dickens. He still read widely in twentieth-century literature, however, making mention specifically of Yeats and Cummings, and expressing his excitement at discovering Robbe-Grillet. He also read and commented on the available literary reviews. His own writing was growing in strength, evincing an increasingly subtle use of tone, a greater control of rhythm, and a more vivid sense of the expressive possibilities of imagery. He was honing his craft, interweaving external circumstance and internal impression, the material actualities of daily life and the subjective response, exploring in depth the themes of absence and exile, the intoxications of fleeting love, and the sensuous particularities of existential experience. He continued to publish in literary journals, with poems appearing in *Purple Renoster* and *Anglo-Welsh Review*, and entered negotiations to have poems included in anthologies to be published by Heinemann and Penguin.

Nortje took his poetic craft seriously, paying careful attention to its formal qualities. His Journal records his experimentation with voice, rhythm, internal rhyme and half rhyme, and conveys his regard for rigour as opposed to flaccid emotionality, applauding 'intellectual professionalism' and dismissing what he calls 'pissing all over the walls of the mind' (Journal 88, Unisa). He argues that the 'vitalising criteria' of poetry are its newness and autonomy, and claims, rather ingenuously, given his own practice of drawing on personal experience, that 'medium precedes message' (Journal 68, Unisa). In respect of its formal structure, Nortje's poetry was out of tune with the looser, more open forms of poetic expression that, under the influence of Beat poetry, were popular at the time. His poetry was also out of tune with the taut, imagistic forms of expression favoured by many contemporary poets. He did not affiliate himself to any particular school of poetry and worked in isolation from any community of poets. His was a lone voice, divorced from the mainstream. He tended, on the whole, to write to a confessional and conversational style, engaging the reader directly as a kind of alter ego. In addition to poetry, Nortje also ventured into other forms of writing. Much earlier in his life, he had written dramatic pieces. He also continued to express interest in narrative writing, and refers to short stories and at least one novel that he was working on.[7] These dramatic and narrative pieces have not been located, and perhaps never will be. However, it is likely that the narrative sections and diary entries of his notepads and Journal were intended as sketches towards projected narrative pieces.

A letter from the Department of Education and Science in the United Kingdom in May 1967 informed Nortje that, were he to be appointed as a full-time teacher, his qualifications would entitle him to the status of 'qualified teacher', and that a probation period of twelve months applied to satisfy the Secretary of State of practical proficiency. This letter indicates that Nortje was exploring the possibility of teaching in the United Kingdom. He would have had until 30 July 1967 to find a post, after which his visa would have expired. There is no indication that he was considering further study. If he were, he would have had to secure financial support, which would have been difficult to obtain. His financial support from Jesus College terminated at the end of July. The only way in which Nortje could have stayed in the United Kingdom would have been to find employment or to secure sponsorship for further study. It seems likely that he would have found employment as a teacher. Meanwhile, however, he had also, with the assistance of James Davidson, explored the possibility of teaching in Canada. After meeting the relevant Canadian education officials in May 1967 when they visited London, he was offered a teaching post at Hope Secondary School, Fraser Canyon, British Columbia, some 100 miles from Vancouver, where Davidson lived. Nortje was issued with a Canada Immigrant Visa on 30 May 1967.

England had been good to Nortje, providing a fertile context for the nourishment of his intellectual and poetic exertions. He had found himself in the company of people for whom intellectual existence was a way of life rather than an exceptional achievement. If, in one sense, he had arrived in an environment where he felt intellectually at home, absorbing the culture of books and reading on offer in libraries, bookshops, and literary reviews, in another sense he was more alienated than ever before. At times, he felt his difference keenly, construing relationships as an effect of mutual curiosity rather than of mutual acknowledgement. A part of him remained detached, wary, sceptical, and he seemed sometimes to engage in social interactions as if they were compulsive rituals of pleasure rather than opportunities for shared intimacy. His energy and enthusiasm, his flippant bravura, could not quite expel moments of incertitude and ennui. Above all, however, he was alive to his experience, deeply inhaling the scent of English spring, feeling keenly the warmth of a pub after an evening's chill, the textures of stone walls and immaculate lawns, the solitude and blurred menace of night when psychic ghosts knocked insistently on the door of consciousness, the lassitude of misspent days.

In July 1967 Nortje left England and entered Canada as a 'landed immigrant', a status that entitled him to apply for Canadian citizenship.[8] There are several possible reasons that Nortje might have chosen to take up a teaching job in Canada. Several years earlier, when he had started thinking seriously about leaving South Africa, he had Canada in mind. The fact that both James Davidson and Raymond Leitch were living there would have played a part in his decision. He also appears to have entertained the hope of renewing his relationship with Joan Cornelius. Nortje and Joan had met again in England, where Joan stopped over on her way back from South Africa after having visited her family. They spent two weeks together, during which time, as far as Joan was concerned, the relationship really developed (letter from Joan Ferguson-Roberts to Abu Solomons, 1 April 1989). If Nortje's emigration to Canada was motivated by the prospect of maintaining and perhaps deepening these relationships, he was to be disappointed. On arrival in Canada, Nortje stayed with James Davidson, with whom he soon quarrelled. He also discovered that Joan Cornelius had been involved with another man, and rejected her, saying, 'I've lost interest in Joan' (audio letter from Raymond Leitch, 14 October 1979, citing Mervyn Rousseau). A year earlier he had similarly condemned her when he had written, in a fit of jealous bitterness at her perceived indifference to him, 'may blizzards blast your sterile hollows' (*AD* 169). Nortje's reactions on both occasions can be attributed to his own insecurities.

Nortje took up his teaching post at Hope Secondary School on 1 September 1967. At first he lived on the waterfront at the Gagnon Apartments, and then moved into an apartment above the 'Trash and Trade' second-hand store on Wallace Street, where he befriended the owner and landlord, Alex, with whom he would spend weekends eating, drinking Lamb's Navy, and swapping outrageous anecdotes. He was granted a School Teacher's Interim Certificate valid until 30 June 1971. A letter from The College of Education, University of Toronto, dated 2 December 1968, indicates that Nortje had satisfied the academic requirements for admission to the course leading to the Interim High School Assistant's Certificate in English, suggesting that he would have had to complete this course if he wished to be granted a permanent teaching post. He made a good impression as teacher, inspiring pupils with his passion for literature and satisfying the headmaster with his subject knowledge and class organisation. His love of music found expression in his involvement with the school's Listeners Club. He came across as self-possessed, personable, and private, generally dressed in a semi-formal style in jacket and tie, and exquisitely correct in speech, urbane, like the Oxford graduate he had become. As in the past, however, his professionalism and dedication during the week contrasted with his binge drinking and dissipation over the weekend. The Hope that Nortje would have encountered was a small and isolated town of rugged natural beauty, of burly foresters and gruff miners, and of muscular outdoor sports. It was hardly the centre of cultural and intellectual pursuit for which he had yearned in South Africa and to which he had grown accustomed in Oxford. That the quiet rhythms of a small town existence and the bracing health of the wild outdoors did not preclude despair is evinced by the suicide of Robert Storey, a friend of Nortje's, in 1969. The poetry testifies to Nortje's sense of confinement during his years in Hope, and describes how 'the rich valleys regiment with ease / my scope, confine my art' (*AD* 273). After two years of having been cut off from the world he had known before, Nortje tendered his resignation from Hope Secondary School and relocated from the BC interior to central Canada.

When he left British Columbia in June 1969, Nortje moved to Ontario, where, on 1 September 1969, he took up employment at Alderwood Collegiate, a secondary school in Etobicoke, Toronto. His passport, which had expired on 20 October 1968, was renewed until 20 October 1971. On arrival in Toronto Nortje stayed with Raymond Leitch in an apartment on Lawrence Avenue West, before taking up residence at 222 Roncesvalles Avenue. Leitch's wife later informed Raymond that during Nortje's stay he had been in the habit of taking drugs such as amphetamines and barbiturates (audio letter from Raymond Leitch, 14 October 1979). The poetry likewise speaks of Nortje's predilection for a 'yellow pill' to 'calm fright' (*AD* 358). It is not clear at what point during his residence in Canada Nortje came to use pharmaceuticals regularly, but by the end of 1967 he seems to have developed a dependency. Official assessments of Nortje's teaching at Alderwood Collegiate continued to express satisfaction with his performance, but he was in fact heading for a nervous collapse, exacerbated, perhaps, by the suicide of Carrie Rousseau in the latter half of the year. The poetry conveys a wan sense of solitary emptiness, of failure to establish meaningful relationships with others and with his physical and cultural environments. 'The heart is a stone in water' (*AD* 334), he writes. On the surface, however, he appeared to be as ebullient as ever, entertaining friends with lively letters full of wry observations.

In January 1970 Nortje was compelled to take sick leave from teaching for what appears to have been a nervous condition. He moved in with the Reed family at 106 Balsam Avenue. Olga Reed, a history teacher and colleague of Raymond Leitch, who was an English teacher, took Nortje into her care. Evidently, she tried to wean him from his dependence on tranquillisers, staying up and talking with him until late at night (Davis, *The poetry of Arthur Nortje* 7). At the end of February 1970 Nortje went to London for a month's holiday, enjoying his reunion with this 'city of the heart' (*AD* 337). On his return to Toronto he terminated his teaching contract on grounds of ill health. He had been employed at Alderwood Collegiate for seven months. At the same time, he made enquiries about further study. After initially rejecting his application to enrol for an MA degree, indicating that he would first have to complete an honours degree, the University of Toronto did offer him a place. Nortje had meanwhile also applied at Jesus College to enrol for a BPhil degree, and was likewise accepted. He decided in favour of Jesus College, indicating subsequently that a degree from Oxford University carried the greatest possible prestige (letter to Olga Reed, 31 October 1970, Unisa). Olga Reed opposed his decision to return to England as she felt he had not yet recovered fully from his illness (Davis, *The poetry of Arthur Nortje* 8).

The theme of alienation haunts the poetry of the Canadian years. Whereas the poetry written in Oxford had invoked, albeit often as a regrettable absence, relationships with others, the poetry written in Canada invokes a sense of permanent severance from others. Nortje characteristically uses a group of related terms, specifically 'correspondence' and 'symmetry', to denote relationship. The terms are significant as they extend the notion of relationship to include not only the relation between man and woman, but also the relation between self and other, inside and outside, subject and object, and between contrary aspects of the psyche. What Nortje pursues is a healing relation that will knit together the fragments of self. The Canadian poems intimate that such integration is obviated by the way in which consumerist culture objectifies and dehumanizes the self. By reinforcing a narcissistic relation between the self and its objects of desire, consumerism encourages the formation of a monolithic and therefore paranoid self, rather than a dialectical and adaptable self. A sustained satirical note enters the poetry, and is often directed against the speaker himself and his participation in the very culture he abjures. The poetry pays close attention to local and domestic detail. In counterpoint to this immediacy, and in juxtaposition to the parochial concerns, there are poems that take account of epochal events, such as the war in Vietnam. Often the evocation of the particular and the reference to the general, the microcosm of everyday life and the macrocosm of trans-national events, coexist. During this period, Nortje's poetry was published in *African Arts* and anthologised in *Modern Poetry from Africa*. His poems were also read on the BBC Radio programme African Writers' Club in March 1970. The journal he had started in Oxford in 1965 had lost impetus in Canada. The final entries comprise largely transcriptions of older poems going as far back in time as his student years in South Africa. It seems that Nortje was deliberately gathering his work into one definitive book of poetry.

In Canada Nortje ceased to be a student, which he had been almost continuously since leaving school, and was forced to adapt to the routines and disciplines of a working life. He enjoyed his subject and performed well in his role as teacher. It is clear, however, that he was having difficulty sustaining the life he was leading. From the outset Hope had been a temporary solution. Nortje had been able to obtain a teaching post in Canada because teachers were required in outlying places, but he would never have been able to settle down in Hope. The town was too small and parochial for his needs. He required the cosmopolitan excitement of the city, which is why he had enjoyed London so much, more even than Oxford. Toronto seemed to offer what was lacking in Hope, but by the time he arrived in this second largest Canadian city, his psychological state was extremely fragile. Olga Reed's home provided a safe environment where he might recover, and he appreciated Olga's ministrations and developed close friendships with her family members. He was assimilated into the Reed household just as he had been assimilated into the Rousseau household many years before. Participating in family events such as day outings, dinners and birthdays seemed to restore his psychic equilibrium. He had lived a solitary existence for many years, alternately between reclusive study and riotous socialising, though the opportunities for the latter had diminished in Hope. Driven back upon himself in the absence of a supportive social network, devoid of family or close friends, he had begun to rely on pharmaceuticals to fill the gap. Olga's care seemed to change all that, and he appeared, temporarily at least, to rediscover an appetite for life.

Nortje's return to England signalled, for him, 'the most / beautiful of revivals' (*AD* 367), yet within six months he would be dead. He was granted a twelve-month permit when he arrived at Heathrow airport in July 1970, and initially he stayed in London, probably with Cosmo Pieterse at 51 Lady Margaret Road. In the beginning of October he took up residence at 147 Walton Street, Oxford, where he befriended Donald Arthur, a fellow lodger in this rather dismal looking, Industrial Age, dark brick apartment block. The degree for which he had enrolled covered nineteenth-century literature and required extensive reading of Carlyle, Mills, Dickens, Tennyson and other voluminous writers. He would be very busy with academic studies. Nevertheless, he was immediately drawn into his own poetic activities. At the invitation of Arthur Ravenscroft, editor of the *Journal of Commonwealth Studies*, he read his poetry at the University of Leeds on 11 November 1970, and, on the following day, addressed a postgraduate seminar on the problems that black writers encounter in white-dominated society. At this meeting he rejected 'the taking of lives in open insurrection' as a political solution to state oppression in South Africa (letter to Olga Reed, 27 November 1970, Unisa). Ravenscroft expressed his satisfaction with the event and conveyed his growing admiration of Nortje's poetry, which he said repaid careful reading (letter from Arthur Ravenscroft, 20 November 1970, Unisa). Nortje was also invited by Dennis Brutus to participate in a 'Voices from Africa' poetry reading at the University of London on 12 December 1970, in celebration of Human Rights Day. The aim of the meeting was to explain to students what it was like in South Africa. This meeting would have been political rather than academic and, given the large number of exiles in London, might have been hostile to Nortje's pacifism. It is significant that it was in his capacity as poet that Nortje was drawn into issues surrounding South Africa. The dilemma, for him, was the extent of his willing involvement. Some months before in Canada, he had written, 'some of us must storm the castles / some define the happening' (*AD* 361). This suggests that he did see a role for himself in the political struggle in South Africa, but as a witness and an interpreter of political events rather than as an activist.

Nortje had begun to receive serious recognition as poet. Over the years, his poems had been published in several journals. The broadcast of his poetry on BBC and his participation in the poetry reading at the University of Leeds means that he was beginning to assume a visible public presence as poet. In addition, plans were underway for the inclusion of a substantial number of his poems in *Seven South African Poets*. Nortje was also consolidating his intellectual career with his enrolment for a BPhil degree. Conceivably, a future academic post was in sight, or at least a position in a prestigious school. Had Nortje decided to return to South Africa on completion of his degree, he would almost certainly have been able to secure a post at his former university or at a teacher training college. The prospects on an artistic and professional front looked good. Whether Nortje would have wanted to return to South Africa, and whether he would have had a choice in the matter, short of seeking political asylum in England, is unclear.

It would seem that Nortje's attitude towards, and involvement in, the liberation struggle remained ambivalent. In South Africa he had grown up in poverty and had registered the impact of apartheid policy on society, not only in an intellectual way but also in an existential way, in terms of his person, his very body. He had been barred from white institutions and had smarted under the restrictions imposed upon his academic and literary aspirations. The South Africa he had come to know was stupid and brutal. Many of his close associates were activists and some of them had been persecuted by the South African regime for their radical political activities. There are moments in the poetry when Nortje gives vent to feelings of outrage and vengeance, as when he says 'I will fall out of the sky ... / and in broad daylight perpetrate atrocities / on the daughters of the boss' (*AD* 374). His decision to go abroad had been motivated by political conditions in South Africa. Once he had left South Africa, he continued to identify himself in relation to his homeland as an exile. Nevertheless, as evidenced by his half-hearted involvement with the Joint Action Committee Against Racial Injustice (Jacari) at Oxford University (Journal 147, Unisa), he was not the type of person to give himself wholeheartedly to a cause. He was an individualist and did not want to be dragooned into thinking along party-political lines, but he did want to make a meaningful contribution to the freedom struggle in South Africa. Thus, before he left Hope for Toronto, he and Raymond Leitch had planned to form a political grouping of some sort (letter to Mervyn Rousseau, 22 August 1968, Unisa), an idea that was never actually pursued. Nortje was torn between his commitment to the liberation struggle and his inability to yield entirely to the demands made by this struggle. He was an intellectual and a poet, not a bureaucrat or a soldier. The ambivalence caused immense guilt. Particularly towards the end of 1970, on his return to Oxford, and possibly under the influence of the anti-apartheid movement, Nortje felt that he had indulged himself and squandered his life while his countrymen suffered. He cries out, 'convict me for my once burning ideals / my brothers' (*AD* 393), and admits, 'I myself have lost / sight of the long night fire' (*AD* 392). His last poems, written in the Little Exercise Books, are full of existential and political despair.

It is unclear whether Nortje could have continued legally to remain abroad. His United Kingdom visa was valid until July 1971 and his passport was valid until October 1971. Presumably, his visa would have been renewed as long as he was either studying or working. As the BPhil degree extended over two years, the visa would have had to be renewed. It is not certain, however, that his

South African passport would have been renewed, as the passport stipulates that the holder could forfeit his or her citizenship through continued residence in a foreign country. Moreover, Nortje still had an obligation towards the South African Department of Education either to return to a teaching position or to repay his bursary. Although Nortje had signalled his intention to apply for citizenship of the United Kingdom when he arrived in Oxford in 1965, by leaving the country in 1967 he had forfeited his opportunity to do so, which he could only have done after a period of five years of continuous residence. It is unlikely that he faced imminent deportation. However, it is also unlikely that he would have been able to gain citizenship of the United Kingdom without having first to return to South Africa. Nortje was in the habit of periodically destroying all his correspondence, so it is impossible to reconstruct accurately what the situation was concerning his continued residence in the United Kingdom. He was under no immediate pressure to leave, but perhaps the prospect of a future departure weighed on his mind. There is an additional suggestion that he might have wanted ultimately to return to South Africa, but as a British citizen (Arthur Donald reminiscence, Unisa). Whether the South African government would have allowed him to return under these conditions is uncertain. In a letter to Olga Reed, Nortje claims that he intended to return to Ontario after completion of the BPhil degree, and that his immediate problem was not related to passport or visa but to the financing of his studies, particularly as regards the second year of study (letter to Olga Reed, 31 October 1970, Unisa).

Nortje had planned to visit the University of London on Thursday 10 December 1970 to finalise arrangements for the poetry reading to which Brutus had invited him. Perhaps he also wished to use the occasion to clarify his political role with the South African exile community in London. On Tuesday evening 8 December he had dinner with friends in Oxford, and then went to his favourite pub, The White Horse in Broad Street, where he watched the Muhammad Ali and Oscar Bonavena boxing match on television. In a wager on the outcome of the fight, which went to Muhammad Ali in a fifteenth-round knockout, he won as many as ten bottles of beer, probably Newcastle Brown Ale, a favourite brew. He arrived back at his lodgings at about half-past eleven and engaged Donald Arthur in conversation, asking him to wake him the following day as he had an appointment to keep. On Wednesday morning Donald knocked on Nortje's door and went to work, thinking that this would be sufficient to wake Nortje. Getting no answer from Nortje's room on Wednesday night and again on Thursday, Donald assumed that Nortje had gone to London earlier than originally planned. On Friday morning, when the cleaner arrived, Donald asked her to unlock Nortje's door. At first, it appeared to the cleaner that Nortje was asleep in his bed. Donald investigated more closely and discovered that Nortje was dead, lying face down in a pool of vomit and blood. The autopsy subsequently revealed that Nortje had ingested around twenty-five barbiturate tablets. The coroner's report returned an open verdict, saying that the tablets had been sufficient to induce a coma but had not necessarily killed Nortje. The report went on to say that the evidence was consistent with suffocation due to inhalation of vomit. The precise time of death could not be determined.

Nortje had not displayed suicidal tendencies to any of his acquaintances. However, as his last poems testify, he was, once again, in crisis. In earlier poems he had often evinced despair. Perhaps the most serious crisis was the one recorded in a poem of early 1967, where Nortje, objectifying himself in the second person pronoun, says 'your wrists can stain razors' (*AD* 207). Several years earlier, in 1964, using a similar image, he had mentioned casually in a letter to James Davidson that he had recently come close to slitting his wrists (letter to James Davidson, 15 April 1964. Unisa). The last poems are not necessarily more despairing and suicidal than some earlier poems had been. On the contrary, many of the later poems convey an emotional flatness, a sustained bleakness, a complete evacuation of self. Yet it is precisely these indicators, in retrospect at least, that provide a sense of the extremity of Nortje's existential desolation. Raymond Leitch had detected Nortje's fragile state of mind after receiving a copy of the poem 'All hungers pass away' written in November 1970, a few weeks before Nortje's death. Years later Leitch still felt guilty that he had not acted on his unease and given Nortje more emotional support. Not for the first time, he had been angry with Nortje,[9] and had not bothered to respond (audio letter from Raymond Leitch, 14 October 1979, Unisa). This is not to say that Nortje did commit suicide. There is no evidence of a premeditated act of this nature. Nevertheless, he had ingested a large number of barbiturates. Might he have done so accidentally? Was he perhaps seeking relief from emotional pain, consuming the capsules until the pain ceased, without thinking consciously of suicide? Was he seeking some intense experience? Hard evidence is lacking. What resonates, though, are the ambiguities and contradictions of Nortje's life, between his European and his African affiliations, between his private life and his social life, between his intellectual engagement and his emotional detachment. These contradictions were transformed into a poetry that employs not only irony but also paradox to convey the complexity of his inner struggle. 'I have given all to / be the nothing that I want to be', he writes, 'so close are births to deaths, so terse our sojourn' (*AD* 164).

Nortje's way of resolving, or of attempting to resolve, the tensions in his life was to write about them. Talking about the schism of exile, he asks 'What substance around the foreign body / can pearl it smooth, what words can make me whole?' (*AD* 159). It is as if he hoped that the creation of poetic unity would precipitate psychic unity, that the pursuit of aesthetic wholeness would bring about the integration of conflicting aspects of the self. Where it is not a case of psychic integration, it is a case of overcoming loss, emptiness, incompletion. 'Moving from place to place I always have / come some way closer to knowing / the final sequence of the song that's going / to master the solitudes night can teach' (*AD* 193), Nortje says. The question is not whether Nortje was able finally to 'master' his solitudes through writing poetry. Rather, the question is whether the poetry amounts to a significant 'sequence of ... song', whether it invests these solitudes with a meaningful structure, whether, that is, it addresses existential issues in an aesthetically satisfying manner.

Nortje's funeral service was held in Jesus College Chapel on 17 December 1970, a day after what would have been his twenty-eighth birthday. Friends had flown in from Canada and driven up from London to pay a final tribute. Afterwards, Nortje's remains were taken to Wolvercote Cemetery and buried. Dennis Brutus delivered the funeral oration, saying that Nortje 'knew the hardships and squalor of ghetto existence on the fringes of society', but that he 'never accepted the denials that apartheid society tried to impose on him'. He went on to say that Nortje 'lived life fully, relishing it, perhaps over-compensating for the denials he had known in his motherland and with an irreverence logical for one who had been denied cultural roots in his own society' (funeral oration, 17 December 1970, Unisa). A few months later, in February 1971, a memorial seminar was held at St Antony's College, where Nortje's poetry was discussed by a group of interested academics and students. Nortje had travelled far from his homeland in pursuit of his academic and literary aspirations. Oxford University had nurtured his talent and had given him hope that he might realize his potential. It is fitting, therefore, that the university should have honoured his memory in this way.

For a couple of years after Nortje's death poems continued to appear in journals such as *Strumpet*, *Sechaba*, *Gloucester Green*, *The Literary Review* and *Poetry One*. A substantial number of poems were anthologised in *Apartheid: a collection of writings on South African racism by South Africans* (1971), *Seven South African poets: poems of exile* (1971), and *Poets to the people: South African freedom poems* (1974). Two collections of Nortje's poetry were published, *Dead roots* (1973) and a supplementary volume, *Lonely against the light* (1973). The Arthur Nortje Poetry Prize was established in South Africa to commemorate his achievements. Literary articles on his life and work began to surface in scholarly journals, and several dissertations on his life and work have been written.

Nortje's mother, Cecilia, died on 26 June 1989, aged 80, after having spent her last years living with her daughter Susan in Sanctor, Port Elizabeth. She had outlived her son by almost twenty years. There was little that she remembered about him. One gets the sense that she had not really known him, that he was a stranger in some ways, or possibly just strange, having existed for most of his life outside her realm of emotional and intellectual experience. Those in Port Elizabeth and Cape Town who still remember Nortje speak unanimously of his intellectuality, his penchant for poetic quotation, his disciplined work habits, and his capacity for hard partying. More than one person claims that, despite the conviviality, there was something remote about him, also something quite wilful and difficult. Acquaintances from Oxford remember the seriousness with which he approached his craft of writing and the intensity with which he lived his life, as well as his essential privacy. Former students at Hope Secondary School recall his inspiration as teacher, his personable and professional manner (McLuckie and Tyner). Between the fractures of these memories, between the lines on the pages of documents, between the facts and reconstructions of the biographical account, the real life, the singular existence, slips away. 'I am / the fragrant air in the cocoon that is vacant' (AD 163), he had said.

Notes

1 'Untitled'.
2 Cf reminiscences by Raymond Leitch, Arthur Donald and Richard Rive in *Lonely against the light*, 'Arthur Nortje: The wayward ego' by Hedy Davis, 'Arthur Nortje: forging links between poetry and society – Canada 1967–1970' by Abubakar Solomons, and 'The raw and the cooked: Arthur Kenneth Nortje, Canada and a comprehensive bibliography', a bio-bibliographical sketch by Craig McLuckie and Ross Tyner.
3 Cf 'A critical analysis of the poetry of Arthur Kenneth Nortje' by Raymond Leitch, 'The poetry of Arthur Nortje: a critical introduction' by Hedy Davis, 'Engagement, alienation and self-discovery in the poetry of Arthur Nortje' by Abubakar Solomons, and 'A biography of Arthur Nortje, with emphasis on the South African years 1942–1965' by Shaheed Hendricks.
4 The University of South Africa (Unisa), Pretoria, contains the largest collection of Arthur Nortje's holdings. This material was collected and deposited at Unisa by Hedy Davis. The National English Literary Museum (NELM), Grahamstown, has photocopies of the journal, some letters, poem manuscripts deposited by Dennis Brutus, a recorded interview with Peter McPhedran, Hope, and an audio recording of a lecture on Arthur Nortje by Dennis Brutus. I have also gained access to material collected by Abu Solomons and Shaheed Hendricks, including letters and audio recordings of interviews with, among others, James Davidson. I have not cited each use of these sources in the text, only where I have referred directly to a source or where the information may be contentious and therefore in need of documentary evidence.
5 I have relied on the audio recordings of interviews mentioned above, as well as audio recordings of interviews I have conducted with Tyrone Yon, Rita Rousseau, Mervyn Rousseau, Ambrose George, Abu Solomons, Sybil Hitzeroth, Jonty Driver, David Bowen-Jones, Robbie van Vuuren, Mrs Halford, Desmond Moodaley, Michael Cornelius, and David Evans, among others.
6 Such quarrels occurred with Albert Smith, James Davidson and Raymond Leitch.
7 The Journal contains several references to these narrative pieces. Several years later, in a letter to Mervyn Rousseau dated 3 July 1970, Nortje again referred to a novel he was working on, tentatively entitled 'Natural children'.
8 [Eds. Nortje was one of 1 366 South Africans (albeit Nortje applied from London, England) to emigrate to Canada in 1967. Although this was the largest number of South African immigrants to Canada in any year between 1956 and 1974, it still represented just 0,6% of total immigration to Canada in that year. Immigration from Africa as a whole constituted 2% of the 1967 total, higher only than South America among continents. (*Historical Statistics of Canada*. 2nd ed Ed F H Leacy. Ottawa: Statistics Canada, 1983.)]

9   In a letter to Louis Rousseau, dated December 1968, Nortje speaks of having restored his 'reputation' in the Leitch household, indicating a fallout of some sort. NELM.

Works cited

Davis, Hedy. 'Arthur Nortje: the wayward ego', *The Bloody Horse* 3 (January–February 1981):14–24.

Davis, Hedy. 'The poetry of Arthur Nortje: a critical introduction'. MA dissertation, University of South Africa, 1983.

Hendricks, Shaheed. 'A biography of Arthur Nortje, with emphasis on the South African years 1942–1965'. Honours long essay, Vista University: Port Elizabeth, 1996.

Leitch, Raymond. 'A critical analysis of the poetry of Arthur Kenneth Nortje'. MA dissertation, University of Toronto, 1975.

McLuckie, Craig W & Ross Tyner. "The raw and the cooked': Arthur Kenneth Nortje, Canada and a comprehensive bibliography', *English in Africa* 26.2 (October 1999):1–54.

Nortje, Arthur. *Lonely against the light*. Ed Guy Butler. *New Coin Poetry* 9.3&4 (September 1973).

Nortje, Arthur. *Anatomy of dark: collected poems of Arthur Nortje*. Ed. Dirk Klopper. Pretoria: Unisa Press, 2000.

Solomons, Abubakar. 'Engagement, alienation and self-discovery in the poetry of Arthur Nortje'. MA dissertation, University of the Western Cape, 1986.

Solomons, Abubakar. 'Arthur Nortje: forging links between poetry and society – Canada 1967–1970', *AKAL* 1.2 (August 1989):10–12.

Chapter 2: Nortje and nature

Amanda Bloomfield

Many poets, particularly the Romantics, have used the seasons of the year as a
device to describe the setting or mood of a poem. Poets such as John Keats and
James Thompson write about seasons and celebrate the beauty of nature by
recording their reactions to it (*English Romantic Poetry and Prose* 4–10:1202).
Arthur Nortje is similar to the Romantics in this respect since he utilizes all
four seasons throughout his poetry to convey the same ideas. His use of the
seasons is not limited to this criterion though, as he also uses them to discuss
racial issues, his feelings of exile, and his lack of hope in the future. As a South
African who was detached from his homeland Nortje was plagued by feelings
of isolation as well as guilt for being a distant survivor of apartheid (Gagiano
325). His poetry is imbued with overtones of grief and sadness for the country
he is separated from and his inability to find a place to call home (325).
Overall, Nortje's use of seasons in his poetry reflects both the climate and
setting he is writing in as well as the deeper emotional and psychological issues
that he was confronting.

In *Anatomy of dark*, Nortje mentions one or more of the seasons in over
seventy poems. The poems dealt with here have been chosen for the way they
are used by Nortje to indicate setting, race and identity. One of the most direct
ways he uses seasons in his poems is to denote the setting of the poem itself.
Since this is the more simple and obvious way he uses seasons, discussion here
is brief. The more complex and metaphorical aspects of Nortje's use of seasons
involve his examination of race, politics and exile. First, then, an example of
Nortje's usage of seasons is 'Wayward ego', the last poem he wrote, where he
positions the speaker 'occupying the peeling bench of an autumn day' (*AD*
400). By mentioning that it is autumn, Nortje is able to evoke the colours and
temperature of the day to the readers as we view the speaker sitting on a park
bench. In Nortje's 'In recovery', a poem he wrote early in his career as a writer,
he writes of recalling memories of past romances as the speaker states to former

lovers, 'From you and you I bear these memories / of tenderness and violence, quick bright laughter. / An autumn day with milky cloud / returns the scenes' (122). In this instance, the autumn day is the background in which the speaker remembers past events under a serene autumn sky. In 'Draft history', Nortje describes soldiers falling in battle 'after a thundery summer' (260). Here, he is using summer to create the setting of the battle and uses the 'thundery' nature of summer storms to parallel the violence of war. In 'Dangerous silences' Nortje mentions both winter and autumn to establish the setting. As the speaker looks up at the sky, he sees that 'Between the snow peaks barred / cloud blooms against the shard / of winter sky' (275). At the end of the poem Nortje describes the persona as walking 'among the washed stones, old self, light under heaven, making noises in the autumn' (275). The setting in this poem is constructed first by the winter sky and then by a reference to the 'old self' of the speaker as he remembers walking in autumn. Finally, in 'Goodbye to She of the beautiful island', Nortje uses summer to describe the scenery as the persona thinks about leaving England (236). The speaker reminisces about his attachment to England and he states that the 'Tide brings you home in summer light', conjuring an image in the eye of the reader of the Atlantic Ocean in the warm glow of summer (236). On a simplistic level then, Nortje uses the seasons to give a sense of the setting of the poem. By describing the details of the seasons in so many of his poems, Nortje mirrors the Romantic poets, who wrote of the beauty of seasons. The main difference between them is that Nortje uses seasons not just to describe the beauty of nature's cycles, but also to express more complex issues, such as race and his own problem with his identity.

The two main seasons Nortje uses to discuss race are autumn and winter. As a coloured person, Nortje plays with the idea of leaves in autumn as representing his group. This is evident particularly in his poem 'A house on Roncesvalles, Toronto 222' (354). The first section of the poem positions the speaker inside his house on a cold winter day, wanting and trying to write. He states, 'hesitant about whether / to fetch out pen and paper / I wonder will thought dribble' (354). We know it is winter outside as the speaker talks of the 'windowpane ice-cold to my survey / saving my fingertips I test with my knuckles' (355). The next words from the speaker parallel his mention of leaves and snow in the following section, and reveal that he is using winter and autumn to suggest race. In lines 11 and 12, he states that even though he is touching the cold window with his knuckles it 'is what a corpse under the first / snowfall has no earthly need to do' (355). The speaker, feeling like a corpse under the snow, then has to remind himself that he is living. He states in a parenthetical section,

(I the living take account
of anatomy and function:
runnels from the nose

... I sneeze and relish
    the warm coils of the soul's home realizations). (355)

The speaker is reminding himself of his corporeal self to counteract his feeling of being like a 'corpse' under the first snowfall.

It is at the beginning of the second stanza that the speaker's contemplation of seasons and race becomes evident. He looks out the window and sees 'city leaves in late October / when the blood and gold tones of autumn / cower under crowns of white' (355). Although, the speaker is talking about the natural setting, there could also be an implied comparison between the autumn leaves under snow and a coloured South African writer living in a cold climate. Being unaccustomed to such frigid weather, it is fitting that the speaker would feel like he was 'cowering' under crowns of white or was a 'corpse' under the snow. On a deeper level of racial symbolism, the image could also be reflecting the speaker's alienation from the whites in Canada and his inability to establish community. He is detached and cowering from whites in Canada, while perhaps also hiding from whites in South Africa. This latter inference comes only in light of the biographical information on Nortje. Like his persona, he was in exile from his homeland and was a lonely person hiding from community in Canada (Gagiano 323). Under the previous section, the speaker also sees the cowering of the autumn leaves beneath crowns of white as a positive thing compared to 'smokestacks belching fumes in a wasteland / of freight trains and beef factories' (*AD* 355). The speaker states that it is better to hide under the snow or white people in Canada than to live in the 'wasteland' conditions he remembers from another place of residence, or perhaps in South Africa. At the end of the poem the speaker mentions that 'snow on the mute boughs' is less marvelled at than 'the walk in the moondust' (356). The speaker is saying that the world 'made a marvel' of men walking on the moon, but they do not marvel at the endurance of those under apartheid or other types of oppression. In order to reinforce his message, Nortje uses the boughs that are 'muted' under the snow in winter to represent the oppressed, while the snow represents the white oppressor.

In the parenthetical section below the speaker accuses those who ignore the strength of the oppressed as he states, '(these are not the respecters of trees / who burdened us with plastic bags of rocks / to plant in planetariums)' (356). In other words, the speaker is being critical of the world for being more interested in moon rocks than in the fight for basic human rights. He concludes, with a tribute to those who survive under oppression: 'under the grime and slime the heart beats non-stop / apple strong' (356). The heart of those persevering is 'apple strong', perhaps because the speaker believes that one day the boughs will be free to produce fruit when the snow is not weighing them down any more. This poem, then, can be viewed as an extended metaphor about the oppressive political systems. Nortje uses seasons in the poem, such as autumn and winter, and their features, such as leaves and snow, to indicate not just his own position as foreigner in a cold climate but as part of racially oppressed groups. The poem is, as the speaker states, 'a secular poem' that 'will note / unpalatable truths' about the world's attitude to racist regimes (356). The speaker feels some sense of blame ignoring the issues too as he claims ' I am he who / let the ornaments fade / because of the dog days that were upon us' (356). In other words, he became comfortable in his position outside white oppression, and neglected to persevere against it.

Nortje uses the images of bare boughs, winter and leaves again in another of his poems, 'No change' (95). Here, the suggestions about race are in direct connection to South Africa. The speaker declares that:

Leaves lose no colour
this or any
season in
(and winter's funny!)
good hope Cape
Peninsula (95).

Here, the speaker suggests that the 'leaves lose no colour', or that in the Cape, the coloured, black and Indian people are always viewed as lesser humans. Whereas the speaker in the previous poem could relate himself to the coloured leaves in autumn because he is a coloured person in Canada, the coloured people in South Africa are not allowed to change. In this instance, Nortje uses winter in a different way from the previous poem as the speaker states here that '(and winter's funny!)' in the Cape (95). This statement causes the reader to give pause and think why Nortje would choose to use the word 'funny'. His purpose may be to parallel winter to the whites in South Africa; that as the seasons change, they stay the same and winter is funny because it is not so different from any other part of the year. In this way, winter as funny has a connotation of strangeness, not hilarity. It also suggests that winter is what is necessary for change, implying that the whites controlling the situation are allowing no social change to come. Contrasted to the previous poem, Nortje uses winter, leaves and bare boughs here in a different way. Instead of using snow as a metaphor of oppression, he is using the lack of it as a sign of the stubbornness of apartheid in South Africa. The scenery never changes; the oppression remains the same.

The leaves here are not used in connection with Nortje's own identity as a coloured person but are more symbolic of captivity as they always stay in the same place and are the same colour, not being allowed any freedom from their position. In this way, they symbolize the racially oppressed groups in South Africa who are locked into a system. From a macro perspective, the leaves may also represent whites as they have locked themselves into the system that allows no change of colour either, further entrenching their ignorance. The 'bare boughs' that 'are rare here' imply not just the natural event of leaves falling but that the boughs are also symbolic of humanity (95). That the coloured leaves always cover up the bare boughs reflects the reality that racially oppressed groups are not seen for their own humanity. Instead, the whites always see them as different, connecting again back to the idea that whites, as a wintering force, are the ones who could bring change and begin to see the bare boughs or the oppressed people's humanity.

The political nature of the poem is only reinforced by the third stanza, which portrays a specific and common type of government violence in South Africa. The speaker states 'Boots on the door / in the black of night' (95). The speaker is not just suggesting general violence here but is referring to the method the government used to arrest political and social activists against apartheid (Thompson 199). These lines then detail the repression of those who would bring change to the system. The next two lines accuse the world of its ignorance to these events as the speaker says, 'Rest of the world / sleep out of sight' (*AD* 95). The second half of this line causes the reader to finish the cliché, 'out of sight, out of mind'. In other words, because the outside world is not there to witness the events, they feel no weight on their psyche. The poem ends with the statement, 'No change: we stay strange', signifying, as suggested through the leaves not losing colour and winter not coming, that just as the climate in South Africa can be unchanging, so too the political climate remains static (95).

Nortje uses seasons and their elements in similar ways. He describes leaves as both coloured and changing colour, signifying political change or a lack of it. In both poems he employs winter as an image of white oppression and the lack of it as the white's resistance to change. As well, bare boughs are used to indicate humanity. The two poems differ significantly in the tone of their message though, particularly because of the time and place in which they were written. 'No change' was written in May 1964 when Nortje was still in South Africa (95). This may explain the more explicit political nature of the poem as opposed to 'A house on Roncesvalles, Toronto 222'. The latter poem was written in Toronto in 1970, after Nortje had been gone from his homeland for five years. This may explain the more convoluted political nature of the poem, as Nortje is still deeply aware of the problems in South Africa but is also having difficulty facing his own identity as an exile (Gagiano 325).

An image that emerges repeatedly throughout his work is his exiled self, represented through the windswept leaf in autumn. As mentioned, he connects his race to a fallen leaf, one that has changed colour. The fallen leaf driven by the wind, though, is an image Nortje presents to explain his own position as exile, since it represents something that is disconnected from its home. It has no roots, another prevalent image in Nortje's writing, as it is tossed about with no direction or purpose. Nortje's picture of himself in this form is clearly expressed in 'Chelsea visit' (*AD* 152). We are presented with the image of the leaf in the first stanza as the speaker describes the river bank:

Dim among mists a starfish floats, the sun
of London autumn, leaves with everything.
The wind has found its trembling orphans' nooks,
though some, soft with the weight of rain, are trodden
pulpy in the concrete of embankment (152).

If we are to explore Nortje's idea of his exiled self as similar to that of a leaf,
he is offering us two positions for himself here. One is that the wind has
somehow found the leaf, a 'trembling orphan', a home or a nook to be sheltered
from 'the weight of rain'. Given that Nortje wrote this poem in London in
1965, he would have been new to England and is showing through these words
his hope that the wind has found him a nook in that country (152). Yet the
second half of the first stanza indicates Nortje's fear that as an exile from his
homeland he will not be able to find a position of shelter in any country, but
will be driven about endlessly, finishing 'trodden / pulpy in the concrete of
embankment'.

This fear of ending up as refuse is echoed in Nortje's last known poem,
'Wayward ego', where the speaker states that:

Nights on the streets find us windswept ...
under the sky that buffets whatever's moveable;
or awash in the city tide,
or swimming between the rage of bottles,
floating in muck, flotsam and tossed jetsam,
rockbottom smelling the gutter (400).

Through the speaker's words here, just as in 'Chelsea visit', Nortje's fear of
having an exiled position resulting in a transient and useless life is evident. He
is fearful of ending up as trash or pulpy waste on the side of a hill, and being of
no consequence to anyone or anything. However, while he sees where his
future may lead, he feels that he has no control over it. The last stanza of
'Chelsea visit' articulates his response to his unrooted position as exile when
the speaker states,

What does not go but for some grace?
The arching rainbow arcs a problem spectrum.
I seek no answers, cradling your muddied face,
so far together have we come from home. (152)

In other words, he views himself as having no control over his position, and
therefore he seeks 'no answers' to his future. Instead he withdraws into himself
for survival as he cradles his own 'muddied face' and says to his reflection, 'so
far together we have come from home' (152). The image of the muddied face
implies that he has accepted that the wind will not find him a nook but that he

will finish in a 'trodden pulpy' state. Even though he says he is not looking for answers, he offers himself one when he resigns himself to fate as an answer in itself.

Eerily, in one of his very early poems, Nortje predicts his own future in 'To a friend departing for Canada' (6). At this early stage he has already identified himself with falling leaves and expresses, perhaps unknowingly, what he sees his position in life to be as the speaker states:

> Remember me to the leaves in fall
> falling like millions of black shadows
> silhouetted against the terrible red wall
> flowering out from the sunset
> which talon or claw cannot buffet with blows
> and none of us forget.
> Remember me perhaps despairingly. (8)

In light of his eventual suicide, his words may as well be to those reading his work after his death instead of just to the auditor. By associating himself with leaves, he believed he would not be 'buffeted' by 'talon or claw' since he would always be a moving target. However, as we have seen in his later poems, Nortje still felt buffeted by the wind and had not found a way to escape conflict, whether politically or within himself. This conclusion to his life echoes his qualitative plea, 'Remember me perhaps despairingly'. Memories of him are to be full of despair since his resignation to fate positions him as an eternal exile from his home, himself, and others.

Overall, Arthur Nortje uses seasons in a number of ways in his poetry. Structurally speaking, he uses all four seasons to generate mood, time and setting. Thematically, he also employs seasons to explore issues around race and politics, as well as his own position as an exile. Specifically, around these issues, Nortje evokes images primarily through the seasons of autumn and winter, exploring their contrasts and using their elements such as snow and leaves to represent humanity and identity. Like the Romantic poets of the eighteenth and nineteenth centuries, Nortje was observant of his environment, but he used nature to question his life, not to find answers to it. He leaves the answers to fate. In contrast, John Keats reveals through his poem 'To autumn' that he looks to seasons to find wholeness (*Romantic poetry* 1202). The speaker in the poem asks this season, 'Who hath not seen thee oft amid thy store? / Sometimes whoever seeks abroad may find / Thee sitting careless on a granary floor / Thy hair soft-lifted by the winnowing wind' (1202). To Keats, the seasons have answers for those who are searching 'abroad'. For Nortje, though, the cycles of nature are working against him as in his poem 'Winter: Oxford'. Here, the speaker feels stalked by winter as he states:

You, chill-faced winter, follow leering along
the trail of gobs that weigh my cobwebs down.
On porcelain thrones of cubicles I've sat
to think away an exile long impoverished.
Who can pay for my safety now,
and why is it so ineffable? (*AD* 206)

To Nortje, the answer to his position in exile is beyond his comprehension. He is distanced from the seasons, which cannot offer him safety, leaving him isolated and abandoned, until as his last poem, 'Wayward ego', tells us that there is 'not even crackle of leaf / or a wild flurry of spinning' (400). He sees that the autumn wind has not found a home for him, and does not bother to try any more. Nortje's expression of nature's acquiescence points to the poet's own decision to give up on life as well. Altogether, Nortje uses seasons in his poems to reflect setting as well as his problems with identity and his position as an exile. With his ultimate detachment from seasons being illustrated in his poetry, we can also see his spiral down towards an eventual detachment from life itself.

Works cited

Gagiano, Annie. 'Arthur Nortje', *Dictionary of literary biography: South African writers*, vol 225. Detroit: The Gale Group, 2000:322–327.

Keats, John. *English Romantic poetry and prose*. Ed Russell Noyes. New York: Oxford University Press, 1956.

Nortje, Arthur. *Anatomy of dark: collected poems of Arthur Nortje*. Ed Dirk Klopper. Pretoria: University of South Africa, 2000.

Thompson, Leonard. *A history of South Africa*. New Haven: Yale University Press, 2000.

Chapter 3: Bodiographies: writing the body in Arthur Nortje[1]

Sarah Nuttall

> Black residue ... night thing!
> Arthur Nortje, 'Transition', 1965

> Shields of bone, the moist glands, membranes,
> bulbs of flesh and hair roots breed again,
> propagate themselves, protect, renew ...
> Arthur Nortje, 'Memory merchant', 1966

> The body is our general medium for having a world.
> Maurice Merleau-Ponty, *Phenomenology of perception*

Until recently, much work on the post-colonial body has focused on what could be called macro-processes of the embodied self: the body of the self in relation to the body of the Other, the body of exile, and the body as a site of multiple political and social inscriptions.[2] Important as this work has been, it has often left aside those textual markings of the body as lived flesh in its fully anatomical dimensions – as a body in parts, made up of sensory organs.[3] It has left aside the body as flesh and bones, as soft and hard, as surface and volume; the body as densely packed interior – liver, kidneys, heart, cavities, vessels, fluids – and as breath, odour-like, beyond the material, the anatomical. It has left aside such a body in parts with its eery, individuated agencies and its imagined loci of self-knowledge when in fact a number of writers and poets (in particular the work of Soni Labou Tansi and Dambudzo Marechera) have inscribed such a body in their work.[4] In this essay it is *this* body, this anatomical and material body, its parts, potentialities, territories, limits that I would like to consider as a means of elaborating less well traced fields of cultural enquiry. I do so by discussing the poetry of Arthur Nortje, who left behind an oeuvre of over 400 poems, published for the first time in *Anatomy of dark* (2000). The title, which is also a line from 'Midnight and after' (*AD* 42), offers a compelling frame for Nortje's preoccupations, though critics have yet to take up the fully anatomical or fleshly dimensions of his work. Nortje, as the title intimates, and as David Bunn (1996) has pointed out, takes his own body as a site of extended reference and complex embellishment in his poetry. In this essay I build on Bunn's work, on the fuller suggestiveness of the readings that Nortje's imaginary and material 'anatomies' offer us. Nortje's poems are largely autobiographical reflections on his self and his body. They offer us a comparative commentary on a Foucauldian process of 'self stylization', of work performed by the self on the self (1994). Nortje's is a body in parts, a site of individuated organs which take on complex valencies across his work.

His biography is currently being written, but until it is published we are left with relatively little knowledge of Nortje as a person. Rive, in his memoir *Writing black* (1981), describes Nortje as someone who 'identified himself so completely with his writing that to be critical of his poetry was to be critical of the man himself. He was his poetry.' Rive, too, refers to Nortje's 'intensity' (97); others such as Brutus (1970) point to his personal and poetic 'over-compensation' and 'irreverence' (26); critics frequently mention what they see to be an 'excessiveness' in his style[5]. Such readings, though based on some truth, also tend to contain what is most compelling and original in Nortje's work.

The seeds of Nortje's biography as well as the evidence from the poems reveal that the particularities of his ancestry, both coloured and Jewish, his exposure to high apartheid,[6] and his intense engagement with his writing all shape his poetic persona in profound ways. That his racial origins took on powerful valencies for him in a race-obsessed context is clear not only from the multiple senses his work brings to the notion 'anatomy of dark', as we will see, but also in explicit apellations of himself as, for instance, 'dispersed hotnot, disparaged jew' (*AD* 391). While much writing on the body histories of both Khoisan and Jew has sought to show the symbolic potency of the links between the corporeal body and the body politic,[7] Nortje's work takes us beyond the meta-symbolic dimensions to the 'flesh and bone' histories, the potent imaginary anatomies, of such bodies as they invent and imagine themselves. His work takes us into a less well rehearsed terrain of anatomical and fleshly agencies and subjectivities.

I begin with a set of close textual readings of some of Nortje's poems, to elicit what he means by these notions of 'anatomy' and 'flesh'. I then consider his work in the context of wider conceptions of writing the body and flesh. I conclude with a set of reflections on the relationship between the body and poetry writing. In the course of my argument I track three questions in particular. What are the specific materialities of the body that Nortje brings to light, and what are their potentialities and limits? What valencies do the body and flesh take on in Nortje's work in relation to conceptions by, say, Merleau-Ponty and Foucault? What are the concepts of the self that emerge out of these understandings of the body and the flesh?

Bodiographies

'Bodiographies' are narratives of self centred on the lived body in which the body is figured less as an object inscribed with the social and the political than as a subject actively contributing to the production of meaning. That Nortje's poetic consciousness is informed by a visceral response to the world, and a powerful set of bodily anatomies, is evident from two early poems that he wrote when he was twenty-three. The first is 'Apartheid' (1965), of which this is an extract:

Winter parades as a mannequin.
The early scene looks virgin.
We sway past in a Volkswagen.

Nothing outwardly grieves,
so luxuriant are the trees.
Leaf-rich boughs ride past with spring's ease.

Yes, there is beauty: you make
the understandable mistake.
But the sun doesn't shine for the sun's sake.

Flame-sharp, it beats casual
sweat from my aching skull
And the May winds are mechanical.

A bird's clean flight
exhibits the virtues of light.
I skulk in a backseat, darker than white. (*AD* 130)

Nortje is interested in the notion of a masking ('winter parades as a mannequin'), in which the natural world, as Bloomfield notes, masks the social world, and in particular the extremity of the apartheid system. He juxtaposes a sense of outward beauty and an inward aching, in this case the beauty of the natural world versus the aching, suffering body. It is the skull, the bone of his body, that aches, and the bones and their saliencies will come to form a domain or materiality of the body that recurs in Nortje's poetry. The sun is not just the sun, in a mimetic sense ('the sun doesn't shine for the sun's sake'), but a whole world of light and white, in which he is dark. Thus there is something unnatural here ('the May winds are mechanical'). The poem reveals the lyric mode which Nortje favoured and was schooled in, the landscape of which would increasingly turn out to be that of his own body, a kind of corporeal topography. That the author's own body takes the place of an extended geographic reference, Bunn has argued, may be because the sheer impossibility of civil society under apartheid undermines his ability to use conventional landscape paradigms in his poetry. While this is one important reason for his writing taking the form it did, it doesn't fully account for the specific materialities of the body that Nortje chose to write within, and their specific histories within but also preceding the apartheid period. Nortje's increasing focus on the body and in particular the 'flesh' can be seen in 'Catharsis', written the following month:

The flesh, soft and debauched, finds
darkened room its harsh miasma:
bloodless air assumes awareness
of terror, regret enough's enough.
O so the self disgust descends
on lids in unsedation, shamed
my lashes glitter with dark tears.
Can the sour mouth smoothly speak
love, the bloated tissues kiss you sweet?
For this the limbs lie quivering,
The soul at near-dawn sweats. (131)

The poem is written in part as a lament against the loss of his girlfriend, Joan Cornelius, who emigrated to Canada in 1964 (the last two lines of the poem read: 'your image is the one thing real / to you is my whole being given'), whom he describes in 'One for Joan' as being caught in an 'intricate survival' (240). It also reveals to us in more detail the bodily registers his work would increasingly take on. If 'Apartheid' develops one materiality of the body around the bones, in 'Catharsis' it is the notion of the flesh that is introduced. The flesh is further qualified by both 'softness' and 'debauchery', perhaps softness as a result of debauchery. Unlike the domain of the skeleton, the skull, here it is that of the muscles and liquids of the body, its channels of articulation ('blood' and 'tissues'). The 'mouth' is disaggregated into its anatomical parts – it is a conundrum of 'bloated tissues' which cannot be sure to be able to speak (love) or kiss. It exists in a contradictory state, able yet here unable to speak, an orifice on the boundary of a body and a self mired in self-disgust and in danger of being silenced by the psyche. The word 'can' reinforces the sense in this poem of a crisis of the body's potentialities and thus of the self. In the penultimate lines, Nortje writes that 'the limbs lie quivering': here too the body seems to be in a certain state of 'deregulation' – taking on qualities and attributes that are not usual. Thus the body appears under serious threat of not being able to fulfil any co-ordinated function – of ceasing to be itself. In the last line, Nortje introduces a metaphysical dimension ('the soul'), pointing at the same time to an inversion of the body and the soul in the phrase the 'soul sweats'. The soul takes on a function of the body, complicating the relationship between the materiality and non-materiality of the body.

'Catharsis' is set in the night, the 'near-dawn', as many of Nortje's poems of exile would come to be (there is a thematic continuity in terms of his representations of the body between a number of his poems of 'home', such as this one, and his poems of 'exile').[8] While the word 'dark' often invokes its racial sense in Nortje's work,[9] it also carries a continual reference to the night. In its challenge to the senses, the night emerges through clusters of motifs and images: night and violence, night and sexuality, night and pleasure, night and solitude. The night, echoing the metaphors of the body, is a play on the inside and the outside, both a time of retreat from the outside to the inside, though this represents for Nortje intense solitude and loneliness – but also takes other forms – the seeking of pleasure, entertainment and distraction, not least through drugs (Schlor 1998). As we see explicitly in the extract below, these rich languages of the night merge increasingly with the nocturnal city itself: here, it is the metropolis of London that produces the body, his body, as its effect and vice versa:

> City, calling.
> A 'clear, calm night'. Stars that pierce
> the skin with tiny flitters. Veins
> breathe. My bones are manly. (*AD* 233)

The night city calls to him in a web of skin and veins, its lights the stars that pierce the dark. The city itself is the backdrop and the metaphor for the drug he is taking: the piercing of the skin, the penetration of the flesh and the flutters of sensation produce little explosions (stars) within the body's dense liquidity. Nortje writes the circuits of bodily sensation and experience, and suggests, as he does so often in his work, the materialities of selfhood and self-exploration. The veins here suggest impulsivity and bodily force, they are energy channels which make the body move and feel; as the drug takes its course, they become the internal distribution systems of an enhanced subjectivity.[10] Just as in 'Catharsis' the soul 'sweated', so here another inversion of bodily functions takes place: the 'Veins / breathe'. In contrast to all of this are the bones, central architecture of the body, sites of articulation and disarticulation, less mobile in comparison with the constant interchangeability and mutability of the other sensory organs, some of which take on functions not usually their own.

In 'Message from an LSD eater' he takes 'a trip / beyond the moon, past violet stars, through luminous sound waves / invisibly travelling the year's kaleidoscope' (210) but also feels himself 'being buried in mud, life-locked' (212) as he comes down from the high induced by the drug. A landscape of sea and land, life and death, is enacted upon, encased by his body, experienced internally rather than as external to the self. Other poems, such as 'Fragment in acquired England', are even more suggestive of the floating phantasmagoric world of the night he inhabits:

> What do you know of my night meditations,
> vigils, ordeals, odysseys in metropolises?
> When out of nightmares I wake wet as a fish
> into dawn, eyes puffed, my mouth
> raw with survival, the hair of life
> streaming upon the hollows, domes of the flesh
> flayed, grazed, torn, gashed and battered
> in a million operations of discovery
> kaleidoscoped phantasmagorically. (161)

Nortje's metropolitan 'night meditations' reveal an intense visceral land-scape of 'domes' and 'hollows'. Here, again, is the mouth, at once bodily and conceptual, encoding concerns about uncontrollable and contradictory forms of human subjectivity. Inside the mouth is the tongue, which can move in and out of the context of the body, and extend not only the linguistic but the material boundaries of the self; thus it constantly threatens distinctions between the classical and the grotesque body (Mazzio 56). The violence of the flesh ('flayed, grazed, torn, gashed and battered') also constitutes a 'discovery'. Nortje's intense histories of the flesh, his bodily vistas of the night, are also the changing vistas of 'exile', 'metropolis' and 'diaspora'. While the word 'survival' in the extract above speaks to the isolation and loneliness of exile which Nortje articulates in many poems, and while 'exile' is without exception the register in which his poetry has been discussed by critics, there is much to suggest in his 'night meditations' that his is also the more ambiguous figure of the stranger,[11] whose bodily 'discoveries' are also the discoveries of a 'different urbanity' (Donald 1999), part of claiming a right to a 'living city', a phantom city of projection and introjection, to a style of living in the present, as well as the past which his exile continually conjures up. In the process he is beginning to invent, through his bodily histories, a new kind of diasporic African person. In addition to the powerful framework of exile, as discussed in Gagiano's chapter, Nortje's work has much to tell us about the still latent histories of diaspora in the African context. Many of his poems invoke a London steeped in the culture of the sixties: the Beatles, LSD, Kennedy, Vietnam and space journeys, a technological and globalising age – although as Michael Chapman (1979) rightly points out, few are wholly successful in fully exploiting these utterly new images of his age. Yet it is true that many of his poems, such as 'Cosmos in London' (*AD* 175) and 'London impressions' (188) reveal a familiarity with and even an embeddedness in the city which still has to be adequately discussed by critics.[12]

In 'Fragment in acquired England', Nortje seems to be commenting on the body's capacity to access the realm of the 'not real', in particular by juxtaposing the notions of 'nightmare', 'phantasm' and 'kaleidoscope'. Each suggests ways a topology of the body fashioned from its otherwise invisible impulses and drives, giving it disturbing and nocturnal[13] a wheel of illusions, too, built from changing phases of bodily life. The medium of translation between these differing realms of the 'not real' may be drugs, as many of his poems suggest. Yet it is not only drugs that link these different domains in Nortje's writing. The medium of the real and its other are also mediated by moments on a continuum of sleep and waking. Though sleep is mentioned relatively seldom in the poems, what is more clearly articulated are the moments after sleep, in waking, in which the body appears to him in a way that he wasn't aware of before ('domes of flesh', etc). It is in these moments when the body is illuminated in particular ways that he makes 'a million operations of discovery'.

The poem also reveals to us other persistent visceral indices of Nortje's corporeal landscape. He refers in a number of his poems, for instance, to fish. In 'Fragment in acquired England', the reference operates as a relatively simple metaphor for the wetness of his own sweat, born of his fear ('I wake wet as a fish / into dawn'). But in a poem written near the end of his life called 'Visceral nightmare (a visitation)', for example, he extends this imagery:

> Laid out on marble slabs the prosperous fish
> dribbling watery veins of red
> lie with disconsolate bulbous eyes.
> Uneviscerated, you
> yet plead and pay
> at the meat counter
> for a piece of rump
> or a pound of liver
> or a beef heart whole! (389)

The poem was written in Oxford, when Nortje was nearing his death. The fish are 'prosperous' yet 'disconsolate', a reflection perhaps of his experience of Canada, and its reputedly sanitizing consumer culture, which he captures in another poem:

> Met by an antiseptic stare
> a void grin from the unknown
> you pocket pills at cold counters where
> white rubber shoes pass down
> cosmetic aisles ... (287)

In contrast with this antiseptic environment is the viscerality of the fish's body, all red veins and bulbous eyes, dribbling from its orifices. Perhaps it is his own viscerality, the liquidity of a body that dribbles and drips, too, which he sees in the fish, as this extract from 'A house on Roncesvalles, Toronto 222' suggests:

> (I the living take account
> of anatomy and function:
> runnels from the nose
> find a shallow grave in Kleenex: seems
> the flesh which breeds it cannot cope;
> in bedrooms likewise drips
> honey resin from the taut torso;
> through the root seep
> tonic juices
> the groin sweats ... (355))

In 'Visceral nightmare (a visitation)' he describes himself as 'uneviscerated' – as one whose entrails have not been removed, who has not been disembowelled, from whom an organ has not been taken – yet who wants, with desperation ('plead and pay'), to ingest meat – organs. This is part of an increasing focus in his poems on food, eating and ingestion. As Bunn writes, Nortje becomes trapped in corporeal self-loathing and begins to represent his personal torment through an 'economy of references to the body, diet and eating. As the self-disgust increases, so too it starts to be associated with food, his weight and ingestion' (41). Thus in one poem Nortje writes: 'afraid of reflections I creep past the mirror / and boil two eggs' (*AD* 258) and in another: 'Mere diversions, a Chinese meal perhaps' (267). In 'Visceral nightmare', the imagined ingestion is all the more bloody: rump, liver, and the heart. What is this spectre of eating the heart? In its materiality and its capacity for metaphoric overdetermination, the heart is the seat of life and heat – via its arteries it communicates life to the whole body – and thus of the fleshly, affective body. Eating the heart is an especially fearsome and symbolic image. Eating an animal's heart has a slightly cannibalistic edge to it; it conjures up the spectre of eating a human heart. There is a sense in this poem that Nortje is seeing his own body through the lens of animal parts. Francis Bacon once observed, 'We are meat, we are potential carcasses. If I go into a butcher's shop, I always think it's surprising that I wasn't there instead of the animal' (Sylvester 46). It is the commonality between his own body and that of an animal that Bacon's comment illuminates: both are bundles of muscle, flesh, nerve and sensation, and exist in registers of physical flux. Nortje's poem too seems to move between the animal body and his own body, almost as if it is the organs of his own body that he will be ingesting. Other images in his poetry suggest killing himself, killing *his body* in particular. In the extract below, note the word 'poison' and how the word 'dead' is explicitly highlighted by the line break: 'Kidneys are cesspools, the liver slithers / in poison chemicals. But isn't the dead / lock of the heart the flashpoint to consider?' (*AD* 209). Thus there is a connection between ingestion and death in his poetry. Nortje's references to 'rump', 'liver' and 'heart' may also be read in wider registers. In several of his poems he writes of himself as a kind of vacuum: he is 'disembodied as a cloud' and describes himself in terms of the 'heart's diffusion' (190); he is the air in a 'cocoon that is vacant' (163). Later, the self is less halo or cocoon than hardly there at all: of the landscape he sees from his window in a hotel in Hope, Canada, he writes that it confines his art and 'is not worth / consideration even now to win back selfhood' (273). In the last poem before his death he writes: '... I am most alive and revitalised / when self's dead' (400). In the context of this emptying out of self, ingesting body organs may be a kind of perverse attempt to 'produce an interior' in the face of increasing loss of self, of subjectlessness. David Hillman (1997) has shown how producing an interior for the body is often linked to the production of inwardness. References to the visceral interior of the body taken as a whole – heart, liver, bowels, kidneys, etc – he shows, are often linked to the production of the mental interior, of the individual's private experience, of a corporeal inwardness. The body's interior, as a whole, has an important place in the comprehension of subjectivity.[14] Jonathan Sawday (1995) wonders whether an intense engagement with the interior of the body is a mark of the moment when the body finally becomes not 'the body' but 'my body' (*AD* 15). For Nortje, it appears at this point rather as a response to a self he can hardly feel any longer.

On the one hand, as we have seen, the body, and in particular the 'flesh', is a site of 'discovery' for Nortje. Yet in these images, too, the flesh is central to a set of intimations which can only be read as a process of killing, and attempting to resurrrect, the body and the self, the body as self. Nortje, not unlike Foucault, is interested in how certain experiences of the flesh relate to expanding notions of the self. He could be said to have performed a set of operations on his body, his flesh, as a way of transforming his understandings of his self. For Foucault, the main interest in life and work is to 'become someone else that you were not in the beginning' (Miller 328). Perhaps in a different kind of world, with a different set of techniques for approaching the self, Foucault speculated, a human being might no longer feel compelled to punish and sacrifice him or her self – 'in order to become what one is' (324). Foucault's speculations were part of a deepening perplexity in his own work about what the self *is*. Foucault's experiments with his self, as a body, as flesh, especially through sado-masochistic gay sex in an age of Aids, late in his life, were also part of a fascination with death as a site of truth: 'If I know the truth I will be changed', Foucault said in 1982, ' 'And maybe I will be saved. Or maybe I'll die' – he burst out laughing – 'but I think that is the same for me anyway' ' (358).

While there are some similarities between the trajectories of the two writers, Nortje's experiments with the flesh and his 'self-stylisations' are different from Foucault's in significant ways. His project of self-discovery did not exclude experiments with self-destruction, although, significantly, such a project was also crucially a response to racism. Like Foucault, he was interested in following his body and his mind to their 'psychoboundaries' (241), as he puts it in one of his poems. In some of his last poems, Nortje reveals, as Chapman has pointed out, a complicated need to vindicate his 'sins'. Foucault was also engaged in a complex attempt to remove himself from, while still implicitly relying on, a Catholic notion of the flesh as belonging to the domain of sin. Though he tried to shift away from such a notion, Foucault, in his writing at least, powerfully signals to a tradition in which the body is the locus of sin (see *The history of sexuality,* 1979). Nortje, in two extracts from late poems, writes: 'in wild pursuits, life of the libertine: / do not repent, confess, seek remedies. / The bourgeois sinners are banned from where I've been' (*AD* 369).

And

Love of perversity, rage and vice,
unknown to all who live complacently,
drive me to lunacy, compel confessions
I am loathe to make were I at Peter's Gate. (371)

Thus Nortje asserts that he has been to 'places' where others haven't been, that are 'unknown' to others. At the same time, he reveals that he hasn't been able to escape the notion of the forbidden ('perversity, rage and vice') and the need to 'confess' his deeds. In the last line above, he refers to the moment of final judgement ('Peter's Gate') where some are banished and others are elected to the heavenly realms. What emerges is a further suggestive contradiction in Nortje's readings of the flesh – on the one hand it is the site of discovery and exploration, and a way of thinking and writing the self, new kinds of selves, into being; on the other is the need, near death, to confess to his 'transgressions'. His poems enact multiple discourses of the flesh, including the difficulty of finally releasing the self from the certain longstanding histories of the flesh which reside in vocabularies of renunciation.

Writing the body

The section above shows us the instability of the meanings of the 'anatomy' and 'flesh' in Nortje's writing. In this section I want to consider his work in relation to wider conceptions of writing the body and flesh. In particular I reflect on his 'bodiographies' in relation to the work of South African scholar Alexander Butchart in *The anatomy of power: European constructions of the African body* (1998) and in relation to that of French philosopher Maurice Merleau-Ponty, whose phenomenological conception of body and flesh contains much worth revisiting in this context.

Butchart tracks a shift in European views of the African body from a surface of nose, teeth, skin and hair in the seventeenth century to a body with volume (an anatomical interior possessed of such organs as the heart, the lungs, the spleen, the kidney or the brain) by the nineteenth. While the former denied the notion of individual subjectivity associated with the interior of the body, the latter fabricated the interior of the African body as a 'pathological anatomy' to be studied by missionary medicine. 'A new episteme and a way of functioning,' writes Butchart, 'emerged that played less *upon* the bodies of Africans than *through* them, mapping a set of relations between medical practice and the African with a body of organs and a soul: the African as an anatomized body' (76). By the late nineteenth century, the notion of the 'African personality' with the African psyche as a possible object of knowledge as the effect of a psychiatric gaze emerged. The focus here was on the relationship between the internal space of the African mind and the external space of the environment – rather than on the problematisation of the nervous system.

While Nortje was 'coloured', an identity which carried specific psychic and bodily trajectories of its own, he would also have thought of himself as 'black' (as multiple references in his poetry confirm)[15] within the broad parameters of the apartheid binary, so that the spectre of the African body and its anatomical history would have been one of a set of frames that informed his consciousness. We might also see how his work on the body and its imaginary and material anatomies situates itself differently from European constructions. In the latter, as Butchart shows, one finds a pathological anatomy of surface (nose, teeth, skin, hair) and depth (heart, lungs, spleen, kidney, brain) and of a relationship between inside and outside which is tied to the construction of an 'African personality' and psyche. Nortje's anatomies have to do with other bodily axes – the flesh and bones, and the boundaries of the body as places of discovery and reflection (rather than sites of social engineering). Moreover, the instability and complexity of Nortje's conceptions of anatomy and flesh work to unfix the pathologizing gaze of European constructions. While at times the flesh, for instance, signifies kidneys, liver, the heart and meat at others it is as if the flesh is 'desire' – or, beyond the muscles and sinews that would seem to constitute it:

What troubles the flesh leaves the bone
sorry. Is it heart's desire, or what? It is
loneliness, believe me, despite the attachment
of muscles, cling of tautened sinews. (*AD* 91)

The flesh, then, may constitute feelings, the psyche; in the poem below it is described as 'spirals of agony'. Bones, by contrast, are sites of 'articulation', structure, words:

Whether the fates will choose to twist
this clothed flesh into spirals of agony
round the entrenched and articulate bones
or whether the Paraclete

will intercede for such a one as I
dispersed hotnot, disparaged jew. (391)

I will return to the notions of flesh and bones that Nortje develops in this poem, but for the moment I want to turn to the work of Maurice Merleau-Ponty, and his reflections of the subjectivity of the body and the flesh. Merleau-Ponty (1962) contests empiricist accounts of the body that treat it as an object, a 'thing', a *tabula rasa* onto which socio-political inscriptions are made. He examines the 'lived body' or the body as subject in its physiological, psychological, sexual and expressive modes. This 'lived body' he derives from a notion of the 'flesh of the world':

> That means that my body is made of the same flesh of the world (it is perceived), and moreover that this flesh of my body is shared by the world, the world reflects it, encroaches upon it and it encroaches upon the world ... they are in a relation of transgression or of overlapping this also means: my body is not only one perceived among others, it is the measurement of all, of all the dimensions of the world. (1968:248)

The living body is not a separate entity in a world external to it but rather is of the same stuff as that world. When he says that 'our body is our medium for having a world at all', he means it is not a fixed given, yet its anchorage in the world nonetheless consists of an interconnected web of relations with the human and the non-human, the cultural and the natural. It is an inexhaustible sensory world that we do not possess; an intersubjective fleshly world (Bigwood 108).

Merleau-Ponty writes from within a tradition of phenomenology which contested the idea of a subjective self reflecting on an objective world exterior to it (the Cartesian perspectivalist gaze) and aimed instead to gain intuitive insight into essences (sources of existence and meaning). For Merleau-Ponty, though, as Martin Jay (1994) has argued, it was not so much a question of evoking pure essences as about exploring 'impure existence' – in which everyday life and the lived body are centrally important (268). Derrida would later see such a view as complicitous with a Western metaphysics of presence.[16] Yet Merleau-Ponty's notion of bodily 'sentience' may in fact reveal the limits of post-structuralism's culturally inscribed body, and the quasi-rationalist account of the body upon which it relies.

Merleau-Ponty says 'my body is the measurement of the world' (249) but for Nortje his body *is* the world – or at least becomes the world. It is not that 'the world' disappears in Nortje's work, but rather that there are multiple worlds – not 'a world' in the phenomenological sense. Nortje accesses the world in its conventional sense and in that process his own body also becomes the world. Merleau-Ponty, too, still has a cosmological notion of body and flesh: they are a cosmos, universal in their being. But Nortje writes in the black body and *its* histories of the anatomy and flesh. Finally, Merleau-Ponty's notion of the flesh is more metaphorical than Nortje's – the former is more interested in 'the senses', 'the touching itself, the seeing itself of the body' (249), as he puts it. Yet, he says, it is by the flesh of the world that one can understand the 'lived body'. Nortje offers us such a lived, situated, contextualised body – beyond what Merleau-Ponty himself perhaps had in mind.

An organism of words

Merleau-Ponty says 'I do not bring together one by one the parts of my body; this translation and this unification are performed once and for all within me: they are my body itself ... the same is true of a poem or novel although they are made up of words ... a poem, though it has a superficial meaning translatable into prose, leads, in the reader's mind, a further existence which makes it a poem' (149). The process of expression, when it is successful, does not merely leave for the reader and the writer a reminder, it brings the meaning into existence 'as a thing at the very heart of the text, it brings it to life in an organism of words, establishing it in the writer or the reader as a new sense organ, opening a new field or a new dimension to our experience' (182). Merleau-Ponty's 'organism of words', establishing a 'new sense organ' in the reader, is related to his idea that he possesses the word as one of the possible uses of his body ('I reach back for the word as my hand reaches towards the part of my body which is being pricked; the word ... is part of my equipment'). Here is the text as bodiography: it has a 'heart'; it is an 'organism' with 'sense organs'; and these enable 'experience'.

In an example from Nortje's work, the 'poem' is metaphorically related to images such as a snail, a fish (with its own visceral associations, as we have seen, across Nortje's work) and a 'glittering nerve'. As 'nerve', the poem is compared to a sense organ, recalling Merleau-Ponty's formulation:

> The poem trails across the ruined wall
> a solitary snail, or phosphorescently
> swims into vision like a fish
> through a hole in the mind's foundation, acute
> as a glittering nerve. (*AD* 243)

In other poems, the depiction of poetry and words is less metaphorical and more traumatically tied to the body: in the last stanza of 'Shock therapy', a poem in which he refers to 'madness', 'dementia' and 'nihilism', he writes:

> Spreadeagled in the blue gore on the page
> or tightening the words to pearls of sweat
> that the busy brain fosters from a latent life,
> shock is the stilling therapy for the poet. (347)

Here is an image of the poet lying abandoned on the body – the flesh – of the page ('blue gore'), where words become sweat; are sweated. Dameron writes of this extract: 'the stuff of life is what Nortje fashioned into poetry. And in turn, Nortje seemed to believe that the creative impulse saved him from madness and allowed him to come to terms with himself and his experiences' (162). Yet the images of meat, flesh and sweat suggest that it is more than 'the stuff of life' that is being imaged – it is a deepening sense of the body which emerges from these lines as the 'impulse' from which creation is coming. In the following image we return to the architecture of bones and flesh in the genesis of 'verse': 'how the glut / of worms in meat has forced verse from my bones' (372). Bones, 'clean' in relation to the corrupted ('worm-ridden') flesh, are again the sites of words, articulation, an architecture of poetry. But the relationship between the two – flesh and bones – is not so distinct: it is the 'meat', too, that has forced poetry from the bones. It is the body, its agonies, its corruptability, which produces words, poetry. Finally, in a poem which repudiates poetry, while in the process of creating poetry, Nortje adopts a somewhat suicidal or at least self-destructive stance: 'I bred words in hosts, in vain, I'll have to / bleed ...' (377). We are back to the pre-death intuitions or intimations which inhabit Nortje's later poems. Three months later he was dead.

Conclusion: selves

Elaine Scarry, in her work on the body in pain (1985), points out that in attempts to describe such a body, recourse is almost always made in language to an 'as if ...' structure, often using metaphors of agency and damage ('It feels as if my arm is broken at each joint and the jagged ends are sticking through the skin' (15)). The same is not true of psychological suffering, which, unlike pain, is susceptible to verbal objectification and is habitually depicted in art. But, Scarry notes, some writing, some literature *can* be centrally and uninterrupt-edly about the nature of bodily pain, and thus is able to capture aspects of such a body in a truly instructive way. So too it would seem that the nature of body as anatomy and flesh can be pressed open within writing. Nortje's work offers such a sustained reading as to be newly instructive to us beyond the broadly metaphoric representation of psychological suffering; his work differs from that of fellow South African writer Bloke Modisane (*Blame me on history*, 1963), who frames the corporeal constructions of the black body in largely metaphorical terms.[17]

I have said little about the *form* of Nortje's work, for Volk and Ojaide's chapters do that. Yet Rive's phrase 'he was his poetry' suggests an investment in writing which carries with it the needs of the subaltern body and psyche so as to mark those styles of the fragment with different political and aesthetic energies. Words, Nortje reveals in his poetry, are traumatically tied to the body, his body – and are seen to emerge from the body, are pressed upon by a particular and visceral history. It is true that he reveals this more strongly through content than through the innovations of form.

Nortje's work, however, brings into focus not only the lived body, in its dimensions as anatomy and flesh and the agencies of a body made up of parts and processes, but also a body which is affected by, but could also be said to exist beyond, the inscription of 'the social'. The body produces meaning beyond the sociological inscription – although, as Roy Boyne (2001) has so eloquently put it, this is not a straighforward issue to theorize:

> The body is a public matter. Bodies are social phenomena. From the sociological standpoint, experience of pleasure, pain, hunger, thirst, touch, smell, sight, hearing, taste, growth, decay, strength, weakness, movement, or stillness. The rough and the smooth, the hot and the cold, the wet and the dry, sharp or blunt: embodied experience is social experience ... Interiority, then is, it might appear, a franchised operation ... The double subjugation of interiority and exteriority within the social realm is pervasive. Our bodies are not our own. This social enclosure is not, however, entirely sealed. There are leakages; there is excess; there is the time of the body, a corporeal time, different from the time of social organisation. (106-107)

Boyne goes on to say that the 're-territorialization' of the body by society, and paradigmatically by sociology, is a networked strategy which parallels the denial of subjectivity within the main traditions of social thought. We can see the extent to which our bodies are not our own, but also the potential for leakage out of this social framing, in any number of ways. This points to the body beyond the social, to the time of the subject beyond linearity.

This body, this self 'beyond the social', as explored in Nortje's extraordinary poetry, takes on special significance in South Africa, where through a long and violent history, the political authorities have acted and thought as if the black body belonged to them – to do with which what they wanted. It also places at the heart of post-colonial cultural fields of enquiry the sentient, sensuous, gendered being of flesh, nerves and sinews – doomed to death in the end. As such, it insists that we revisit in all our thinking the body's special presence, knowledge and powers.

Notes

1 A version of this chapter was delivered at 'Versions and Subversions: International Conference on African Literature', 1–4 May 2002, Humboldt University, Berlin.

2 See, for example, Salman Rushdie (*Imaginary homelands,* 1991), Homi Bhabha (*The location of culture,* 1994), Stuart Hall ('Cultural identity and diaspora', 1990), Francoise Lionnet's 'Inscriptions of exile' in her *Postcolonial representations* (1995), Paul Gilroy's recent work *Between camps* (2000) critiques race, a central tenet of post-colonial criticism.

3 An interesting exception is the work of Achille Mbembe in *On the postcolony* (2001) and in particular his essay 'The thing and its doubles'. In this essay the political body of the autocrat is brought back, re-harnessed, to the realm of the ordinary body – in order to ask questions of its power. In Mbembe's work there is a double movement in relation to the body and power: there is the profanation of the absolutism of power as represented by the body of the autocrat, a body that denies its own anatomical formations and the dethroning of such a body through its own vulgarity, representative of the vulgarity of power.

4 Jane Bryce, in her essay 'Inside/out: body and sexuality in Damdubzo Marechera's fiction' (Viet-Wild 1999) goes some way towards writing in such a body of individuated parts and agencies.

5 Michael Chapman writes for instance: 'His work contains much that is excessive. He is often too close to his subject and he lacks the critical sense to eliminate unnecessary epithets, nauseous scatological references and banalities generally' (66).

6 [Eds. Post-1949 National Party electoral victory race laws; sometimes referred to as grand apartheid].

7 See for example Steven Robins, 'Silence in my father's house: memory, nationalism and narratives of the body' in *Negotiating the past: the making of memory in South Africa*. Eds S Nuttall & C Coetzee. Cape Town: Oxford University Press, 1998.

8 When one looks across his oeuvre, 'exile' is not always the overarching frame that it has been taken to be in his work. Matters of aesthetic and personal 'temperament' play a part as well. On the other hand, one could also advance the argument that living in South Africa for a black person in the 1960s and 1970s would have been like living in a state of internal exile, an exile from within as dictated by a system of what has sometimes been called 'internal colonialism'.

9 These are just some of the phrases Nortje uses: 'dungeon black, I am your property' (3); 'the darkness grins with utter force' (13); 'inhabitants of inky ghetto years' (41); 'go among dark things rather to know them' (58); 'wrong pigment has no scope' (171); 'God's stepchild' (178); 'black stepchildren' (194); 'black bull' (303).

10 I derive this idea from Gail Kern Paster's 'Nervous tension' (1997). About notions associated with the 'vessels' of the body she says that 'by bringing order and connection to bodily substance, their networks help to constitute what we might call the early modern subject's imagined physiology of self' (112).

11 'You smoke, beginning again among strangers' (155).

12 In these poems he brings his observations of London back to the lens of South Africa.

13 Foucault writes that the capacity to fantasize gives every human being 'disturbing and nocturnal powers ... as if haunted by a daimon'. He describes taking LSD as a 'swarming of phantasm-events' (Miller 223).

14 Nietzsche reminds us that physiology and subjectivity are ineluctably linked, and that in any interpretation of human endeavour 'we must start from the *body* and employ it as a guide' (1968:289). 'Your entrails,' he writes, 'are what is strongest in you' (1976:234).

15 Nortje, as Chapman (1979) has pointed out, often aligns himself with the black majority in a mode of resistance to white rule, while also naming the specificity of a maligned 'coloured' identity as when he refers to himself as 'dogsbody' and 'buffer' (see 'Dogsbody half-breed', *AD* 344).

16 Its implication in a metaphysical tradition was reinforced by what Derrida saw as its equally problematic faith in the primacy of speech over writing (1973: 78). Yet for Derrida, too, there is no way to purge language of its sensory entanglements (hence his refusal to be cast as a

simple anti-Enlightenment thinker). He reveals a special fascination with the complicating role of the non-visual senses (note his stress in his readings of texts on tactile textures with hinges, breaks and crevices) (Jay 512).

17 Modisane responded powerfully to the corporeal constructions of the black body by the colonial and apartheid gaze. He takes sex and the sexualized body as the place from which he reacts to racism and his own racialized subjectivities. But for him, the sexual is largely a metaphor for dispossession in which the anatomical and fleshly body only seldom appears. For example, the distortions that the trauma of racism causes are reflected in the ritual revisiting of a perversely pleasant pain. The full obscenity of apartheid and its devouring memories can only be captured through a literature of debasement: images of frustrated sex, or sterile sex.

Works cited

Barnett, U. *A vision of order: a study of South African literature in English (1914–1980)*. Cape Town: Maskew Miller Longman, 1983.

Berthoud, Jacques. 'Poetry and exile: the case of Arthur Nortje', *English in Africa* 11.1 (1984): 1–14.

Bhabha, H. *The location of culture*. London and New York: Routledge, 1994.

Bigwood, C. 'Renaturalizing the body (with the help of Merleau-Ponty)' in *Body and Flesh: A Philosophical Reader*, ed D Welton. Oxford: Blackwell, 1998.

Boyne, R. *Subject, society and culture*. London: Sage, 2001.

Brutus, Dennis. 'In memoriam', *Research in African Literatures* 2.1 (1971): 26–7.

Bryce, J. 'Inside/out: body and sexuality in Marechera's fiction' in *Emerging perspectives on Dambudzo Marechera*, eds F Veit-Wild & A Chennels. Asmara: Africa World Press Inc, 1999: 221–234.

Bunn, David. 'Some alien native land': Arthur Nortje, literary history and the body in exile', *World Literature Today* 70.1, (1996): 33–44.

Butchart, Alexander. *The anatomy of power: European constructions of the African body*. London: Zed Books, 1998.

Chapman, Michael. 'Arthur Nortje: poet of exile', *English in Africa* 6.1 (1979): 60–71.

Dameron, C. 'Arthur Nortje: Craftsman for his muse' in Aspects of South African literature, ed Christopher Heywood. London: Heinemann, 1976: 155–62.

Davis, H. 'The poetry of Arthur Nortje, a critical introduction'. MA dissertation. Pretoria: Unisa, 1983.

Derrida, J. *Speech and phenomena and other essays on Husserl's theory of signs*, transl D Allison. Evanston: Northwestern University Press, 1973.

Donald, J. *Imagining the modern city*. Minneapolis: University of Minnesota Press, 1999.

Foucault, M. 'Technologies of the self' in *Michel Foucault. Ethics: subjectivity and truth,* ed P Rabinow New York: The New Press, 1994: 223–251.

Foucault, M. *The history of sexuality.* London: Lane, 1979.

Gilroy, P. *Between camps. Nations, cultures and the allure of race.* London: Penguin, 2000.

Hall, S. 1990. 'Cultural identity and diaspora' in ed J Rutherford. *Identity: community, culture, difference.* London: Lawrence & Wishart, 2000: 222–237.

Hillman, D & Carla Mazzio. *The body in parts: fantasies of corporeality in early modern Europe.* New York and London: Routledge, 1997.

Hillman, D. 'Visceral knowledge' in *The body in parts: fantasies of corporeality in early modern europe.* New York and London: Routledge, 1997: 81–105.

Jay, Martin. *Downcast eyes: the denigration of vision in twentieth century French thought.* Berkeley and London: University of California Press, 1994.

Klopper, Dirk ed. *Anatomy of dark: collected poems of Arthur Nortje.* Pretoria: University of South Africa Press, 2000.

Leitch, R G. 'Nortje: poet at work', *African Literature Today* 10 (1979): 224–30.

Lionnet, F. *Postcolonial representations. Women, literature, identity.* Ithaca and London: Cornell University Press, 1995.

Mazzio, C. 'Sins of the tongue' in *The body in parts: fantasies of corporeality in early modern Europe,* eds D Hillman & C Mazzio. London and New York: Routledge, 1997: 53–79.

Mbembe, A. *On the postcolony.* Berkeley: University of California Press, 2001.

Merleau-Ponty, Maurice. *The phenomenology of perception.* London: Routledge & Kegan Paul, 1962.

Merleau-Ponty, Maurice. *The visible and the invisible,* ed C Lefort, transl A Lingis. Evanston: Northwestern University Press, 1968.

Miller, James. *The passion of Michel Foucault.* Cambridge, Mass: Harvard University Press, 1993.

Modisane, Bloke. *Blame me on history.* London: Thames & Hudson, 1963.

Nietzsche, F. *The will to power,* trans W Kaufmann & R J Hollingdale. New York: Vintage Books, 1968.

Nietzsche, F. *Thus spoke Zarathustra.* In *The portable Nietzsche,* ed and transl W Kaufmann. New York: Penguin Books, 1976.

Paster, G K. 'Nervous tension' in *The body in parts: fantasies of corporeality in early modern Europe,* Eds D Hillman & C Mazzio. London and New York: Routledge, 1997: 107–125.

Rive, Richard. *Writing black.* Cape Town: David Philip, 1981.

Robins, Steven. 'Silence in my father's house: memory, nationalism, and narratives of the body' in *Negotiating the past: the making of memory in South Africa,* eds Nuttall, S & Carli Coetzee. Cape Town: Oxford University Press, 1998: 120–140.

Rushdie, Salman. *Imaginary homelands: essays and criticism* 1981–1991. London: Granta, 1991.

Sawday, Jonathan. *The body emblazoned: dissection and the human body in Renaissance culture.* London: Routledge, 1995.

Scarry, Elaine. *The body in pain: the making and unmaking of the world.* New York and London: Oxford University Press, 1985.

Schlor, Joachim. *Nights in the big city.* London: Reakton Books Ltd, 1998.

Sylvester, D. *Interviews with Francis Bacon.* London: Thames & Hudson, 1980.

Chapter 4: What do you expect?: oration in Nortje and spitting images

Richard Volk

Throughout his life Nortje was a peripheral character, if not because of his 'mixed breeding', then surely because of his life lived, for lack of a better term, in exile. Consequently much Nortjean scholarship has framed him in postcolonial terms, aligning him with issues of marginalization, race, and alienation. No doubt, themes in Nortje's poetry support these contentions. What this theoretical framework implies, however, is the influence of one discourse upon another; the artist becomes a filter through which a text is refined, and the experience is extrapolated from and regarded in relation to experience outside of itself. In short, a palimpsest is presented to the reader from which interpretation is gleaned. As suggested by Nuttall in the previous chapter, in the case of Nortje the body is the site where this is most notable. Fluidic language runs throughout Nortje's work, with an emphasis on the oral as locus. Spitting is one such image that is particularly frequent and apt because its implications are multifaceted: aside from its immediate (poetical) connotations, spitting reflects the vigour required for a politically resistant voice, as spitting is an extension of self; manifests Nortje's bitterness and melancholy as bile; and challenges the reader in its distinction as socially stigmatic, thereby empowering the effect of the poetry not only by shocking the reader, but also by undermining hierarchical constructions of class by maculating notions of prim priggishness.

The editor's preface in *Anatomy of the dark* states that critical studies have revealed a tendency in Nortje's poetry: a consistent opposition to social oppression, including not only apartheid rule of South Africa of the 1960s, but also forms of racist and economic oppression Nortje encountered while exiled in England and in Canada. In terms of this tendency, the poetry is associated with a literature of political resistance (xxv). Regardless of the fact that his exile was self-inflicted, Nortje was a maverick who spoke out against the inequalities of life as he saw them. He writes 'My weapon is vapour' (44), and in 'Exploration' he tries to 'belch ... miasma' (112) like a martyr. There is a social responsibility implicit in his identity as a writer that reminds the reader that beyond the distracting form of poetry he intends to speak truth: 'Not that I spit of deceptive lustre' (137):

> honesty has sprouted;
> in the bullion tube of its [his] midas gullet
> the world can't swallow the acid that will save it
> hence the bitterness that bleeds
> from the mushroom of my tongue whose root is frantic. (263)

The larynx in this excerpt is golden, reflecting the quality of words that are spoken in search for truth. Compare this to the reference to Nelson Mandela the lawyer, 'who because of the golden words that sprang from his black mouth / languishes in a stone cage' (373), itself reminiscent of Nortje's depiction in 'Autopsy' of his mentor and teacher Dennis Brutus, whose imprisoned 'luminous tongue in the black world / has infinite possibilities no longer' (197). Like all poets, words are Nortje's ammunition, and they are what motivate and invigorate him: they are ontological to him. But there is a political danger in such close identification with the word:

> I squeeze from discoloured glands
> the terrible meaning of glum juices.
> The world is regarding me with a bull's eye. (157)

Nortje's curse is that he is a target for disseminating truth as he sees it, particularly as viewed from the periphery in the then polarized society of South Africa. Through words not only does Nortje identify himself in a Wittgensteinian and Saussurian sense of an otherwise empty and arbitrary world of significations, but he inveighs against oppositions, iniquities, and counterdiscourses as well. In 'Year of the monkey' Nortje states that his 'words drip like essence' (282), indicating the contingency of *mots justes* on being. Expression of the poet is inherent to his purpose; as a poet is both connected to and acknowledged by his words, so do words define the poet.

Spitting is also a projection of self. In this way, spitting is in accord with Nortje's political responsibility as a writer and herald of truth. In 'Bodiographies' Nuttall claims that cultural studies focus too immediately on 'marco-processes of the embodied self: the body of the self in relation to the body of the Other, the body of exile, and the body as a site of multiple political and social inscriptions'. Her argument proposes a more provincial examination of the body, one that is more local. In this light, the image of expectorating is hardly surprising for Nortje, a man self-reflexive and intense, so much so Richard Rive doubts Nortje ever cared he was listening (*AD* xxx). Egestion is an impetus in both a literal and figurative sense:

Here I stand in the most
beautiful of revivals, freshened into
lovesong tenderness, cool and lyrical
with no halfway feelings, no
dryness in throat, because
I breathe you. (367)

Here the other is inspired by the narrator. It must be noted that the lack of
dryness in the throat contrasts the throat of the persona in 'Everywhere I looked
was me', a title whose line is reflected in the first line of 'Mirror prison of the
self' (388–389). Such emphasis on the mouth and its functions further links
the place of articulation to the manner of articulation by reminding the reader
of the purpose beyond the stanza:

About action all we know revolves
around the easy friability of words:
or alternately despair composes life
into the suicidal statement of a gun. (22)

This is where conflict takes place for Nortje. The oral is the locus from
where he determinately spits his words into the wind's vortex (135). For Nortje,
the oral identifies the self. It is from where breath, drool, spit and even vomit
emit, and is the site where 'there is never work without resistance' (346).

A further effect of Nortje expectorating is that of hawking out impurities.
The golden imagery 'in the bullion tube of its midas gullet' incorporates not
only images of his smoking ('I must kick the poetry habit, / gold stains haunt
my fingers' (177)), but more prominently the four humours' yellow bile, an
image his poetic voice returns to again and again. In 'Bile and sympathy'

Adrenalin spurts through channels of fluorescence,
and green in a morning gullet leaps the bile.
Through the flowering mouth of Venus flies gall
blacker than the century's decadence. (382)

The end of the poem reveals that 'September's ending scarcely embitters
me. /Horror and love produce this melancholy', attesting to the symptom of
yellow bile. Beyond the obvious relation that bile has to excess, the reader is
told that this melancholy stems most likely from a jilted love, perhaps national
or something more intimate (as found in Nortje's unrequited relationship with
Joan Cornelius): 'desire grew until / love turned lucifer: / the aftertaste was
acid' (103). Troubled and sleepless, 'bitterness proliferates / as I lie breaking
wind / swallowing my spittle' (43). Here the attempt to clear the system of sour
experiences conveys a struggle within, another tendency in Nortje's poetry

critics are quick to note (xxv). Nortje's internal struggle can be likened to fighting a disease that must be fought, for conceding to the welling up of the bitterness is defeatist:

> we who have been tarzaned, o my
> brothers
> will find the air acidulous
> the muse expired
>
> the senses whimper in these brutal times
> should the tongue not shrill its bitterness. (348)

One can see the necessity of Nortje to voice the melancholy within himself as therapeutic. Loss of country is synonymous with loss of love, and has identical dire consequences:

> the loveless essence
> remains the empty
> nights and years, husks of the exile.
>
> The soul has left
> its slim volume
> of acrid poems only (128)

Note this haunting final stanza, and how its tone and its content reflect much of Nortje's legacy.

The power of resistance to efficiently project the self beyond the self via spitting, while simultaneously purging the spume that has accumulated within himself, illustrates Nortje's profound understanding of words. He exemplifies this lexical sensitivity by playing on words to achieve greater effect, such as inserting a lacuna in a word to create two morphemes while keeping the character order identical, as found in the title 'Alter native'; or punning, as found in the allusions to *Revolver, rubber soul,* and *A hard day's night* in 'To John, Paul, George and Ringo' (209–210). His awareness extends to etymologies, enriching his words and extending images: 'Or smoked hashish ... You lie like an assassin [hash eater] in wait for the moon' (207). Nortje projects words with deliberation, like the persona in 'Basement reflections', who 'spits his words like poppy seeds' (296). Spitting is an appropriate way to express himself, not least owing to the word's onomatopoeic value. Spit, used as a verb, is ejective, carries behind it force, and contains within itself denotative power. To utter 'spit' is to (nearly) perform the action. Significance is found within the plosive morpheme, exterior to sentential syntax. The appeal of this to a poet is one in which the word is loaded, hearkening to Keats: 'Poetry should surprise by a fine excess and not by Singularity' (69). Spitting and other hydrodynamic images in Nortje's poetry saturate and energize the lines, with some queer constructions. In 'For Sylvia Plath', the narrator's 'pen bites like a bullet', and 'venomous words are spat from the fire' (184). The image of embers borne from a hissing fire are married with poisonous words to evoke the pernicious potential of expression. 'Kaffir tongues spit mirth' (99) in the same textual world where the 'periscope of the listener's eye / is misted by the spittle of the ocean' (284). The people Nortje passes on the street drool from their orifices (209); midday news pours from the transistor (53), smokestacks belch fumes in a wasteland (355), and he wonders if thoughts will 'dribble while the radiator weeps into its coils' (354).

Images of spit and bile have another purpose to Nortje. By delving into the vulgar, antisocial, and even taboo aspects of bodily fluids and orifices Nortje is able to establish a repertoire with all people, creating a lowest common denominator, a platform upon which his message may be understood more easily if not with increased interest. Crassness often triggers in the reader catharsis or shock, allowing more impact to the words. Here the author is reminded of the one-time quiddity of shock, *Mad Magazine*, with the words on a pull-out wall poster 'No spitting on the floors or walls', itself an echo of an earlier time when the signs on the streetcars of Ottawa in the thirties and forties read 'No spitting / Défense de cracher' (Stinson). Spitting and other forms of excretion are regarded as dirty, and Nortje capitalizes on this to aid the impact of his poetry by jarring the reader out of complacency. In 'Philosophy,' he writes: 'Metaphors blossom in the blood-spoor of purge ... Thus lyrical, evocative I wish to be' (181). His 'words spew through the sewers / in the company of beer cans', and 'Shock therapy' contains the lines 'tightening the words to pearls of sweat/that the busy brain fosters from a latent life, / shock is the stilling therapy for the poet' (347): 'spasm of guts, stagger and grab / the door: brown spew' (100). Defamiliarization of the reader is intended on the part of Nortje, but there is also a conceit at work when he states:

What is mundane I wish to make sublime.
What ordinarily moves upon the ground
can rise and rainbow, shooting from the slime,
can grow in revelation, can transcend. (370)

Thus, 'One can see marvels in devil's excrement' (371) when 'the glut / of worms in meat has forced verse from my bones' (372). Nortje often mixes the grotesque with the palatable, culminating in a dichotomy manifested as conflict: 'The smelly and the raw / crowds that disgust me are also the ones I adore' (369), or 'Expectorate politely in your chamber pots' (369–370). He blurs the binary oppositions of attraction and repulsion and asks 'Who can distinguish / the dialogue from the graffiti?' (212), yet he also undermines dominant discourse by using coarse imagery: 'afterwards puke at stench from the bucket / gorged with old history excrement-yellow' (37). With words charged with exile he repents the 'gritty memories' and apologizes for spilling 'across your borders' (176–177), but perhaps this is merely a rhetorical device by Nortje to set the reader up for another shock, for 'At the top there is nothing / but a hole that leads back, into the bowels' (245).

Nortje's work is rife with oral images. By providing images of fluids, he adds depth to the poetry, giving a life of sorts to the lines. This extension of self suggests an unusual investment with the reader, but one which is intimate. Insight is gleaned by the persona excreting substance; given that Nortje is a highly reflexive poet fuelled largely by emotion, the locus, method and even substances of excretion offer clues to the nuances of a marginal and currently enigmatic poet. By resorting to the base functions of the human animal, Nortje bares all, reminding the reader that oppositions, conflicts and inequalities are merely constructs of discourse. To spit in one's eye is an awakening; what Nortje asks of the reader is the humility and wisdom to recognise his intentions as true to the human condition.

Works cited

Keats, John. Letter to John Taylor, 27 February 1818. *Letters of John Keats,* ed Robert Gittings. Oxford: The University Press, 1970.

Nortje, Arthur. *Anatomy of dark: collected poems of Arthur Nortje,* ed Dirk Klopper. Pretoria: Unisa Press, 2000.

Nuttall, Sarah. 'Bodiographies: writing the body in Arthur Nortje'. See the previous chapter in this volume.

Stinson, Fred. Personal interview. 6 June 2002.

Chapter 5: The politics of national identity in the poetry of Arthur Nortje: poet, coloured, South African[1]

Kwadwo Osei-Nyame Jnr

[A]rt has a changing scope and it may be just as well not to try to define sharply what's inside and what's outside of it ... truth exists only as a product of historical becoming.
  Theodor Adorno (3–4).

What substance around the foreign body / can pearl it smooth, what words can make me whole?
  Arthur Kenneth Nortje (*AD* 159).

There can be no doubt that Arthur Nortje, 'poet,' 'coloured,' and 'South African', was primarily a poet of exile who was estranged from his native homeland. Nortje often turned to nostalgia in his poetry to re-affirm his identification with his nation. In the poem 'In exile' Nortje describes himself as 'vaguely anxious' and projects his situation as one whose 'soul decays in exile' (*AD* 171) away from South Africa. The contradiction of the situation is, of course, that Nortje yearns in the poem for a home that instead of being a place of solace and a safe sanctuary is actually one of intimidation and oppression. 'In exile', written in 1966, illustrates the ideological paradoxes of Nortje's writing, or what Klopper describes in *Anatomy of dark* as a 'spectre of loss and fragmentation' that is also 'the very basis of consciousness' in Nortje's writing (*AD* xxvii). The list of poems by Nortje that deploy nostalgia includes 'In exile' (1966), 'Draft history' (1967), 'Poem: South African' (1970) and 'Native's letter' (1970).

Nortje's poetry contributes to a critical discourse on South African society, culture and politics that formed part of the collective struggle to resist the dominant and overbearing institution of apartheid. Disillusioned with the sense of dominant nationalism of the apartheid Afrikaner government of his time, a counter-discourse of 'black' nationalism nevertheless remained for Nortje a viable ideology.[2] Nortje was aware, for instance, that he was writing for and speaking on behalf of 'a disaffected community who, in the past' had 'shown themselves eager and willing to be counted among those calling themselves as South Africans' (Venter 1974:xiv).

For Nortje, the alienating environment of exile becomes visible only when it is imaginatively counterposed to the space of home – South Africa – from which he is absent. It is this ideological purview that informs 'Return to the city of the heart':

Far from my native town and soil
it is out of the blue
nostalgia that I land tranquil.
Toward this world having come
after all is an achievement (*AD* 338).

In this poem, as in the many others Nortje wrote in the years in which he became increasingly vocal about the politics of black consciousness, his poetic discourse is illustrative not only of what Klopper has described as verses of 'existential and political despair' (*AD* xxii). Nortje is also writing out of an increasing sense of boldness in self-affirmation. As Klopper notes, for example, Nortje's creative vision was a product of 'a consistent opposition to social oppression, including not only apartheid rule of South Africa of the 1960s, but also forms of racist and economic oppression' he 'encountered while exiled in England and in Canada' (*AD* xxv).

Nationalism is the basis upon which Nortje's commitment to South Africa and his attachment to the nation were founded. He might not have been active in anti-apartheid movements such as the African National Congress (ANC) and the breakaway Pan-Africanist Congress (PAC); nonetheless his poetry appropriates revolutionary rhetoric and discourse in sympathy with the movement for black liberation. That he himself obviously considered his work revolutionary is evident in his mode of narration. In a statement that is reminiscent of Frantz Fanon's much-discussed theories on violence, decolonisation and revolution, Nortje asserts in his 1962 poem 'The exiles silenced' that 'violence', when it 'delays too long, paralyses its active self' and 'unveils only fangs' that are inevitably 'superficially' oriented 'scares' (*AD* 22).[3] Es'kia Mphahlele has observed that 'Towards the end of the sixties, poetry emerged from among young students who, as members of the South African Students' Organisation (SASO), were hauled before the courts to answer to charges of inciting people to violence through their verse' (Mphahlele 56). When he wrote 'The exiles silenced', Nortje was just out of school and was an angry young black man, who, as Alvarez-Pereyre argues, composed 'poems which most effectively expressed the deeper reality of the sixties'. As a result of the power of his poetry, Alvarez-Pereyre contends, Nortje's death became the 'tragic symbol' of the times (Alvarez-Pereyre 22).

This argument is confirmed somewhat by 'Mother republic', a poem in which Nortje inscribes the figure of the African mother as a broken body, a product of the culture of violence that the South African state represented around 1960, when the poem was written. The persona of the poem describes the numbness and inertia that is imposed on him by the overbearing apparatus of the South African state. The embodiment of the nation or the state as an oppressive instrument for its peoples is articulated thus: 'Through dungeon-mesh the barbed wire spikes / Your crop of toil-potatoes wrung / From rains of blood – now blind me / Too, and numb ...' (*AD* 3). The elliptical nature of the narrative – the fact that Nortje refuses to close it – is reflective of the extent to which the story of state brutality is a continuous one. The Sharpeville massacres had already happened by the time the poem was written. Thus Nortje demonstrates how he was a product of the culture of resistance of the times: 'Mother, my muscles feel nothing, but temptation / To succumb ...' Yet succumbing or yielding to the dominant and oppressive system remains a mere 'temptation' (5).

Nortje might not have been a political activist, yet he can be described as a public intellectual whose poetry reflects a politicized consciousness. 'The exiles silenced' is a self-reflexive statement on the role of the intellectual, or the artist or poet in his community. Interrogating the prevailing notion that 'actions speak louder than words', the poem comments ironically: 'About action all we know revolves / around the easy friability of words' (22). This reflects the poet's scepticism regarding the customary bifurcation of theory and praxis. Nortje's ruminations are particularly significant because the 1960s saw writers of protest in South Africa becoming increasingly vocal in their demands that equality and independence be granted the black majority. This political agitation occurred at the same time as the Afrikaner state became more repressive and intolerant.[4] Nortje's desire for revolution and change in apartheid South Africa also permeates the openly contestatory discourse of 'Change,' which was published in the same year as 'The exiles silenced.' It is a narrative that begins with an inquiry on 'what change would mean' (*AD* 23) and remains assured by the end of the necessity of 'engineering change' (*AD* 23). Here, as elsewhere, Nortje validates political rhetoric and almost equates it with revolution when he asserts: 'Words burn in me / flailed by you' (*AD* 23).

The ideological project of 'Dogsbody half-breed,' written in Canada in 1970, and which ostensibly displaces Nortje from the immediate cultural, socio-economic and political centre and at the social and physical margins of his country is again a powerful claim for identification with the nation. Particularly as far as a critical South African historical discourse is concerned, Nortje legitimizes a narrative of black self-awareness. In this poem many of the categorical markers and descriptors that subtend colonialism and imperialism are present. Nortje talks, for example, about the 'magnet of exotica that draws / sailors from their holds, blood from the sword' (*AD* 344) in a clear reference to the manner in which the South African landscape was plundered as a result of Boer and Afrikaner adventure and expedition. The reference to the Zulu also alludes to the mythical power of the African nation that resisted Boer nationalism.

In producing such fictionalized historical narratives, Nortje's poetry gestures at a fundamental fact. Although coloured and therefore inhabiting a specific locale within the South African racial imagery, he is speaking for the oppressed majority as a whole. Venter's observation on the nature of identity politics within apartheid society is instructive here: 'The rumbling political content of 16 million black souls who share their shores and their aspirations is, in reality, only an extension of what is called the coloured problem, magnified in essence, finality and interpretation of the law' (Venter xiv). One has to take issue then with a comment that Alvarez-Pereyre makes when comparing the work of Nortje to that of some of his contemporaries – older poets like Anthony Delius, Dennis Brutus and Cosmo Pieterse, and those closer to Nortje in age and time like Oswald Mtshali and Mongane Wally Serote. Showing the different ways in which the work of the 'coloured' Nortje and the 'black' poets Mtshali and Serote have been shaped by the ideology and politics of apartheid, Alvarez-Pereyre observes that:

> Although Nortje belongs to the same age group as Mtshali and Serote ... a world separates them. His preoccupations, his themes, his style and his 'accent' are all different. It is a question of personality, certainly, but also of circumstances: Nortje, a Coloured, encountered fewer social and racial handicaps than his two contemporaries, brought up in the Transvaal; he started school earlier than they did and was able to go to university. (Alvarez-Pereyre 1984:155)

Clearly, the poetry of 'coloured,' white' and 'black' South Africans, as Alvarez-Pereyre convincingly demonstrates, is significantly shaped and informed by the peculiar socio-economic, cultural and political circumstances of the individual poets and their respective ethno-nationalities.

Yet it is possible to collectively distinguish the ideological value of the poetry of these writers in terms of their common politics of resistance. If as a result of official racial classifications and hierarchizations Nortje appeared to be more privileged than the average black person in South Africa because he was coloured, being coloured was equally problematic.[5] As a 'young coloured woman who had fallen pregnant' by a 'white student', Norjte's mother, Cecilia Nortje, suffered racial discrimination (*AD* xix). Like Bessie Head, whose mother was ostracized for having an affair with a black man, Cecilia Nortje's crossing of the racial border in marriage was considered an ' 'illicit' union', and her marriage no doubt failed partly for this reason.[6] Nortje is emphatic about this in 'Dogsbody half-breed' where in direct reference to his mother he asserts: 'Maternal muscle of my mixed-blood life / with child were you heavy, with discontent rife' (*AD* 344).

As a result, Nortje himself suffered.[7] In 'Dogsbody' Nortje refers to himself as 'hybrid' (*AD* 345), thus ruminating on his split subjectivity and the combination within him of white and coloured ancestry. Coloureds were and are as traumatised as blacks. Each group may experience arguably different levels of oppression, but as a politically conscious artist Nortje was aware that oppression, whatever form it takes, always triggers for the individual or the group debilitating forms of self-fragmentation and anxiety. If any privileges accrued to him by virtue of his being coloured, he rejected them by speaking against a system which historically had always invented tags and labels for all those it considered Other.[8]

What is important, then, is Nortje's awareness that he was representing an oppressed group among other oppressed groups within the South African nation. Moreover, though officially designated as 'coloured', Nortje's ideological vision encompassed the historical oppression that South Africans as a whole had faced.

Merely by virtue of his being a coloured individual who sought to free himself from the domineering political apparatus of the South African state, Nortje spoke on behalf of many others, and particularly the oppressed black majority. Here it is possible to compare Nortje to Bessie Head, another coloured South African exile, who wrote:

> If I had to write one day I would just like to say *people is people* and not damn white, damn black. Perhaps if I was a good enough writer I would still write damn white, damn black and still make people *live*. Make them real. Make you love them, not because of the colour of their skin but because they are important as human beings. (Head 1990:6)

The transgressive ideological value of Head's statement lies in the fact that her critique of a rigid racial system is not done only on behalf of her fellow coloureds, but is generally reflective of the aspirations of all oppressed South Africans seeking liberation (Goldin 1987:178).

That Nortje saw the identity that 'coloured' represented as embodying a contested realm of negation and self-validation is encapsulated in the tension generated in the self in 'Solving the crossword', a poem in which Nortje uses the deprecating word 'kaffir' (*AD* 58). In this despondent poem, he describes himself as a 'half-shattered' body who has to grapple with the 'old symbols' which lead to 'depression'. In a gloomy and ominous statement he asserts: 'I quite start to believe that death is the answer' (*AD* 58). However, seen against the poem's title it is evident that Nortje, although tormented and anguished, refused total self-annihilation – as the gerund attests, he was in the process of finding an answer.

Further to the politics of racism and exclusion, Nortje proclaims in an apparently banal statement that in South Africa the 'wrong pigment has no scope' (*AD* 171) for secure existence within society. Although the poem seems to state the obvious and the aversion towards racism has by this time become routine, one is nevertheless reminded of the agonizing statement with which Bessie Head begins *A woman alone*:

> There must be many people like me in South Africa whose birth or beginnings are filled with calamity and disaster, the sort of person who is the skeleton in the cupboard or the dark and fearful secret swept under the carpet. The circumstances of my birth seemed to make it necessary to obliterate all traces of a family history. (Head 1990:3)

Equally noteworthy is Nortje's ability to evoke the much-maligned Dark Continent as part of a deconstructive narrative in 'Return to the city of the heart,' a poem in which he associates himself not only with South Africa but with the African continent as a whole albeit in a language of paradox and self-irony: 'as a cool drunk, Afro-Saxon bred / winsome intellectual (ex / Dark Continent – congratulate me here)' (*AD* 339). Nortje is alluding to the fact that moving from South Africa to England and to a place like Oxford could be perceived as a journey from barbarism into civilisation. However, he makes it clear that to adopt this stance would be tantamount to rehearsing the stereotypes of colonial discourse. Thus he writes that 'I am back ... / wishing not to appear soulsick, washed up, blackmailed, whitewashed' (*AD* 339). These lines were written after Nortje had experienced a different kind of exile in Canada. Not only does he invert the psychological make-up of a colonial discourse, by describing himself further as 'footsore and war-weary' (*AD* 339), he forces his readers to recognize his mounting awareness that there is no substitute for home (South Africa). The phrase 'abortive America' (*AD* 339) captures this homesickness succinctly as it becomes a synecdoche for all of Nortje's experiences in exile. Nortje has produced a narrative that deconstructs the colonial myth of the Dark Continent.

Nortje's physical and psychic alienation and marginalization are usefully examined through Edward Said's argument that if exile is a condition over which displaced people have very little control, then it is mainly because the exile

> ... must have the independence and detachment of someone whose homeland is 'sweet', but whose actual condition makes it impossible to recapture that sweetness, and even less possible to derive satisfaction from substitutes furnished by illusion or dogma, whether deriving from pride in one's heritage or from certainty about who 'we' are. (*AD* 407)

Alvarez-Pereyre makes a similar argument when he describes how Nortje's poetry follows a time-honoured tradition of exiled South African writing:

> Then came the day when Nortje in his turn took the road of exile. Legally as a student, but it was in exile all the same: in order to find happiness, he would have to find a way to blot out the past, to forget everything the emigrant takes with him in his luggage, everything he has left behind. This man exiled from himself, *this outsider in his own country*, uproots himself ... There only remains, then, the bitter taste of conditional freedom, that of the man without a country. For the passport issued by the oppressor is in no sense the key to some kind of citizenship; it is hardly even a door half-opened onto an elsewhere scarcely more satisfactory than the here denied him. (1984:154)

Alvarez-Pereyre is correct to argue that Nortje, like others before him, was a 'man without a country'. Nevertheless, it is also the case, as David Bunn (1996) observes, that it was the 'dramatic, tidal return of an exiled and sequestered population' that led to 'the emergence of a new nation' in South Africa in the immediate post-apartheid years (Bunn 1996:33). One way of further elaborating Bunn's argument is to say that the experience of exile within South African identity politics, as much as it is informed primarily by notions of alienation and displacement, also has firmly anchored within it perpetual legitimations and affirmations of emplacement.[9]

Nortje continually projected himself as a voice of his nation and as a critic who was aware of the complicated history of inequality and racism that defined him as an outsider. Nortje, a product of the tradition of resistance to apartheid represented by the likes of his tutor, Dennis Brutus, affirmed himself as a South African even in the face of palpable marginalization from his country.[10] Consequently, South Africa, always overtly politicized, remains a major referent in his poetry. In poems such as 'My country is not', 'Poem: South African', 'Exit visa', and 'Dead roots' – in which Nortje describes himself as 'a dispersed hotnot' and a 'disparaged Jew' (391) – he stakes an important claim for identification with his nation. These poems depict exile as a paradoxical condition, one in which the exiled critic, writer, artist or poet simultaneously appeals to and legitimizes exile's opposing signifiers and markers of identity formation: home, nation, national identity, nationalism.

I have so far argued that nothing illustrates the tensions and ambivalences of Nortje's imaginative vocation better than the fact that although his poetic itinerary derives first and foremost from a personal experience of exile and isolation, the sense of community and nation-ness in his poetry is also very largely foregrounded. Consider also the simultaneous articulation of displacement and emplacement in 'Native's letter,' a bitter but somewhat controlled diatribe in which South Africa becomes 'my dear land' (*AD* 361). The opening sequence of this poem, an oxymoronic passage that reflects the generally apocalyptic and utopian impulse of much of Nortje's writing, includes South Africa among the 'habitable planets' that are 'unknown or too / far away from us to be / of consequence' (*AD* 360). When Nortje, whom Ursula Barnett includes among the South African poets who refused to 'create in the stifling atmosphere of censorship and harassment' wonders what the exile must do 'To be of / value to his homeland' (*AD* 361), he reaches the conclusion that he will have to 'delve into mythologies perhaps' to 'carry on memories apocryphal / of Tshaka, Hendrik, Witbooi, Adam Kok / of the Xhosa nation's dream / as he moonlights in another country' (*AD* 361). 'Native's letter' was written just before Nortje's death in 1970. However, it is evident that even at that point, despite his having been so long in exile, Nortje was determined 'to let no amnesia' (*AD* 361) about his nation overcome him.

Clearly, although he is describing South Africa from the viewpoint of an alienated individual, Nortje affirms his place in the country from which he is exiled by demonstrating his knowledge of the nation's history and its mythology. This contradicts Bunn's argument that '[d]espite his desperate effort to find equivalences, there is for Nortje no mythopoeic frame of reference that can help him process the South African landscape' (Bunn 1996:39). It is not the case either, as Barnett argues, that 'like all the black writers who left South Africa, Nortje never thought of himself as anything but an exile' (Barnett 1983:86). Given his obsession with his homeland, and his engagement of South African national mythology, it is important to bring Nortje to the fore as a poet of the nation. This is more so as Nortje's poetry is commendable for being an all-inclusive endeavour at nation building. In examining his mythopoeic cosmology, or the mythical universe from which he draws, the cautious reader is struck by the juxtaposition in the poet's obviously fertile imagination of the legendary Chaka the Zulu and other individuals who obviously occupy important spaces in the tradition of coloured and Afrikaner mythology. It should also be noted, however, that the specific reference to Chaka in 'Native's letter' is indicative of Nortje's desire to inscribe the black body within a South African historical imagination and national memory that is noted for its exclusive and dominant ideological practices. Nortje repeats this conscious ideological manoeuvre in 'Draft history,' where he declares his aim 'to show a black mane at the nape / under the oppressor's stolid pity' (*AD* 260).

Such self-conscious ideological postures help counter a dominant white-settler nationalist discourse that would deny black and coloured South Africans a place in history. Nortje's fictional account coincides ideologically with the historical analysis of South African society provided by Bernard Magubane in *The political economy of race and class in South Africa*:

> The African people are struggling not only against the illegal forms of the
> white settlers' social practice, but also against the all-embracing, universal

exploitation they experience under capitalism. They are challenging a history of violation that goes far beyond the juridical, into that which is economic and social as well. (1979:xii)

While it may be easy to question the descriptor 'African people' given the complex nature of racial hierarchies and the 'caste' system in South Africa, I have already demonstrated that Nortje's writing contests racialist and capitalist oppression as a whole, particularly in the sense in which a conglomerate of oppressed saw themselves pitted against a dominant minority in South Africa. Although he did not personally experience the kind of exploitation of black or African labour he describes, he writes: 'I am aware of having spent ... the last ounce of energy for the master of my salt' (*AD* 344). By referring to the 'overland / expansion into farm and mine' (*AD* 344) of the South African landscape, Nortje speaks on behalf of dispossessed South Africans generally.

Nortje's creative documentation of the plight of the oppressed peoples in South Africa reflects the argument by Amritjit Singh that while '[t]he dominant group in any nation-state often resorts' to 'mental or cultural ellipses, and to general forgetfulness' to legitimize itself at the expense of others, marginalized individuals and groups often empower themselves against this mode of domination via self-empowering counter-discourse of resistance (Singh et al 1996:5). It is a politically conscious Nortje who condemns the actions of colonialism thus: 'your bastardies, abortions, sins of silence / those marooned, dragooned, those massacred or shackled / by your few chosen from the many called' (*AD* 344). When the narrator evokes the memory of 'the growers of wine / beyond whose vineyards stretched the purlieus' before 'there was an overland / expansion of farm and mine,' Nortje reveals his knowledge that the gradual colonization of South Africa went hand in hand with the exploitation of African labour. Again, when the poem describes the 'ammunitioned' settlers who penetrated 'the heartland' (*AD* 344) of South Africa, Nortje is registering the simple fact that the nineteenth-century colonial wars in South Africa 'gave the white settlers the best lands and a considerable measure of control over African labour' (Magubane 1979:9). As Magubane further argues,

African labour was exploited in a constantly changing environment as the development of mines and farms, of secondary industries and towns changed the methods by which the conquerors secured their surplus. The mountain of labour legislation, beginning with master and slave codes, is an indispensable raw material for understanding the politics of racial inequality in these changing circumstances. (1979:9–10)

Nortje found it important to interrogate apartheid away from the country because he considered his writing to be part of a counter-discourse of South African nationalism and as a narrative of contestation of a dominant discourse of nationalism.

To comprehend Nortje's political vision, which is reflective of his general participation, even immersion in the debates and discourses that sought to define a South African national identity between the 1960s and the 1970s, it is useful to remember Adorno's argument that works of art do not 'leave the real empirical world behind, producing a counter-realm of their own, a realm which is an existent like the empirical world' (Adorno 1986:2). Instead, as Adorno contends, 'aesthetic form' is always invariably 'a sedimentation of content', so that even what seems like 'pure art' derives from 'external content' (1986:7).

Critics have sometimes found it difficult to see the connection between Nortje's aesthetics and his politics. In his otherwise illuminating discussion of Nortje, Klopper contends that:

> Ironically the very complexity of Nortje's vision also forms the basis of what may be seen to be his poetic failures. If Nortje characteristically endeavours to relate the external circumstances of his life to his inner experiences, if he seeks to articulate the ways in which the personal and the political, the social and the subjective are interrelated, it is not uncommon for communication to break down in the poetry, leaving the reader bewildered by what appears to be *an incommunicable, subjective experience in which the objective referents appear to be absent.* (*AD* xxviii; emphasis added)

Klopper cites the last four lines of 'Interruptus' to illustrate this argument:

> The universe's now gloomed
> calisthenic sense calls for
> circumstances of the soul poem:
> render not trivialities. (*AD* 285)

I would suggest that the 'objective referents' that Klopper cannot identify in this poem are to be found in the socio-cultural, economic and political forces of domination that regulated the lives of Nortje and many like him. This is implied also in the ideological tenor of Nortje's self-conscious tirade against the unease that he feels about his 'universe' or his world. Consider carefully, again, the poignant and distressing statement: 'The universe's now gloomed / calisthenic sense calls for / circumstances of the soul poem.' This is a deeply existential discourse that emanates from Nortje's alienation from and disillusion with his society. Nortje's pithily stated imperative that 'the soul poem: / render not trivialities' unravels some of the tensions and ambiguities that inform his ideological project. Both in his imagination and in real life the world is gloomy for generating a constricting ambience. The issues at stake here are a set of interconnected factors – alienation, disenchantment, the unsatisfactory politics of Nortje's time and various unmentioned causes of disaffection.

It is by paying attention to such particularities that we can draw connections between Nortje's voyages of self-discovery as he moved first from South Africa, then to England and Canada and back to England. To locate Nortje's writing within the historical conditions of his lifetime, even to evoke some of the specific cultural and political experiences which shaped and informed his identity as an exiled South African national or citizen is also to engage with what Adorno, in 'Art, society, aesthetics' describes as 'the intrinsically historical nature of aesthetics' (Adorno 2).[11] Adorno contends that 'True art challenges its own essence, thereby heightening the sense of uncertainty that dwells in the artist.' As such 'Art becomes a qualitatively different entity by virtue of its opposition, at the level of artistic form, to the existing world and also by virtue of its readiness to aid and shape that world' (2). Although in all respects Nortje's life and the creativity that issued of it were dominated by the torment and exasperation of self-fragmentation and self-debilitation, his was also an art that in Adorno's terms sought to 'shape' the world.

Notes

1 The terse and captivating phrase 'poet, coloured and South African,' is taken from Jacques Alvarez-Pereyre: 'If you live in solitude, then you must as well choose your own. On 8 December 1970, Arthur Nortje, poet, coloured, South African, "took" his own life. Nortje's poems read like a story: the story of the 1960s, his own story. A story in the form of poems, of fragments of a diary, of letters. Poems in the form of a malaise, of 'ill-being' ' (Alvarez-Pereyre 154).

2 Al J Venter, xiv, provides information on how The South African Population Registration Act (No 30 of 1950) and Proclamation R123 of 1967 had ensured that coloured South Africans were classified 'negatively' as a 'minority group'. However, as Goldin argues, 'Coloured identity does not necessarily correspond with the official classification' by the South African government. '[M]any people reject the official race designations' (178). The same might be said for the notion of 'blackness' as inferior. See Magubane (1996).

3 Frantz Fanon, whose *The wretched of the earth* is seen by many to be *the* manifesto for a Third World revolution, begins his chapter 'Concerning violence' with the following statement: 'whatever may be the headings used or the new formulas introduced, decolonisation is always a violent phenomenon' (Fanon 27). In citing Fanon I do not mean to repeat the stereotype that he was an apostle of violence. For a serious critique of misrepresentations of Fanon, see David Macey, *Frantz Fanon: a life*. Fanon's theories on violence have been misrepresented. In his stimulating biography Macey corrects such mis-impressions.

4 Consider, for instance, Lewis Nkosi's argument:

> Sharpeville was the culmination of a political turmoil during a decade of extra-parliamentary opposition ... Sharpeville and the brutal massacre of unarmed Africans marching to a local police station brought us bang into 1960 and into a different era altogether. Henceforth the times will be troubled indeed! (6)

5 Even those of Nortje's experiences that we are not privy to and the historical circumstances that dictate them are partly conveyed in Venter's interview with a randomly selected coloured man:

I asked a Coloured man to explain what he understood by being classified Coloured; he shrugged his shoulders and hesitated a moment before answering: 'Problems, real problems,' the man said seriously. Then moments later he added: 'Who really knows what a Coloured is? They classify us, they categorise us according to their ideals and they keep us apart from the rest – in our own interests – we are told. Then they move us out of our homes, our villages and towns and churches. But unlike Africans we are not Xhosa or Zulu or Sotho. We are South African. Our culture, our language, even our way of life is South African. What else are we but South African? God knows, enough of us died for South Africa during two world wars'. The man shrugged again (Venter 1974:1).

6 See Note on author, Bessie Head, *A woman alone: autobiographical writings.*

7 See Alvarez-Pereyre: 'Nortje suffered from an existential anguish which perhaps had its roots in his very early childhood, but which was fostered and developed by apartheid, and which goes far beyond any geographical setting' (*AD* 162).

8 See Goldin: the term coloured 'until the turn of the twentieth century, generally referred to all non-European people ... The official Cape census of 1875 included in the category 'coloured' all "non-European" people, including "Kafir proper" (*AD* 158).

9 My argument goes against the general grain of Bunn's argument, which locates Nortje *primarily* as a poet of exile.

10 Brutus decried Nortje's 'timidity' in his poetry, but equivocated when confronted by Cosmo Pieterse, and described Nortje's work as indicating 'a tremendous willingness to grapple with reality' (Duerden & Pieterse 1972:60, 61).

11 Among 'the bewildering array of impressions' which form tropes in Nortje's work, Bunn lists the notes on 'exile, his aesthetic theories, drinking bouts, film plots, sexual encounters, the imprisonment of South African friends', and 'even the excruciating pain caused by his piles' (33).

Works cited

Adorno, Theodor. *Aesthetic theory,* eds Gretel Adorno & Rolf Tiedemann. Trans C Lenhardt. London: Routledge & Kegan Paul, 1986.

Alvarez-Pereyre, Jacques. *The poetry of commitment in South Africa.* Trans Clive Wake. London: Heinemann, 1984.

Barnett, Ursula. *A vision of order: a study of black South African literature in English, 1914–1980.* London: Sinclair Browne; Amherst: University of Massachusetts Press, 1983:26.

Bunn, David. 'Some alien native land': Arthur Nortje, literary history, and the body in exile', *World Literature Today* 70.1 (Winter 1996):33–44.

Duerden, Dennis & Cosmo Pieterse eds, *African Writers Talking.* Oxford: Heinemann, 1972: 51–61.

Fanon, Frantz. *The wretched of the earth.* Trans Constance Farrington. Harmondsworth: Penguin, 1967.

Goldin, Ian. 'The reconstitution of coloured identity in the Western Cape,' eds Shula Marks & Stanley Trapido, *The politics of race, class and nationalism in twentieth century South Africa*. London: Longman, 1987:156–181.

Head, Bessie. *A woman alone: autobiographical writings*. Selected and edited Craig MacKenzie. London: Heinemann, 1990.

Macey, David. *Frantz Fanon: a life*. London: Granta, 2000.

Magubane, Bernard Makhosezwe. *The political economy of race and class in South Africa*. New York and London: Monthly Review Press, 1979:xii.

Mphahlele, Es'kia. 'Landmarks of a literary history in South Africa: a black perspective', eds Michael Chapman, Colin Gardner, & Es'kia Mphahlele, *South African English literature*. Johannesburg: Ad Donker, 1992: 37–59.

Nkosi, Lewis. *Home and exile and other selections*. Longman: London and New York, 1983.

Nortje, Arthur. *Anatomy of dark: collected poems of Arthur Nortje,* ed Dirk Klopper. Pretoria: Unisa Press, 2000.

Said, Edward W. *Culture and imperialism*. London: Vintage, 1994; Chatto & Windus, 1993.

Singh, Amritjit, Joseph T Skerrett, Jr, and Robert E Hogan. 'Introduction: Uncle Hansen's children: Are they?', eds Amritjit Singh, Joseph T Skerrett, Jr, and Robert E Hogan, *Memory and cultural politics: new approaches to American ethnic literatures*. Boston: Northeastern University Press, 1996:3–18.

Venter, Al J. *Coloured: a profile of two million South Africans*. Cape Town: Human & Rousseau, 1974.

Chapter 6: Arthur Nortje's technical accomplishments

Tanure Ojaide

Arthur Nortje died at a young age; his work received little substantive attention in his lifetime. Posthumous criticism coincided with the publication of *Dead roots* and the selection of his poems for anthologies. Since then the poet has received the attention of literary scholars, as noted in Appendix B bibliography. Nortje's relatively short poetic career – a decade – together with his mixed background in the apartheid South African situation and his later expatriation to England and Canada have kept him off the screen for long. However brief his literary career, it was very intense and makes him comparable to Nigeria's Christopher Okigbo, a poet who died young, but had a lasting impact on his national and continental literatures. There is now an adequate body of work from which to glean his achievements.

As a person of mixed blood (a *kleurling* in Afrikaans) in apartheid South Africa, Nortje was a victim of the apartheid system that he wrote against, much like his mentor, Dennis Brutus. Nortje's expatriation did not remove him from always wrestling with or tackling the socio-political, spiritual and psychic problems arising from the country he left and the problems of which he internalized (see the chapters by Klopper, Nuttall, Volk, Osei-Nyame and Gagiano). His poems in London for Cosmo Pieterse and thoughts of Robben Island testify to this. His imagination always bore the South African situation wherever he found himself. Revisiting his poetry, the critic notes its relevance to place and its deserved position in South African and African literature. Nortje cuts a mark in African literature in technical accomplishments that mere longevity of career does not. I thus intend to discuss the technical achievement of his poetry, which learning, practice, passion, thematic intensity, and other factors bring about.

Many of Nortje's poems are problematic editorially. The poet sent many to friends, who, after his death, submitted them to editors for publication. Such poems might have held the status of work in progress for Nortje. To make matters worse, Dennis Brutus and Dirk Klopper have taken liberties with the poems (*AD* xxxii). For instance, I suspect that 'Everywhere I looked was me' and 'Mirror prison of the self' are the same poem at different stages of composition and might not have been completed. Brutus did not follow chronology in his arrangement of *Dead roots* (quoted in *AD* xxxi–xxxii). Besides, some of the poems are rough drafts 'appearing exclusively in the Notepads, the School Diary or the little Exercise Book' (*AD* xxiv). So, the critic of Nortje's poetry has to deal with the poems as they are published with the understanding that one is dealing with versions of poems that might not be final. Nonetheless, Klopper's *Anatomy of dark: collected poems of Arthur Nortje*, the most comprehensive extant collection, is the primary text.

Two approaches recommend themselves in the discussion of Nortje's technical accomplishments in his poetry. As a result of the carefully dated poems that editors have tended to arrange chronologically as Klopper has done, one strategy is to see the poetry as developing technically from the early poems in South Africa to the expatriate poems in England and Canada. The other strategy is to take a holistic view of his poetry, which, irrespective of period, carries the technical skills of a fine poet. I intend to use the two strategies simultaneously. I use the term 'technical accomplishment' to mean poetic techniques, stylistic features, overall use of language that includes images, figures of speech and sound, and form. As is common to most poets, in Nortje's poetry content conditions style and form (and, as Hewson and McPhail's chapter shows, reader responses). Thus, while the focus will be on language, style and form, the poet's ideas, feelings and themes will necessarily be touched. Klopper, for instance, in recognition of this symbiotic relationship between content and form, observes:

> If Nortje characteristically endeavours to relate the external circumstances of his life to his inner experiences, if he seeks to articulate the ways in which the political and the personal, the social and objective, are interrelated, it is not uncommon for communication to break down in poetry, leaving the reader bewildered by what appears to be an incommunicable, subjective experience in which referents appear to be absent. (*AD* xxvii)

While I dispute Klopper's view of a breakdown in communication in Nortje's poetry, I agree that complex ideas and feelings seek expression in similarly complex language and form.

Nortje's poems, despite occasional editorial variations, easily fall into three groups that time and place accentuate: the poems written in South Africa between 1960 and 1965; the expatriate poems in England and Canada written between December 1965 and 1969; and the last poems written also in Canada and England in 1970. There are variations and developments within these set periods. What is significant is the impact of each environment and personal or historical moment on the poet's imagination. Time and place colour his imagination and each setting inspires a series of poems that bear a particular mark that reflects a specific experience. The poet's ideas and feelings are results of the intersection of time and place in his personal life. From each environment and period he draws images to reflect the condition of his mental and emotional states. South Africa with its apartheid (as Osei-Nyame's chapter argues) remains the root of the poet's emotional swings. The fractured psyche arises from the impact of apartheid on his mixed blood heritage, a condition that elicits political response and also private response in his alienation at home and abroad. Thus, though he moves from South Africa, the 'state' (in all its senses: governance, emotional, psychic, and so on) follows him everywhere.

Nortje's early poems depict a young and talented poet whose tormented psyche goads him on to write passionate poems in a structurally ordered manner. Like any young writer's work though, his early poems show a reflection of his apprenticeship and a dedication from the beginning of a uniquely personal voice and a poet set on paying as much attention to content as to form. One hears echoes of Dennis Brutus and modernists like TS Eliot and Ezra Pound in the young Nortje. Brutus was the most popular anti-apartheid South African poet of the time and younger writers looked up to him for advice and inspiration. Nortje's indebtedness to the modernists is not surprising either because they were very popular in the schooling days of Nortje, and many African poets of his generation studied these poets and modelled their own works on their writings. When, for instance, in 'Hangover', he writes, 'The sun has now gone under the sunset, / the moon squats with a lonely pallor' (*AD* 76), he echoes Eliot's meditative and chant-like style, lines that also echo Christopher Okigbo's verses in the 'Watermaid' section of *Heavensgate* (*AD* 10–13). McLuckie also observes that 'Mirror prison of the self,' a later poem, opens with an echo of Eliot's 'Gerontion' (*AD* 5).

Brutus might just be an elder brother to him and they share similar situations in the apartheid system, but the senior poet's troubadour image is echoed in Nortje's 'Thumbing a lift'. Nortje, as much as Brutus, was trying to defend his mistress (South Africa) against perpetrators of apartheid. He was thus an errant knight. Brutus's use of words like 'spearpoint' also appears in early Nortje. The militant anti-apartheid atmosphere would have given rise to the use of such terms. After all, the African National Congress's military wing was *Umkhonto We Sizwe* (the Spear of the Nation). It is significant that these possible influences and echoes are mild and Nortje's voice remains undiluted and unique from the beginning.

A trademark of his poetry is the four-line stanza (quatrain). Nortje pays attention to structure and form, which give each poem a sense of cohesion. Both 'Midnight' and 'Thumbing a lift' are illustrative of this. In the former poem, as in many others, the rhyme scheme is randomly patterned – two or more lines rhyme in each quatrain/stanza as in:

Tonight, precisely at that wall
my room's floor pauses in its walk,
throws up a gaze, observes the clock.
Bulb and brandy begin to talk. (*AD* 13)

In the short poem 'Explanation', the rhyme scheme works better in the first
stanza than in the second, which is eye rhyme more than anything else. There
appears to be a conscious effort to impose a rhyming pattern on the second
stanza as a line ends with 'by' to run on to the next line. The rhyming of 'by'
and 'simplify' as of 'appetite' and 'yet' are rather strained. 'After study',
indicative of the poet's quick grasp of form, shows a special rhyme scheme –
abba cddc:

Felt hat under the raids of many blind
flies under the globe which holds me under:
brown study love makes loneliness foster.
Absent and silent you have been in mind.

To have exchanged your love for one
with surer prospects I could conspire:
but where in the world are those we desire?
Life's love to prove is the long delusion. (*AD* 115)

The poem also contains alliteration and in-rhyme such as 'love' and 'prove'.
There is further use of alliteration in 'Gnomic'.

Nortje also uses three-line and five-line stanzas to structurally pattern his
poems. A few like 'Soliloquy' are in uneven stanzas. As 1963 runs out, with
effects of wine, women, and perhaps drugs, the disciplined craft is loosened as
if the persona is bursting out of a mould. However, overall, in the early poems
in South Africa, Nortje, while racked by the circumstances of his birth and the
apartheid conditions of the time, attempts to impose discipline on his feelings
and ideas. Nortje's practice is comparable to Dylan Thomas's use of the
villanelle form to control the overpowering emotional reaction to his father's
illness.

In addition to form and structure, Nortje's use of language and imagery
shows a high degree of artistic skill from the beginning. The use of metaphor,
personification, wordplay, axioms and shocking imagery confirms the early
maturity of Nortje's poetry. He plays with words such as in the poem for
Duncan, 'To a friend departing for Canada'. Also to the poet, 'this country is
raindry, havocked' (*AD* 11). 'Raindry' combines two opposite words to denote
the moral aridity of the South African apartheid government. He uses 'havoc'
not in the normal noun form but as a verbal epithet. He is rhetorically
humorous as in 'I'm in love. But why not happy?' (*AD* 61)

It is through the use of metaphor and personification that Nortje's early
poetry gains its strength. In 'We sat', the poet compares his love to a 'mysterious
flower'. In 'Serenade to a Sunday night', the poet says: 'moonbeams drench the

earth with sperm' (*AD* 41). The heart, in 'Initial impulses', is a 'barren ground'. Once in a while, there is the use of similes and metaphors in a mixed manner as in 'Joy cry', where he writes, 'like wind / youth's madness streams through orifices' (*AD* 125). A few examples will illustrate the poet's use of personification. In 'Change', 'Words burn in me' and they 'Often grew recalcitrant, refuse to detonate' (*AD* 23). In 'Poem for a kitchen', the poet writes of 'my healthy socks that hug the feet in nylon, / and underwear that breathes through pores of freedom' (*AD* 115). In 'Compassion', the 'blond / sun kisses the lady on the terrace' (*AD* 124).

Nortje's poetic power is apparent from the beginning in his incisive description of place, time and people. He has an intuitive sense of time and describes specific times of day and night, seasons and the environment around him. Titles of poems such as 'Midnight', 'Serenade to a Sunday night', 'Monday hangover', and 'A milky sunset' illustrate this point. To the poet, 'Anatomy of dark becomes an art / that in silence penetrates upon the rain' (*AD* 42). In these early South African poems, as in the English and Canadian poems later, there is copious reference to time of day, weather, winter, autumn (a structural and thematic device Bloomfield's chapter explores in greater depth), snow, rain, sundown, and plants such as lily and hibiscus. 'Guess all's not well' has many of these time and place observations. In the poetry there are 'muggy afternoon' and 'Belleville 7 am' The sense of detail is also in the description of body parts (as Nuttall's chapter illustrates) – fingers, eyes, and others. Put together, the images, metaphors, and personification, descriptive epithets, and specific details of time, place, nature, and people make Nortje's poetry concrete and sensuous. The lines bristle with vivacity. That is why, even where, as Klopper puts it, the communication breaks down, the energy of the language still pulls the reader along in Nortje's uncharted emotional forays.

If Nortje's South African poems (1960–1965) already show an accomplished poet, the poems in England and Canada (1965–1969) and last poems of 1970 reinforce that view. However, since content tends to condition form, the poet's alienation, new relationships and 'drift' have their impact on the technical aspects of the poetry. Arthur Nortje found South Africa unlivable – he left ostensibly to study abroad – but he was not free of its burden either in England or Canada. As Klopper observes of 1968: 'His poetry during this and the following year is as bleak as the frozen landscapes that hold him hostage. He uses his powers of keen observation to anatomise and abjure consumerist culture in Canada' (*AD* xxii). In 1970, after returning to Oxford, he 'writes poems largely of existential and political despair'. His tormented psyche has bearing on the structure, form and language of his later and last poems.

Being one whose poetry is autobiographical and personal, Nortje's movement out of South Africa to both England and Canada was bound to affect his poetry in content and subsequently in form. The new environment in both countries had its impact on the poet, who responded to the physical and geographical reality as well as to the social and political aspects. The new temperate Western environments and seasons, especially autumn and winter, become the repository of metaphors, which he increasingly draws from to express his bleak and hopeless mind. He is conscious of his new environment, different from where he used to be; hence

Cold of an unknown purity cannot swear
a man from tropical Africa more firmly:
crisp to the soul air's essence filters,
my hushed breath wreathes affirming tacit answers. (AD 152)

Old and new relationships affect his mood. His exile or expatriation cut him physically from his South African home that continued to haunt him and with which he began to make comparisons on *now* and *then*, *here* and *there*. Nortje shows distaste for North American consumerist appetite, a point that Bunn notes:

But silence, too, seemed to surround him once again ... Throughout the journal of his period in British Columbia are references to consumer insanity ... In Canada, Nortje began to talk and write self-consciously of a mass of people there who were divided along the lines of class ... (Bunn 1993 176)

As time goes on, he becomes more tortured in his already racked psyche, a mental prison house. Then he drifts more and more as he indulges in drinking and drugs. The new alienation, comparable to that of earlier poems as in 'Thumbing a lift', grows deeper and more soul-searing, a condition that eventually leads to his death.

It is in light of these factors abroad that Nortje's English, Canadian and last poems will be discussed. Does he lose control of craft? Does he drift and does that affect the form and language of the poems? Despite the fractured psyche, poetry served as a medium with which he attempted to impose order over his life.

Nortje establishes with subtlety the contrast between what he considers 'home', that is South Africa, and England and Canada. England is the 'sheltering island', where 'Gulls squawk among their smutty majesties' (AD 152). 'In Exile' elicits the paradox of the past and present as of home and exile being different and yet similar. Hence, the new place reflects the past, home. To him, 'My heart is / hollowed with the boots passing through' (AD 171), lines which, like Dennis Brutus's in 'Sirens, knuckles boots', remind one of the brutality of apartheid.

The poet carries this contrastive mode beyond geographical replication of past socio-political angst into personal relationships. He no longer loves the lady whose face is now 'muddied', even though 'So far together have we come from home' (*AD* 153). These contrasts enact tension in the poet's imagination, which symbiotically leads to terseness of style. Much of Nortje's poetry in exile carries this tension.

The post-South African poems are obviously more varied in structure and form, a quality that affirms the poet's growth and consistent devotion to craft. While the early poems tend to be mainly structured around quatrains, the poems in England and afterwards are highly varied. The poet experiments with five-line, six-line, seven-line, and eight-line verse stanzas. Besides, there are several prose poems such as 'Walking' and 'Senator's mortuary'. 'America' is organized in two segments as 'epistles'. Furthermore, the poet's vast repertory of form informs not only 'Requiem for a hunter' in the elegiac mode, but also 'Hymn', a prayer-like type of praise poem. 'I lie late' is in jagged lines:

> accumulation drop
> by   drop
>   of my clouded
>   talent
>   as voices rain
>   in the sun
>   or the horn of plenty
>
>   moon fosters
>   fraudulent hopes
>   in neon sculpture
> time makes it clear
> water wherein
>   I should sleep. (*AD* 301)

'Leftovers' is also in this jagged pattern, illustrative of the poet's dismembered psyche. There is even minimalist experiment, as in 'Haiku for H Rap Brown':

> Land built on my back
> so that when I'm standing up
> it is falling down. (*AD* 255)

This is a successful experiment that again captures the poet's troubled state of mind.

The poet must have felt confident and self-assured at this stage of his poetic career and so versatile that he is able to master different forms of the poetic genre. On occasions, as of 'requiem', 'hymn', 'epistle', 'haiku', and prose poems, he has to adjust his register to fit the form and the subject. These poems have become increasingly narrative of happenings around him, observations, and his own experience, which he wants to share with the reader. 'Cosmos in London' and others illustrate this direction.

Nortje's descriptive power intensifies as he describes English and Canadian landscapes. 'Courtenay rocks' is a highly accomplished poem reflective of the descriptive acumen of the poet:

> On the treetrunk looking towards the coastal
> mountains across the noon tide you can see
> sunlit snow, mauve haze, a pastel day
> and try to capture the soul of August:
>
> listenable music of the crabshell
> in the caverns of the rocks with water trickle:
> you may wonder what the crows
> are doing at the water's edge
> curious by the mudholes of crustaceans.
> Evening boats are resting in the beach-house
> above the empty channels. (*AD* 253)

The language of the poem is tactile. In these poems the poet studies the new and foreign landscape and with a painter's skill for details uses words to create a canvas that leaves an indelible impression on the mind. In the poems with broken lines, the poet seems to be aiming at emphasis, even as he pays attention to the rhythm of spoken words.

The poems of 1970 in both Canada and England have an inexorable thrust towards a cataclysmic end. Events of the poet's life, which have resulted in depression, were coming to a head. These poems show despair. To the poet, in 'Ditto love',

> The stint is finished:
> the shrill denunciations have been uttered.
> I have blown my horn sweetly, I have spent
> my loot on dusky beauties. I am back
> on the road doing one-night stands
> trying to sustain a smile
> > (the singer has retired)
> get the time in focus
> > (the drummer defected). (*AD* 340)

He admits to a licentious lifestyle in 'I have drunk up nights', as if at this stage the private and the public masks of the poet have merged into one.

'Nasser is dead' exemplifies the mature Nortje. The poet in many of the last poems is very passionate and no longer wields the discipline of regular stanzas. Simple techniques like alliteration and assonance are subtly integrated into the poem as in 'the Syrians are punished for their impunity' (AD 383). The language is simple but strong. The metaphoric repertory is so vast and well integrated that the poem generates a feeling of exhilaration as in:

> Millions mourn a train longer than the Nile:
> their flood of tears cannot be beaten back,
> and the rich silt is the salt on women's cheeks,
> sweat on the brows of men. (*AD* 385)

'Dead roots' resolves the tension between 'this temporary isle', which could be the poet or England, and Robben Island, the past and the present, which now merge into one vision. Paradoxically, the last poems are more readable and comprehensible, and doubtless attest to the strength of the poet who could not cope with many complications of his life.

Arthur Nortje developed as a poet, though the seeds of his technical achievement sprouted very early and really bloomed into a rich harvest of pleasurable poetry in the last poems. To a large extent, from the beginning the poet sat on a ticking bomb, which was bound to go off. The desperation of his life that he was so conscious of and every new environment created a field of imagination from which he wrote poetry that enraptures the mind and the senses through a high technical accomplishment. The intensity of feelings correspondingly brings forth intensity of expression. In Arthur Nortje, poetic content and form could hardly be better fused into a tense but necessary marriage.

Works cited

Brutus, Dennis. *A simple lust*. London: Heinemann, 1976.

Bunn, David. 'Arthur Nortje', *Dictionary of literary biography* vol 125:170–77, 1993.

McLuckie, Craig W. " 'Breathes there a man?': a note on allusion in Nortje's 'Mirror prison of the self' ", *Notes on Contemporary Literature* 32.3 (May 2002):5–7.

Nortje, Arthur. *Dead roots*. Eds Dennis Brutus et al. London: Heinemann, 1973.

Nortje, Arthur. *Anatomy of dark: Collected Poems of Arthur Nortje*, ed Dirk Klopper. Pretoria: Unisa Press, 2000.

Okigbo, Christopher. *Labyrinths*. London: Heinemann, 1971.

Chapter 7: Pedagogical approaches to Nortje's poetry

Kelly Hewson and Aubrey McPhail

> 'A Poet ... has no identity – he is continually in for – and filling some other Body ...'
>
> Keats, *Letters*

In the 'Editor's preface' to *Anatomy of dark*, Dirk Klopper remarks that 'Nortje's poetry has not been widely circulated'. This, together with the scant biographical information on Nortje, points to some of the challenge in teaching his poetry. Although Klopper and McLuckie and Tyner's biographical sketches in this volume provide a remedy to the latter; nevertheless, information about Nortje's poetic influences and his own poetic theory remains slim. Unlike the poetry of the Romantics or of Adrienne Rich, for example, we have virtually no 'touchstones' that might elucidate the preliminary question as to what the poet thought that poetry in general or his or her poetry in particular was meant to achieve or mean. For some poetry instructors, like Hewson, this presumed lack isn't an issue. For others, like McPhail, it is. But despite our different approaches, we both discovered that questions about Nortje's life and poetics, among other things, invariably come to the fore in teaching his poems to undergraduate students.

English 2235, uninspiringly described in the Mount Royal College calendar as 'a study of selected poetry written in English, with instruction in the writing of critical essays', runs for a fourteen-to-fifteen-week semester in the fall and winter terms.[1] In Hewson's case, the class was an evening one which met for three hours once a week; McPhail's classes in both terms were day classes. (The average number in each class was 30.) Hewson began her poetry class with students putting themselves on the map, so to speak, whether that be geographically, economically, religiously or otherwise. The answers to these questions of location are shared, even enacted, so that a sense of the particular class's community is felt.[2] A sample of responses to the question of location may give you a sense of her class composition: 'science student who left my English credit til the end'; 'I come from Punjab'; 'my parents are from Northern Ireland, but I'm Western Canadian and proud of it'; 'aspiring, totally broke singer-songwriter from a dysfunctional parental unit'; 'I'm from Red Deer but got the hell out as soon as I could'; 'I just got here from Uganda and am staying with my brother and his wife'; 'I'm a Mormon from Lethbridge'; 'a business student who has no time to read novels'; 'Plains Cree mother, European father but I choose to identify myself as a poet'; 'overwhelmed, under-funded single parent'; 'a bartender working 30 hours a week trying not to mess up school this time out'; 'buzzed-out boarder looking for some intensity'; 'an artist at heart who can't earn a living at it, so I'm trying to create an entrepreneurial identity'; 'I came to Calgary from Chile when I was 10'; 'I'm the only one here; my family is in Hong Kong'; 'I grew up in California'; 'I'm in science because my parents forced me to, but I really want to be a writer ...' McPhail's student populations were equally heterogeneous; he began his class by asking students to hand in note cards with some basic biographical information on them.[3] Despite our different methods of identifying our classes' characteristics, we were to find their diversity provided an epistemological apparatus by which to study the relationship between Nortje's poetry and our pedagogical 'experiments'.

Our discussions will consider the three Nortje poems found in the *Broadview anthology of poetry*, the text we have used in our first-year, one-semester courses. This anthology provides adequate footnotes to its poems and brief author biographies, but irritatingly no publication dates. Over two semesters, we asked our students to give a written response to: 'Letter from Pretoria Central Prison'; 'Immigrant'; 'Native's letter'. Mid-way through the first semester, Hewson grouped the Nortje selections loosely with poems about the pain of loss, re- and dislocation and/or imprisonment: Atwood's 'Journey to the interior'; Brand's 'Canto II'; Walcott's 'A far cry from Africa' and Awoonor's 'The first circle'. In Hewson's case, these pre-discussion responses were followed by a class discussion and, after that, a post-discussion written response, the point of the latter to allow the students to chart the difference, if any, between their views on the poems pre- and post-discussion. Were their questions answered? Have other questions emerged? Was initial confusion or incomprehension cleared up? Did the discussion enhance their appreciation of the poem, broaden their reading repertoire ...? She employs this double-sided reading journal to get the students to move beyond a kind of learned helplessness (which often characterizes responses to 'unfamiliar' poems) – 'I don't have a clue what this is about' – to encourage them to develop strategies that help them overcome the obstacles a particular poem may pose. Often those obstacles are simply due to a lack of resourcefulness – 'I don't know what 'salutary' means' – while others are more difficult to manage: 'I want to know who the speaker is, where he is and who he is talking to.'

The students' first introduction to Nortje in Hewson's class, as it often is with other poets, was complete reader response. Thematic context, at any rate, was hinted at by the inclusion of Nortje's poems in the above grouping. The students were instructed to read each poem and, as they were reading, to make explicit the questions arising from it, the obstacles to understanding, any speculations they had about meanings, to note any striking images, anything, in fact, that emerged from their encounter with the poem. McPhail, who organized his course more historically than thematically, presented the Nortje poems to his class near the term's end. They were considered after discussions of some of Heaney's, Ginsberg's and Rich's poems. He guided the students' responses more specifically than Hewson and asked them to try to give an account of what they thought the poems were about. Were any themes apparent? Did any ideas or feelings seem to preoccupy the poet in each or all of the poems? He asked if there were any notable tendencies or, conversely, any surprising idiosyncrasies in Nortje's ideas, images, figures, or tone. He also asked if there were any concerns or difficulties with respect to understanding the poems or the poet. Predictably, the responses varied, but some common hermeneutic threads appeared in the students' unravelling of the poems. And perhaps surprisingly, in McPhail's class, there was little discernable difference in the critical responses between the students who were given some biographical information about Nortje (in the first term) and those who were given none (in the second term). We will return to some of these similarities and differences in our discussion of the poems.

Certainly in literary studies some individual adaptation and effective implementation of the Socratic method is a feature of excellent pedagogy. And especially in poetry classes the balance between framing questions that are sufficiently central to a reasoned understanding of the poem and framing questions that are crudely leading to the student is a delicate matter. We want to invite the students to engage as fully as possible in their own interpretive and critical processes, and yet admittedly, we must lead with questions that, in the service of intelligibility and coherence, often court the danger of impinging on the students' own creative (mis-) conceptions. Mindful of this delicate balance, we not only want our students to identify prominent themes or preoccupations in the poems and to make reasoned inferences, but to invite discussion, generate discovery, augment insights and, hopefully, begin to clarify the poet's own moral, philosophical, political and psychological conflicts. In the spirit of these goals, we offer the following observations, insights, and suggestions for teaching Nortje's 'Letter from Pretoria Central Prison', 'Immigrant', and 'Native's letter'.

'Letter from Pretoria Central Prison' [*AD* 185-186]

Although the students' responses to and interpretations of 'Letter from Pretoria

Central Prison' varied considerably, some salient points of commonality emerged. Virtually all our students considered this poem the most accessible and easy to understand of the three. The following comment nicely captures the essence of the positive responses: 'Wow, I actually understand the theme and language in this poem – everyday language that's easy to understand.' However, a significant number of students also expressed their frustration at what they perceived to be the speaker's ambivalent or neutral attitude towards prison life, and some simply wanted to know the biographical 'truths' concerning the reasons for the speaker's incarceration or the length of his stay and so forth. Here are some of the comments in that vein: 'He seems happy, but I'd like to know why exactly he was there.' 'Two main things are missing: we don't know who received the letter and how he/she is related to the writer, and there's not a trace of what crime has been committed by the writer.' 'I liked this for the common theme, but what is his argument? What does he stand for? What does he believe in?' 'I'm confused regarding his view of jail.' 'He reminds me of Red in *The Shawshank redemption* – the guy who's been in prison so long he's afraid to leave.'

Interestingly, most of McPhail's students assumed this poem to be 'straightforward' with respect to the setting, speaker's identity and, in some measure, the 'purpose'. So it seemed pedagogically prudent to him to disregard the usual kinds of preliminary question designed to give a contextual handle on the poem. So he started with the concerns most commonly voiced by the majority of his students: What is the speaker's attitude toward prison? Why does he feel this way? In Hewson's class, the most frequently asked questions were of a 'truth-seeking' nature. Does the poem reflect 'true' experience? And if the poem isn't 'true', what is the significance of making the prison specific? Is the letter the poem is based on the truth about prison, or is it a reflection of what the writer of it knows the prison authorities want to hear? These questions then led to queries over the speaker's seeming neutrality about his plight and curiosity over the recipient of the letter: 'Is he comforting the receiver the same way Donne's speaker [in *A valediction: forbidding mourning*] is?' 'It sounds like he's writing to a penpal; it's so void of emotion.' Hewson's students also paid a good deal of attention to diction, like the adjective 'insurgent', typically used to describe political action, but here it's describing light and distance. Many loved the image of the 'rifled shadow' greeting the speaker's face, and even without the benefit of a familiarity with Foucault's *Discipline and punish*, many remarked on the atmosphere of surveillance it created.

Several students seemed concerned, perhaps in light of the attacks on New York and Washington DC, on 11 September 2001, about a prisoner being allowed to work with metal. Another wondered what possible work a blacksmith could be doing in a prison. Despite these kinds of mundane question, a number of other readers were struck by the beauty of the alliterative line which has the speaker 'forge' a 'forgetfulness' of more captivating worlds in work that absorbs him. But a brief mention of how Conrad's Marlow similarly praises the efficacy of the work at hand (perhaps as a means of forgetting the 'civilization' left behind or as a buffer against the temptation to indulge Kurtz's terrible freedom) allows us to suggest how the alliterative beauty may, in fact, mask a deep and disturbing ontologic anxiety – that indulging in the freedom of memory may forge new chains of pain and unrest – that 'hammer[ing] metals with zest' to 'forge a forgetfulness' may intimate an attempt to bind the body in fatigue in order to release the mind from the prison house of memory. But the next two lines of the poem seem to suggest a calm acquiescence on the speaker's part: 'The heart being at rest, life peaceable, / your words filter softly through my fibres.' The speaker's apparently antithetical responses reaffirmed the students' general uncertainty as to *his* precise attitude with respect to imprisonment. As one student commented, 'I feel pain in this man but acceptance', or as another put it, 'I'm baffled at what he's getting at. He's almost saying there's happiness in isolation.' And although several students assumed it was a woman to whom he was writing, and that it was *her* words which were 'filtering' softly through him, this still did not sufficiently answer the question of the speaker's apparent ambivalence. At this point the notion of irony of situation may prove helpful. What, then, is good about being in prison? One obvious answer might be that it allows time for contemplation after the 'active hours' that 'fly like sparks in the furnace'. Hence the earlier 'forgetfulness of worlds more magnetic' – forgetfulness of worlds with the extraordinary power to attract – like the larger world of politics – is, perhaps, a necessary condition to reach the kind of mental repose needed to contemplate the more immediate, personal world of human relations. So the prison house of memory turns out to be too general. It may be only one cell in the prison house – the memories of a country in strife and an unjust political system – that needs to be momentarily forgotten so that another's words might 'filter softly' through the fibers of the speaker's soul. This interpretation seems consistent with the rationalizing, ironic tone of the third stanza which most students picked up on.

Here the speaker's activism has been tamed; he's not unhappy; he is 'changed to neutral'; everything's done for him; all is managed, whereas she, on the outside, has to make decisions. And again, perhaps the speaker is rationalizing that, given his imprisonment, (self-imposed?) neutrality is the only viable response to the precarious war between political and personal obligations. However, these issues aside, numerous students simply struggled over the meaning of 'take gaps in pavement crowds' while others indicated the contrast between the disorder of the outside infrastructure (cracks in pavement) and the exercise yard in the next stanza, measured and contained with the 'cleanest stone'. Two students familiar with Austen appreciated her mention and one questioned why the speaker chose to read her. Was it because she too didn't typically fuss over the outside world but confined herself to detailing artfully her particular, closed world?[4] Another student wondered if Austen was chosen and mentioned in the letter strategically, as a sign of the prisoner's 'good behaviour'. S/he read the mention of Austen as an indicator that the prisoner was being 'rehabilitated' or striving to represent himself as such, and hoping that the qualities of Austen's *Persuasion*, as cited in Nortje's poem – 'elegance' and 'agreeableness' – would attach themselves to him.

These thoughts also offer, we think, an opportunity for instructors to raise briefly the thorny question of poetic identity already embedded in the students' remarks. Without risking theoretical obfuscation, one might introduce the prefatory quotation from Keats in order to clarify, examine, and extend the students' own ideas. In his 'Editor's preface', Klopper reminds us that 'the poems often provide insight into Nortje's personal preoccupations at a given time' and of 'the autobiographical nature of his poetry' (*AD* xxiv). And given the title of the poem, it is no surprise that virtually all of the students initially read the poem as a real letter or 'poetic epistle', the 'meaning' of which would be clearer in the welcome light of biographical facts. But when we point out that Nortje was never in Pretoria Central Prison or any other prison, their taste for the truths of biography became an anxious appetite for the internal 'truths' of the poem. This, of course, leads logically to the question of the speaker's identity. Does the speaker have a clear identity that the poem attempts to convey? Or is Nortje imaginatively filling another person's body, occupying the space of another in a kind of sympathetic identification?

With respect to stanza 4, nearly all the students commented on the striking juxtaposition of the beautiful, gentle descriptions of nature with the confinement emblematized by the exercise yard, the wall, the barbed wire, the sentinels' boxes. One student picked up on the phrase 'monastic white flowers' and drew the conclusion that the prisoner's enforced celibacy was affecting his response to nature. Another noted the repetition of 'white' in this stanza and wondered if that was reflective of the fact that the speaker hadn't seen the colour for awhile, that perhaps he was surrounded by an absence of colour. Still others wondered, as did one of McPhail's students, what the point of this stanza was: 'neat imagery, but what's its function?' One of Hewson's suggested it held echoes of Eliot in the sensual delight the speaker was taking in the curling wisps of smoke. This reader likened it to those many introspective moments in 'The love song', particularly the point where Prufrock is momentarily seeking refuge in the yellow fog. Another reader speculated that the speaker wasn't allowed to smoke so was enjoying vicariously the experience of watching another take pleasure in his cigarette.

The postcard quality of the syntax was noted in the concluding stanza. But of more interest to the students seemed to be the idea that one could listen to music and watch movies in prison. One wondered if this was a 'posh' prison. Several noted how accustomed the speaker becomes to routine. Many were glad, finally, to get some sense of whom the speaker was addressing – someone with kidney troubles, confined in a different kind of place, but confined nevertheless. Part of the unintentional humour and risk of reader response comes from misreadings such as the following. The same student who wondered if Pretoria Central Prison was 'posh' responded to Nortje's closing line 'sorry there's no more space' with this: 'What? You mean there's a waiting list to get in?' A good number of students were puzzled by the speaker's desire to have the correspondent date his/her reply, but one was quite moved by this final remark, and interpreted it quite eloquently: that the speaker, being forced to forge a signature of forgetfulness, being forced into neutral, has also been forced into a different relationship with time; it doesn't exist for him in the same ways; he requires a marker.

Hewson felt pedagogically compelled to begin a class discussion with questions designed to elicit contextual responses: Why 'Pretoria' prison? To link prison with South Africa. Many of us a couple of decades older than the majority of students we encounter often have to remind ourselves of the difference between what we consider history and that history from which the bulk of students draw. When we asked our classes what came to mind when they thought of 'South Africa', the overwhelming response was Aids. Several mentioned the high crime rate and one answered 'wicked surfing beaches' but not a single student mentioned apartheid.[5] In giving us the associations they did, they reminded us of the kinds of representation which have shaped their opinions of South Africa. For them apartheid was over; it was not even recent history. So the questions the class raised about the 'truth' of the experience of the poem led easily into some educative possibilities: an 'ancient' history lesson in which one could intervene with one's limited understanding and experiences and the students could build on with library and Internet research.

For instance, Hewson introduced them to Rita Barnard's article in *Research in African Literatures* in which she discusses apartheid as blocking the idea of a nation – that what apartheid did, among other nasty and brutish things, was to strictly regulate who was part of the South African nation and who wasn't. Movements were regulated – blacks restricted to homelands and townships; coloureds to specific areas and whites to whites only areas. The constriction, oppression, repression of apartheid, then, is manifested in the symbol of the prison – the prison becomes a kind of stand-in for the confinement of the South African nation under apartheid (2001:156–157).

Though she isn't much a believer in self-disclosure as a pedagogical strategy (too many past classroom memories of teachers talking about themselves as opposed to the texts or issues, or worse, as opposed to listening to the students), Hewson did talk about her recent sabbatical in Cape Town and a particularly memorable trip to Robben Island, the prison notorious for housing the political leaders of the ANC, the most famous being Nelson Mandela, for 26 years. The prison is now a commemorative site and as pilgrimages were made to it when it functioned as a place of incarceration so they are again.[6] One of the exhibits on Robben Island is called 'Cell stories'. The guides, former political prisoners themselves, walk visitors into a cell where you press a button and listen to a recording of a prisoner telling his 'cell' story. As well as telling their stories, former inmates have left in their cells some *thing* that somehow symbolized their stay on the Island. Encased in a box in his former cell would be the ex-prisoner's particular memento. In one cell there is a saxophone ingeniously constructed from bits of piping, errant wires and drainage tubes. In another there is a comb which an inmate waited for years to possess; in another, the paper of a cement bag upon which the internee did his lessons; in yet another there is a letter. Upon closer inspection, one realizes the salutation and closing are intact, but the entire body of the letter is blocked out. To this prisoner, such 'letters' were the heartbreak of his time there. Through this anecdote, Hewson hoped to impart to the students a more intense sense of how much scrutiny one would be under, that the letters one would send and receive would be so tampered with as to mean nothing. They would be strictly censored, and regulations on how much one could say, what one could say, to whom one could send and how often were strictly controlled.[7] This led to a discussion about the form and tone of Nortje's poem – that perhaps it was structured and imagined as a letter written under such circumstances, with the parameters of the speaker's self-expression rigidly defined, hence its abrupt end, complacent tone, and seeming indifference to imprisonment.[8]

'Letter from Pretoria Central Prison' is important, too, in drawing our attention to political as opposed to the kind of criminal behaviour we as North Americans might associate with grounds for imprisonment. Then we can speculate about what constitutes 'high risk' and who determines, after all, what 'high risk' is. In the South African context, as some students discovered on their research mission, it could be a matter of associating, however loosely, with a member of a banned political party. Whatever the political action this imagined speaker took, it was considered a threat to the regime. To answer the questions of the 'truth' of the letter, it would be worth positing to them whether or not they think a prison to be a place from which one could speak truthfully. And most of the students suggested that perhaps speaking truthfully was what landed some 'high risk political' types in prison in the first place.

'Immigrant' (written in July 1967) [*AD* 248-250]

Both McPhail's and Hewson's classes found 'Immigrant' the most challenging and confusing of the three poems. The general plea seemed to be that more information was needed to enhance their understanding. Not just historical or biographical information, but more clarity in terms of the 'situation' of the poem – to whom is he talking? Who are the 'you's in the poem? Where, exactly, is he coming from and what's his destination?

The opening admonition, for instance, proved quite worrisome to many. What, they wondered, was so threatening about 'Acton at noon' that one shouldn't travel beyond? Interestingly, several misread 'Acton' as 'Action' and wondered what 'Action' one shouldn't be taking beyond noon ... 'Is the speaker saying he should not have left? That he should have stayed in England and before that, South Africa?' 'Why would he not want to travel beyond a place full of [sic] Ayran-nation types and unrest?' asked one student, for whom the notion of immigration is clearly something one need not agonize over. Others picked up on the anger and resistance of the tone and wondered why, if he didn't like the idea of immigrating, he was, indeed, doing so. Hewson attempted to re-align and complicate their responses by reminding them that the twentieth century anyway, if not the twenty-first, was the century not only of wars and bombs, but of the migrant. Invoking Salman Rushdie's *Imaginary homelands*, she reminded her students that never before in history had so many transported themselves from their homelands to elsewhere, and because of the diverse backgrounds of many of their students, McPhail and Hewson were able to engage the class by having those who so wished to share their experiences of what it means to re-locate. And what we all discovered was that immigration involves a tremendous double or triple dislocation – geographical, psychic, and often linguistic. One of Hewson's students perhaps expressed the pain of loss best: 'no matter how awful the state of my place, it is where my heart is'.

The reference to Medicine Hat in southern Alberta was widely enjoyed because recognized. As one student put it, 'at last! I don't have to decode!' But this moment of clarity was immediately followed by disorientation: 'Whoa! Where the hell is Tuskaloosa? And what kind of a flight path is this guy on, anyway?' Several took offence at the speaker's characterization of Canada as a 'bulldozer civilization'. One of the more sophisticated readers, a fan of the beat poets, puzzled through the speaker's linking the trajectory of his movement from South Africa to England to Canada with the movement from puberty to adulthood. Frustrated to harsh judgment, s/he labelled the entire poem 'a masturbatory rant, without the skill ... of Ginsberg'. One of the several singer-songwriters in Hewson's class used associative strategies to make meaning, and mentioned a song by Liz Phair called 'Go west',[9] and suggested that the speaker in this poem, like the persona in that song, 'feels pushed to do something but feels shitty about the move'.

There was plenty of commentary about the next passage, focused particularly on the examination at customs, which to many sounded like a bodily assessment and, most pointedly, on the speaker's concluding metaphor: 'I am an acceptable soldier of fortune.' Hewson's students felt this was one of the key metaphors in the poem, and consequently she devoted a significant portion of class time to exploring it. To label one's self a 'soldier of fortune' is to attach the ideas laden in the term 'mercenary' to one's self. If you consider yourself a mercenary, you're someone who can be bought by or favourably disposed to do the work of a place, a side, which is not necessarily yours.[10] To link 'immigrant' with 'mercenary', as Nortje does, suggested among the following possibilities to her students: often, an immigrant is considered an 'undesirable' or is 'hired' because he or she fits some kind of profile. An immigrant is considered a suitable candidate because the country of immigration believes her to be on its side, working for its side. What the soldier of fortune or successful immigrant linkage suggests is that either, soldier of fortune or successful immigrant, can simply switch attachments from one country to the other; that neither the mercenary nor the immigrant is truly authentically engaged in the enterprise for which he or she has been hired or admitted. This discussion worked effectively to highlight ideas of deracination and uprootedness and served to personalize and problematize the situation of immigration for those assuming it a 'simple' process and one always willingly chosen.

The students picked up on the fact that perhaps the speaker had represented himself as one thing and the Oxford poetry in his bag would blow his cover: 'Why is he ashamed of the poetry? Is he afraid there's no need for artsy-fartsies in Canada?' Or, (and old stereotypes die hard): 'Does he think the Customs guys will think he's gay if they find out he reads poetry?' The point here, though, is that most noticed the speaker has represented himself as one thing to immigration and is making us aware he is more than that limited profile.

The following probably speaks of the students' desire to latch on to something recognizable, but a good number of them wondered what the speaker meant by 'chicken canadian style'. Several expressed concern that a new arrival to Canada was basing his judgments about 'our' chicken based on 'Western Arrow's' version of it. At any rate, at about the ninth stanza, most students identified the poem's tone and geography shift – one even suggested it became a whole new, albeit 'indecipherable', poem. A student with a knowledge of etymology or Greek (or both) talked about the meaning of 'metaphor' being 'transfer': and as the speaker was transferring from one place to another, so the poem itself was undergoing a transfer. Clearly the speaker *is* undergoing a transfer – as he's assessing himself about what he's embarking upon, in 'his mind's customs office', he's making himself sick.

The remainder of 'Immigrant' was barely comprehended. Over and over, the students were wondering who and where the 'you' was. Many were bothered by having their reading interrupted by all the footnotes. One noted the detailed cataloguing of specific geographical regions of South Africa and the repeated questions concerning the 'layers' of South African history, but couldn't figure out who the 'you' was that was 'required as an explanation'. Several gave up all attempts at close reading and 'travelled' to a place where they could make sense: most landed on the mention of 'Saskatchewan' and 'Vancouver' – 'okay, he's in Canada and maybe while he was on the plane he was thinking about Africa, but I still don't get the you and she and now there's another you' – and one landed, not all that carefully, on the mention of whisky. 'Yeah, I can see why he'd want to have a drink; to freshen his breath after being sick.'

There were several attempts to identify the 'you' and 'she' as they appear in the concluding stanza. One reader felt relieved for the speaker when he said 'I find I can read the road signs.' Things, he or she noted, did not have to be translated and were not as unfamiliar as he might have imagined: 'Maybe she is like you.' One student formed an intriguing hypothesis about this line, which ended with a common complaint: 'Maybe the 'she' is Canada and the 'you' is Africa and the speaker is collapsing countries with women. He's then collapsing all women with her and further declaring that all women are all things to all poets? Huh? I have real problems with all this collapsing.' As a result we spent some time as a community of confused but determined readers trying to untangle this final stanza, beginning with this student's observations of collapsing. The 'you', we decided, is metonymic of all women – whether that 'you' be his girlfriend or Africa. Hewson gave them some background on the trope of 'mothering' the land and the consequent (or subsequent) othering of women and wondered whether or not Nortje's speaker is indulging in both idealizing formulations. The line 'all of them are all things to all poets' particularly stuck out for readers, provocatively so. As one student remarked: 'gag, this is as bad as when Tom Cruise says to Renee Zellweger [in *Jerry Maguire*] "You complete me." ' When we explored the image following that line: 'the cigarette girl / in velvet with mink nipples, fishnet thighs, / whose womb is full of tobacco' the students extracted ideas of mothering (one had just read *The white hotel* and was remembering the prologue where the woman's nipples were pouring out milk in ecstatic quantities), whoredom (the fishnet thighs), and death (womb full of tobacco). When we looked at the cigarette girl, we entered into an intriguing discussion about what a cigarette girl, one of the icons of fifties femininity, might mean to a heterosexual male writing in 1967. We speculated that the image might have been conjured up nostalgically. Similarly, we considered what the associations around cigarettes might have been 35 years ago. An examination of cigarette ads from the late fifties/early sixties, championing the allure, sophistication and sensuality of cigarettes, astonished the majority of our classes, who are most familiar with the representation of smoking cigarettes as deadly. The same student who remarked on the collapsing of countries with women suggested that this collapse might mean that all countries, finally, are the same: they centre on commodities – gold in South Africa, tobacco in Canada, so he or she concluded 'it shouldn't be so difficult for this soldier of fortune to switch his allegiances'.

This discussion then led us to consider what position the poet was speaking from which led to lots of fruitful perceptions. We noted the powerlessness of the speaker, as identified by all his questions, and the fact that he positions the 'you' as the one who knows: 'you are required as an explanation'. Many students were piqued by this implicit demand and wondered what it meant. When we let the students know that Nortje himself immigrated to Canada from South Africa because of a South African woman who herself immigrated to Canada, the last half of the poem became clearer to them and all kinds of fascinating exchange occurred. Is she, his 'prairie beloved', going to 'function' for him as Eva, the Hottentot woman, operated for her Dutch masters? As a translator, as a sense-maker? And what does it mean to project this function on a woman? The class then began waking up to the place from which the speaker was speaking: from a set of assumptions about what 'woman' should be. We recognized that even the geography of his and the unnamed woman's homeland is filtered through the speaker's masculinity: 'I approached you under the silver trees. / I was cauterized in the granite glare / on the slopes of Table Mountain ...' And she was the rescuer then: she 'dredged' him from the 'sea like a recent fossil'. Is she going to rescue him again? So it would seem as he travels 'like eros over atlantis (sunk / in the time-repeating seas ...' He's the fossil; he's stuck. He has a need for her, so this 'immigration', we conjectured, is also a male quest that he hopes or imagines is going to play out in the new world as it did in the old – with a duplication of power relations. She's going to be the motivator, the one who will be all things to him: saviour, muse, mother, whore, translator, answerer of questions ...

In this part of Canada, most of us are familiar with the city of Hope, which we assumed to be 'the city of the saviour' referred to in the concluding lines of 'Immigrant', just as most of us in Alberta eat our apples after peeling off the BC (British Columbia) sticker. No student, though, had the mixed pleasure of listening live and ad nauseum, as McPhail and Hewson had when they were eleven and ten respectively, to Bobby Gimbey and his Young Canadians' Centennial song, so they had to hear it, misremembered and incomplete, from us:

north south east west,
there'll be happy times,
church bells will ring ring ring
it's the hundredth anniversary of
con-fed-er-ation
everybody
sing together
CA Na DA
now we are 20 million

And we all imagined the isolation, cynicism and possible bemusement a recent arrival to Canada, a young country, a 'bulldozer civilization', jubilantly celebrating its hundredth anniversary with cross-country train exhibits, an expo, pied-piperish songs, centennial pins, athletic programmes, might feel in Hope, BC, in 1967.

'Native's letter' (Toronto 1970) [*AD* 360-361]

'Native's letter', like 'Immigrant', elicited responses of confusion and challenge from the students. Here are some representative student responses: 'I don't understand this poem at all; you need alot [*sic*] of historical knowledge', 'The

95

poem gives the feeling of 'testing the waters' of a new place', 'Poem seems full of pride, emotions, and patriotism, but I don't know much about South African tribes, so I can't relate to this poem', 'Confusing, wasn't easy to understand', 'Appears to be saying goodbye forever', 'It's just kind of words to me; I didn't understand this poem.' Again, many students voiced their unexamined assumption that the 'truths' of biography and history would provide the key to unlocking the mysteries of the poem. (McPhail's reminding them of Nietzsche's admonition that 'history is the agreed-upon fiction' did little to dismantle their presumptions.) And although our text does provide explanatory notes for what – at least for most of our readers – prove to be cryptic references, most students, nevertheless, insist on the need for further information. For them, as for many novice readers of TS Eliot, the allusive proves illusive. But the exceptions to the puzzlement were telling. A small number of students who apparently did not worry over a history that they couldn't comprehend reflected more on the 'internal' hermeneutic issues: McPhail took his pedagogical cues from them.

We first want to provide the important caveat that the references to Tshaka, Hendrik, Witbooi, Adam Kok and Xhosa[11] do seem to be crucial factors in a felt and reasoned apprehension of the poem. For the purposes of explication, Northrop Frye's insistence on the 'centripetal' or self-referential nature of literature seems naively narrow-minded. With only the two previous poems as 'Nortjean touchstones', some of our students already seem to perceive the importance of place – real and imagined – in Nortje's heart and mind. And as Klopper rightly notes, '[o]ntological struggle does not occur in a vacuum. It is not divorced from questions of race, class and gender, from questions of positionality. Nortje engages at a deeply personal level with issues thrown up by his external circumstances, whether political, social or geographic' (*AD* xxv). And, of course, neither does a poem – especially perhaps one that expresses ontological struggle – occur in a vacuum. Indeed, 'Native's letter' invites a dialogic interpretive approach, a receptivity to the 'relational' quality of the poem: between the external world and existential worry, between the heaves of storm and heaviness of heart. Like the best of Frost, Nortje seems here to ponder the external world in order to illumine his internal one.

Again, mindful of this dialogic impulse and taking his initial cues from those students who reflected more on the poet's ontologic intimations than his affective allusions, McPhail began with two simple questions: What is the denotation of 'native'? On what connotations might Nortje be playing? The difference in the meanings between 'native' as adjective and 'native' as noun leads to all sorts of interesting conjecture as to the speaker's own positionality. What one hopes is that concerns hitherto ill defined and amorphous now move from the backs of students' minds to the tips of their tongues: is he writing as one who sees himself as an original or indigenous inhabitant of South Africa (as opposed to settlers or colonizers)? So, is he positioning himself politically in opposition to his homeland's historical oppressors? Or, similarly, is he writing from a consciousness of colour and positioning himself racially from his white oppressors? Or is he, like the 'natives' of Canada, writing from a consciousness of racial conspicuousness? Given that the poem was written in Toronto before Nortje's return to England, is it an attempted recouping of his homeland in the face of his self-imposed exile? Or is it a kind of poetic rationalization of his vocation as poet in light of his consciousness of being a 'wanderer' – in light of an abiding awareness of never feeling at home anywhere – of feeling like Job's Satan walking to and fro upon the earth but always sensing his own alienation? Is it, then, a poetic attempt to affirm that he *is* a native, that he *does* have a home, if only in his heart? These sorts of question provided a useful point of departure for discussing the poem, but the kinds of response and speculation that they engendered went only so far. Invariably both Hewson and McPhail were forced to return to the exegetical task of close reading in order to satisfactorily address these larger questions and the issues they intimate.

The poem begins with an assertion: 'Habitable planets are unknown or too / far away from us to be / of consequence.' The first question that arises, of course, concerns whether the speaker is referring to habitable planets literally or figuratively – astronomically or geographically (or mentally). Most students perceived that it really didn't matter. The weight of the assertion seems to rest on the word 'consequence'. Habitable planets or places one can inhabit, in any important sense, are too far removed from the speaker, either epistemically or spatially, to be of concern. The following lines then introduce what does concern the speaker:

To be of
value to his homeland must the wanderer
not weep by northern waters, but love
his own bitter clay
roaming through hard cities, tough
himself as coffin nails.

Numerous students read these lines as a(n) (rhetorical) interrogative (even though there is no question mark). They felt the speaker was saying that to be of use, he *must* weep by northern waters *and* love his own bitter clay. Understandable as this reading may be, we ask our students to regard the end punctuation and to suggest why it is important. Students soon appreciate that this is another assertion, and their readings adjust accordingly. A composite paraphrase of some of the students' revised responses would read as follows: 'He is saying that to be of use to his country he must *not* weep by northern waters (one astute student reminded us that much of Toronto stretches along Lake Ontario), but he must love himself and be emotionally or psychologically tough as he goes through cities he finds severe or hostile.' This reading seems legitimate, and it also seems to extend logically the first assertion of the poem.

A number of students admiringly remarked on the phrase 'love his own bitter clay'. One felt the speaker was saying one must appreciate what one has – bitter clay. Another thought the speaker was conveying a kind of general precept: 'acceptance of consequences we can't change; to be of value live in the here and now'. Indeed, these responses seem quite perceptive, but some students also voiced a little perplexity: 'But why bitter?' 'Why clay?' Again, our dictionaries proved useful. Most students initially thought of bitter as a noun, but used as an adjective, as it is in the poem, it can mean not only resentful or cynical, but also vehement or relentless. And clay, as most students know, is an earthy material – pliable when moist but hard when exposed to intense heat. But students were generally surprised to learn that the word 'clay' is also used to distinguish the body from the spirit. Our etymological excursion inspired new and animated conjectures, some in keeping with the earlier impressions but now more precise and, perhaps, more poignant: 'Maybe he's resentful about his body being in Toronto when his spirit is back in South Africa!' Good! 'Maybe he's saying he has to love or accept his own cynicism about being a black man in a mostly white, northern city.' Good! 'Maybe he's saying he has to be vehement about loving his own body; it's a conscious decision not to cry about his race, but love it because it toughens him up.' And so forth. Some students also surmised that the word 'clay' might suggest an earlier pliability in the speaker that now was hardened in response to the 'white heat' of a city that was hard on a black man.[12] In any case, these lines of conjecture seemed to reinvigorate even the admittedly baffled in the class.

However, the first two of the next four lines erected some new barriers to understanding: 'Harping on the nettles of his melancholy, / keening on the blue strings of the blood, / he will delve into mythologies perhaps / call up spirits through the night.' Admitting that we too find the first two lines rather cryptic seemed to put our students more at ease. We note, first, that harping can mean annoyingly or monotonously dwelling on something, or it can mean playing the harp. Secondly, although 'nettles' refers to stinging or prickly plants, 'melancholy' is not always pejorative. Indeed, the Romantics held that melancholy – as intimated in 'Ode to melancholy' – can be seen as an indication or feature of spiritual sensitivity. These considerations both complicate and enrich our understanding of these lines. Hence, harping on the nettles of one's melancholy could mean playing on – in the sense of dwelling on – the thorny aspects of his spiritual sensitivity (or of his pensiveness). He also may be playing on, manipulating, or using that which pricks or rouses his melancholy – whether that melancholy be balm or wormwood. In either case, the same impulse that we saw earlier toward facing squarely, almost stoically, one's external conditions seems apparent here as well. Similarly, although 'keening', which would be to make a sound suggestive of a lamentation, intimates dejection and woe, nevertheless, it leads to the speaker to 'delve into mythologies perhaps / call up spirits through the night'. One need not invoke Frazer's *Golden bough* or Campbell's *The hero with a thousand faces* to adumbrate the effect or efficacy of myth or spirits on the human psyche. The point is that once again the speaker seems to recognize or posit alternatives to his own existential vertigo. And the alternatives he posits are soon particularized; indeed, the general concepts of spirit and myth find an earthly habitation and a name in Tshaka, Hendrik Witbooi, Kok, and in 'the Xhosa nation's dream'.

As an aside, here we want to offer a line of interpretation to the poem that runs counter to the impression that it is rather dark, disdainful, and exudes what one student articulated as a 'heaviness of imagery and ideas'. First, we think it interesting that the speaker admits that the memories of these people (and by extension the events to which they are connected) are 'apocryphal' or fictitious. This may indicate that what is of importance to the speaker is not the *idea* of people and events – the cognitive objectification of humans or history, whether factual or fictitious – but simply the recognition that he has the choice or alternative to 'carry' *others* as subjects with him 'as he moonlights in another country'. And indeed, moonlighting in another country suggests a schism within the self, a self divided, separated from one's authentic or *native* vocation and soil. So here, to carry memories of others that are named is not only to identify particular others but also to identify them dialogically as *for* himself in order to affirm *his* own unique identity as one who will find a place for himself, or as the last line reads, 'define the happening'. As Bakhtin notes,

> It is only in the other human being, in fact, that a living, aesthetically (and ethically) convincing experience of human finitude is given to me ... In the unitary world of cognition, I cannot find a place for myself as a unique *I for myself* in distinction to all other human beings without exception – past, present, future – as *others* for me. (1990:36–37)

Ironically, his marginality as coloured, poet, wanderer may be the very source or grounds for dialogical relation with others, and concomitantly, an ontologic recouping of an inviable self that now 'equally may ... stand and laugh'. Only then, perhaps the poem is suggesting, can the speaker 'have' or own 'cycles of history / outnumbering the guns of supremacy' and hence transcend them. Or, marginality or ontologic fragmentation may lead to authentic identity.

Klopper's remarks seem telling, both for their insight and for what, at least in this poem, seems an incisive exception:

> Nortje's poetry is more intractable than this narrative would lead us to believe. Its vision is more bleak than suggested by a narrative of loss of community and of consequent psychic disintegration as a result of adverse political circumstances. More challengingly, and perhaps more disturbingly, the poetry raises the spectre of loss and fragmentation as constituting the very basis of consciousness. (*AD* xxvi)

We have claimed that 'Native's letter', at very least, insinuates loss and fragmentation, and we have endeavoured to show that the poem does suggest that this may well constitute the basis or foundation of consciousness or identity. But we differ from Klopper's *assessment* of this phenomenon in that given the poem's apprehension of the potentiality of dialogic engagement, we do not think the poem conceives of this as entirely or even predominantly negative. Insofar as the poem offers this potentiality, what it raises is neither bleak, spectral, nor disturbing. So, for the speaker in this poem, 'outnumbering the guns of supremacy' is made possible not through explicit political engagement with power, but through relational engagement with the other, even if only in memory. Indeed, we saw something of this dialogic impulse in 'Letter from Pretoria Central Prison' when the speaker transcends his situation by allowing another's 'words [to] filter softly through [his] fibres'. As Emmanuel Levinas notes in 'Is ontology fundamental?' (contrary to Foucauldian thinking),

> Reflection offers only the tale of a personal adventure, of a private soul, which returns incessantly to itself, even when it seems to flee itself. The human only lends itself to a relation that is not power. (Levinas 1996:10)

And since the speaker has 'lent' himself to a relation that is not power,

> Now and whenever he arrives
> extending feelers into foreign scenes
> exploring times and lives,
> equally may he laugh,
> explode with a paper bag of poems,
> burst upon a million televisions
> with a face as in a Karsh photograph,
> slave voluntarily in some siberia
> to earn the salt of victory. (*AD* 360)

The reference to Siberia seems apt here since, through dialogic relation with an other and its concomitant efficacy to recoup an authentic or native self, even the exile or political prisoner can mitigate external power – slavery – and make it voluntary and so 'earn the salt of victory'. So what seems an expression of disdain or despair, seen in this light, is actually an assertion of triumph. As Hamlet puts it 'there is nothing good or evil, but that thinking makes it so'. Finally, the speaker leaves this dialogic potentiality – and indeed of relation with himself – as a gift to those who also are in the shadow of existential darkness, who are also in need of others:

> Darksome, whoever dies
> in the malaise of my dear land

remember me at swim,
the moving waters spilling through my eyes:
and let no amnesia
attack at fire hour:
for some of us must storm the castles
some define the happening. (*AD* 361)

And there it stands.

As one who has attempted to 'define the happening' of his own peculiar forms of malaise, Nortje gives us a glimpse of an individual wrestling, through his poetry, with some of the most fundamental and perplexing of human concerns: personal identity, politics, morality, alienation and the ubiquitous problem of relation with the other. But as we have seen, Nortje is no nihilist; nor does he leave us merely with an expression of loss and psychic fragmentation or with bitter social, moral or political critique. Although not always immediately apparent or obviously abundant, intimations of some viable alternatives to our situations and potential answers to some of our shared problems are to be found in Nortje's poems.[13] Insofar as Nortje faces these concerns squarely and without cant, we discovered that his poetry proves engaging and illuminating in our college classrooms. In our arrogance or complacency, we're apt to forget, as professors of literature, that these fundamental concerns are present, if often unarticulated or buried even, in our younger students, and it's rewarding to find that with some careful re-reading and strategic prompting, the study of these Nortje poems offers us all an opportunity to share, scrutinize and clarify our positions. And in these outcome-driven times, we see the encouragement and cultivation of critical reading, thinking and communication in our students as one of our significant skills as English instructors. We have found Nortje's poems quite fruitful, if sometimes frustrating, material for sharpening these skills, and we invite others who share similar pedagogical goals to give their students the opportunity to experience this significant poet.

Notes

1 Mount Royal College is in Calgary, Alberta, the southern part of the province, which can be characterized by its blanket political conservatism. 'Canada's leading undergraduate institution', the college is expanding at a remarkable rate. Where it previously specialized in university transfer courses, it now offers applied degrees. It also offers collaborative degrees, one of which is the Bachelor of Arts. Tuition rates are more reasonable than those at the University of Calgary; class sizes are smaller; and modes of delivery are more flexible. From our limited observations some of these features make for a more diverse – in age, experience, class – student population than we've taught at the universities of Calgary and Alberta in Edmonton.

2 One of Hewson's introductory class strategies is to ask her students to arrange themselves, according to their birthplace, from East to West at the front of the room. Not only is this a good ice-breaker – is Stand-off west of Cardston? Is Punjab east or west? – it enables us to see how wide is the world we inhabit and to honour that, intellectually, in our cramped classroom.

3 McPhail was new to teaching poetry and Hewson has been fine-tuning her approach to poetry for nine years. McPhail's style is more formal; Hewson's much less so. On reflection, McPhail thought that making the biographical facts of the classroom public would have been a good pedagogical move, if only to enhance the notion of a community of readers.

4 See Said's 'Jane Austen and empire' in his *Culture and imperialism*. New York: Knopf, 1993:80–97.

5 This may also explain their 'colour' blindness. No student respondent of 'Letter from Pretoria Central Prison' wondered about the racial identity of the speaker.

6 In her article Barnard elaborates on this trope most eloquently. While outlining some of Barnard's points, Hewson also read a section to her class from Mandela's *Long walk to freedom*, which detailed the on-going struggles of his then wife to organize and manage prison visits.

7 See, for example, Dennis Brutus' 'Robben Island sequence'.

8 This led to a broader discussion of form based on several poems in our anthology conceived as letters: Gwendolyn Macewen's chilling 'Letter to a future generation'; Michael Ondaatje's nostalgic 'Letters and other worlds' and William Carlos Williams' pseudo-apology poem, 'This is just to say'.

9 Liz Phair, 'Go west' off *Whip smart*.

10 [Eds: Immigration for Nortje, though sponsored by others, was tied to his teaching post in Hope.]

11 [Eds. The list in Klopper's edition includes a misplaced comma; the name is Hendrik Witbooi.]

12 Assumptions of the speaker's racial identity as black were frequently made in McPhail's class. In Hewson's class this was the poem that generated the only questions about the speaker's racial background in the pre-discussion responses.

13 Hewson often finds that this first-year poetry class consists of a cadre of novice poets. One such student was completely inspired by 'Native's letter': 'He's done it! He's articulated my intuition: that's what *I* want to do: "define the happening", not wait for it to be analysed 10 years from now.' Another of her students had this poignant observation to make: 'I understand the speaker's wish [in 'Native's letter'] to lead his homeland to greatness as he moonlights in another country. When I think of my family's achievements and what I hope mine to be, it sometimes makes me sad to think that they might only be labelled as strictly Canadian achievements.'

Works cited

Bakhtin, M M. *Art and answerability: early philosophical essays*, ed Michael Holquist & Vadim Laipunov. Austin: University of Texas, 1990.

Barnard, Rita. 'Speaking places: prison, poetry and the South African nation', *Research in African Literatures* 32.3 (Fall 2001):154–173.

The Broadview anthology of poetry, eds Herbert Rosengarten & Amanda Goldrick-Jones. Peterborough, Ont: Broadview Press, 1993.

Foucault, Michel. *Discipline and punish: the birth of the prison.* Trans Alan Sheridan. New York: Pantheon Books, 1977.

Levinas, Immanuel. Basic philosophical writings, eds Peperzak, Critchley & Bernasconi. Bloomington: Indiana University Press, 1996.

McLuckie, Craig & Ross Tyner. ' 'The raw and the cooked': Arthur Kenneth Nortje, Canada and an annotated bibliography', *English in Africa* 26.2 (October 1999); 1–54.

Nortje, Arthur. *Anatomy of dark: collected poems of Arthur Nortje*, ed Dirk Klopper. Pretoria: Unisa Press, 2000.

Chapter 8: Arthur Nortje in Canada[1]

Craig McLuckie and Ross Tyner

Much of the criticism written about Nortje's time in Canada relies heavily on the poet's journal of that period, a less than historically specific or accurate document, and the unresearched repetition of a few commentators', at times, subjective accounts. In both instances, a lack of material grounding in and understanding of Canada generally and British Columbia in particular are problematic.

What has become clear about Nortje's experiences in Canada is his professionalism as a teacher, a lack of close acquaintances, a continued linguistic and poetic experimentation (in The Oxford journal), and his evident loneliness and loss (of a sense of home, connections, a lover). The loneliness manifested itself, unsurprisingly, in heavy drinking and, latterly, with narcotics.

Hope, British Columbia

Hope, British Columbia, began as Fort Hope (1848), a Hudson's Bay Company trading post on the Fraser River. In 1858 the Fraser River Gold Rush began. Fort Hope sustained itself through this period but was officially closed in 1892, seven years after the completion of the Canadian Pacific Railway. The settlement survived its commercial closure and was incorporated as a village in 1929. Not until the completion of the Hope-Princeton Highway in 1949 did the community see significant growth. Though, as the table below reveals, the township remained small in size, close-knit in familial make-up.

1966[2]		1961	
Population	2948	**Population**	2751
Households		**Households**	
No of households	826	No of households	768
Avg persons per household	3.4	Avg persons per household	3.5
No hhlds with lodgers	38		
Families		**Families**	
No of Families	703	No of families	671
Avg no persons per family	3.7	Avg no persons per family	3.7
No of families by size of families			
2 person	196		
3 person	141		
4 person	170		
5 person	102		
6 person	58		
7 person	21		
8 person	11		
9+ person	4		
No of families by # children			
0 children	184		
1 child	135		
2 children	170		
3 children	112		
4 children	63		
5 children	20		
6 children	11		
7 children	2		
8 children	2		
9+ children	0		
Avg no children/family (BC = 1.7)	1.8		
Children who live at home			
Total:	1263		
Aged 6	383		
Aged 6–14	586		
Aged 15–18	212		
Aged 19–24	82		

In 1965, two years before Nortje's arrival, part of Peake Mountain descended onto Outram Lake, killing four travellers on the highway. The Hope Slide, as this event is called, evokes a sense of the power of the natural world. The town of Hope is bordered by the Fraser River on the north and west, the Coquihalla River on the east, and the Trans-Canada Highway to the south. It is a small town, nestled among the densely treed, towering hills of the Cascade Mountains. Hope is perhaps best known internationally as the setting for the Sylvester Stallone film *First blood*. Not far from Hope is one of the Fraser Valley's major tourist attractions, the whitewater known as Hell's Gate. These two locales (Hope and Hell's Gate) symbolize the division in Nortje at this time: professional, personable and productive in literary matters during the week; alone, binge-drinking, in crisis on the weekend.

Nortje, according to several commentators, was involved with 'Joan Cornelius, a South African girl whom he met in 1963 when she was still at school, and who emigrated to Canada in 1964, where she became a physiotherapist' (Berthoud 1984:14). This 'affair' became a major motivation in his decision to emigrate to Canada.

Alvarez-Peyrere notes that '[d]eparture for the Great North, two years (1968–69) of which we know only that they were marked by work as a teacher, a deep disappointment in love and a mere four poems from a man who was always writing. For him, external events were not important except in so far as they might have implications for the individual, for the general climate and for the state of mind it causes in the long term.' This perspective on Nortje's literary productivity in Canada has been decisively undermined, as the more than 90 Canadian poems in *Anatomy of dark* attest.

David Bunn, too, presents a negative account of Nortje's time in Canada:

But silence, too, seemed to surround him once again ... Throughout the journal of his period in British Columbia are references to consumer insanity ... In Canada, Nortje began to talk and write self-consciously of a mass of people there who were divided along the lines of class ... During the last two years of his life the old wish for critical objectivity was replaced by an urge to universalize his situation through metaphor and reappraise the past in mythic terms ... [T]wo dismal years in British Columbia ... [Yet, 1970 was] one of the most productive periods of his life. (Bunn, *Dictionary of literary biography* 174)

Even in light of the fact that 'Nortje's "Oxford journal"' is a highly unstable literary document, one that oscillates between different generic paradigms, containing extended autobiographical narrative sequences, a mythopoeic, *Odyssey*-like account of his leaving, transcriptions of letters and poems, even two short vocabulary lists of words to use in erudite company' (Bunn 1996:34), critics continue to rely on its textual evidence in documentary fashion.

What does the complementary evidence hold? An examination of *The Hope Standard* for the period of Nortje's stay shows that enrolments in the school have increased, and that nine of the new teachers are newcomers to the area and the school district (13 September 1967:1, 8), though the town registered a population of 2 948 (Wednesday 15 May 1968:5). Thus, Nortje would not experience as severe a double isolation as one might have thought. Entries for 'Pacific Northwest writers' (for example, Wednesday 28 February, 1968) and other cultural groups reveal his absence, a lack of public engagement outside his professional capacity. Yet, the position and the place, perhaps also the opportunity for a continuing position, have Nortje back to teach senior English (Wednesday 28 August 1968), with high-school enrolment up to 500 students. Nortje was not involved in South African-related events either – at least as far as the public record reveals: no demonstrations, no participation when 'Hope women host visitors from South Africa ...' (Thursday 5 September 1968). In a town that carries its social calendar on the newspaper's front page, where every event gains some mention, Nortje appears only in relation to the two successive appointments. On Wednesday 11 June 1969, on page one, Nortje receives his third newspaper comment: his resignation. Significantly, it is just seven days after this item that Robert 'Mac' Storey's (aged 39) funeral is described (10). Storey is mentioned by Leitch and others in anonymous terms: a 'man he befriended in Hope, BC, committed suicide'. Obviously not a sufficiently strong friendship, as Nortje was neither pall-bearer (Peter McPhedran and Gordon McKay were) nor in attendance; yet, according to his letter to Raymond Leitch he would not be leaving for Toronto until 27 June (letter to Raymond Leitch 5/31/69).

The school district office has a file on Nortje, presumably teaching contracts and so on. Perhaps most useful in the file would be any comments, notes, evaluations by Robertson, so that a sense of career pressures could be built. However, these records are only available with a notarized letter from the next of kin.

The Gagnon Apartments and the locally named 'Trash and Trade' still exist. The latter is a defunct discount store, but its 'apartments', squalid in appearance, remain above what is now a discount carpet shop, on the north side of Wallace Street.

The poetically recorded Hope Hotel stands extant, barring the yearly repainting. Unfortunately the owners during Nortje's time in Hope have moved on, along with the registration records.

The social and political context at the time is summarised in the entry on BC Premier W A C Bennett:

[In 1951] he joined the Social Credit Party, and when the Socreds won a surprise victory in the 1952 election they chose him leader of their minority government. Bennett became the longest-serving Premier in BC history.

His 20 year term was marked by rapid economic growth based on resource development, much of it financed by out-of-province investment, and his governments initiated the building of highways, power dams and railways at an energetic pace. While all of this activity took place, Bennett claimed to be eliminating the provincial debt ... A fervid supporter of free-enterprise, he nevertheless nationalised the ferry system, expanded post-secondary education and created BC Hydro, a Crown Corporation, in 1961. At the same time, Bennett held social spending and labour unions in check. A volatile campaigner ... Bennett retained power with fierce attacks on the 'socialism' of the CCF-NDP [Co-operative Commonwealth Federation-New Democrat Party]. (Bennett 2000:71)

Few commentators on Nortje note the economic and political parallels with South Africa, especially in relation to excluded groups – the indigenous people. Similarly, few commentators have grounded Nortje's sense of Canadian 'consumerist culture' within the economic, albeit resource-based, expansion of his time in British Columbia. 'Material progress through rapid resource development became almost a secular faith' (Barman 2000:341). In context, Nortje lived in a village where 200 families that supplied the workforce for the Giant Mascot Mine (45 minutes away by car) lived. Logging was the primary industry. The populace worked. However, televisions were within the means of most and, as Nortje records in several poems (see for example *AD* 254–205, 256, 263, 265–266, 269, 283, 285–287, 288–291), he was an avid viewer and commentator on the deleterious effects of *American* consumerist culture.

The alienation Nortje felt, too, was due, in part, to his self-isolation. Between Wallace Street (the main street during Nortje's stay) and across Park Street from the old site of Hope Secondary School was a Quonset hut, known as the Igloo, where dances and other entertainments were held. Next to the Igloo were the Bucks Apartments, where 'most of the new, single teachers lived' (conversation with Holly and Jac Smith). Nortje lived away from the school, relatively speaking, and away from his colleagues. Holly Smith remembers him, outside school hours, with 'kids one year out of school; he was rarely with teachers'. Nortje was the only black person in the town; he stood out. Although the secondary school had a fair number of Japanese Canadian and First Nations (ie, Indian) students, there was little mixing.

1967–1968: Student population	
Occupational students	26 (mainly First Nations)
Grade 8:	108
Grade 9:	92
Grade 10:	109
Grade 11:	68
Under-Grads:	21
Grads (Grade 12): (21 girls; 26 boys; 3 Japanese; 44 caucasian).	47
Total:	471 students

In class Nortje is remembered as an excellent teacher, 'immaculate every day; proper', who placed his subject area above politics. Jac Smith, a student in Nortje's homeroom class, remembers the first day: 'he came into the class, took down the picture of Queen Elizabeth and replaced it with a picture of Shakespeare'. Students remember Nortje 'pushing students not just to do the work, but to do their absolute best, considered work' (conversation with Holly and Jac Smith). While Holly Smith remembers 'Living in Hope, we were so far removed from any of that [ie, politics]', she does note that Nortje taught Alan Paton's seminal *Cry, the beloved country*. Poetry that appears in the yearbook, similarly, implies Nortje's international and human concerns, as they influenced his students' subject matter. Linda Langlay's 'A victim of hatred' is about a racially motivated assault that ends 'The Negro boy limped home'. It comprises six quatrains of alternating rhyme. Pat Farrell's 'Future' is about survival, while Randy Mercer's 'Crying' deals with lost love, as does Wendy Reid's 'Love comes'. Roberta Wells' 'Grandpa dropped his glasses' appears to have its inspiration in hallucinogenics. Evelyn Harms, in a prose piece, laments television's effect on 'The death of modern imagination'. Sharon Anderson's 'If I listen' and Wendy Reid's 'Vietnam soldier' cover different aspects of that war; the death of children and black/white relations respectively.

The school had an active recreational roster: Gymnastics Club, indoor and outdoor track, girls gymnastics, boys gymnastics, senior and junior boys and girls basketball, junior girls grass hockey, cheer leading, senior and junior boys soccer, a newspaper group, the school annual group, as well as chess, ping pong, bowling, curling, weight lifting, badminton, photography and the listeners clubs. Nortje sponsored the Listeners.

With the Listeners Club, he was serious, introducing 'new' artists and always analysing the lyrics for their message. The Listeners Club consisted in 1967–68 of Yvonne Magark, Randy Kizuk ('the student who probably spent the most time with him') (conversation with Holly and Jac Smith), Carole Bachinski (in California), Sandra Krasniuk, Evelyn Harms, Lynn Verbeek, Linda Smith, Jean Storey (the daughter of the Robert (above)), and two unnamed members in the school yearbook: Gerry Brindamour and Doug Ratslof. Photographs in *D'Espoir 1967–68* show the as-yet-unidentified album covers of African American musicians.

Socially, in addition to dances at the Igloo, there was the Hope Hotel's bar, though many students worked in the hotel. The school held three 'proms' that year: a Hippy Happening, Christmas and Valentine's. On weekends the younger crowd went drinking at the hotel. The Legion, on the block between Fourth and Fifth Streets, Port and Hudson's Bay, was popular on weekends for dances (see 'Fragment', *AD* 277). Other than those three venues, house parties were the main social entertainment, though these tended to be organized and attended by specific student cliques. Recreational drug use was just beginning in Hope, the 'kids taking them were the experimenters' (conversation with Holly and Jac Smith). There is no evidence of Nortje being seen with this group. Nortje did not participate in sports, nor did he avail himself of the hiking, climbing and skiing available nearby. Rather, when not at work or at home writing, he mixed with the town's youth, often at his apartment. As Jac Smith summarises, 'He was alone, mixing mainly with 19 and 20 year olds.'

Victor Smith. Hope BC

Victor Smith was in Nortje's English class, and was a member of the Listeners Club. He is enthusiastic in his praise for Nortje as a teacher.

How was Mr Nortje as a teacher? *I always hated English, but he made the classes interesting and student centred. It wasn't just rote learning like a lot of the others. You got engaged in what you were studying. Occasionally he'd remind us that we were getting off track and return us to the task at hand. He knew a lot, always responded to questions. He'd have us stand up to make a point, which was beneficial later when we had to do presentations because the fear of that was gone.*

What do you remember of him, his personality? *With a shy Japanese student he was considerate and got her to participate. He was always very smartly dressed and obviously prepared. Outside class, if he saw you he'd exchange a greeting. He made you feel like a person.*

Do you know why he came to Hope? *He said that he'd come to Hope because that's where the job was.*

What other recollections do you have? Was there any sense of his politics? *There seemed to have been a problem with the headmaster, Mr Robertson; students speculated about the 'deal', maybe pot smoking. But, what a teacher does outside class isn't important, if he keeps the class motivated and interested. He knew his stuff. There wasn't anything in the way of talk about South Africa or politics.*

Did you know he was a poet? *We weren't that aware of his poetry or accomplishments elsewhere. He was pretty private. Randi Reid, the student president at that time, would be someone to get in touch with, or Jo-ann Hannah, who was so inspired she did graduate work.*

Victor Smith has two yearbooks and shows pictures. *In the Listeners Club we'd listen to whatever anyone brought, but mostly contemporary music.*

What is significant in these remarks is an obvious enthusiasm for the teacher and a grudging one for the subject. In the 1970 yearbook, under Smith's name is 'Dislikes – English'. One year after Nortje's departure, the grudging taste for English is gone.

Brian Warner, Hope, BC

Principal, Hope Secondary School. Although he was not at the school when Nortje taught there, he was able to present three useful pieces of information: Nortje 'is not one of the characters in the school's anecdotal history of eccentrics'; 'The old school was destroyed by fire in 1972, and many records were lost'; and the names and telephone numbers of people who might be able to assist.

Ms Tama Kawase, Hope, BC

Tama Kawase, formerly Counselor. She said that 'she wasn't aware of a whole lot of writing' by Nortje, that he wasn't involved in many extra-curricular activities like sports or the PTA, but that he had run 'the Listeners' Club' two years in a row. Interestingly, she said that Nortje 'was very dedicated to his teaching, Monday through Friday'. She concluded by directing us to Peter McPhedran.

Peter McPhedran, Hope, BC

Peter McPhedran was a social science and French teacher, a colleague of Nortje's. He was in poor health, but animated about the past.

He stayed first of all ... wasn't he down on the waterfront there, at the Gagnon Apartments first? and then he stayed at a place we called the 'Trash and Trade' it was a ... second hand store downstairs and this guy, a Vancouver fireman, ran this 'Trash and Trade'. There were three or four apartments above; he stayed up there when he was here. What kind of employment contract did he have? Sessional or continuing, or ...? *He would've been continuing if he'd wanted to. It was certainly his own decision to leave, it wasn't ... He was an excellent teacher. He had the kids going on poetry in particular. Poetry and music appreciation were his two big things. He loved music of all kinds. He was a great Beatles fan. As a matter of fact I looked up a couple of the old annuals [1968 and 1969] and he's got a poem in there dedicated to the Beatles in one.* [Mrs McPhedran reading through *Dead roots*: 'they're kind of bleak.']

The story we got was he committed suicide, right? Read out Donald Arthur's description of the Coroner's report and verdict. *Yeah he was a ... I refer to it as a weekend binger. Yeh know, he wouldn't touch anything, well maybe a beer before supper or something, but wouldn't touch anything all week. On Friday night, it was his night to howl so to speak and he would drink quite a bit on Friday night and maybe Saturday, and then Sundays* [Mrs McPhedran: 'but he never ate.'] *he'd cut it off. No he never ate.* [Mrs McPhedran: 'Just drank. He used to come for dinner once a week and he'd help me with an English correspondence course I was taking. He'd come for dinner, and then sit down with the books. He had this voracious appetite; I could never make enough food. It was unbelievable how much he would eat, but then he hadn't eaten all week or weekend. And a lot of people used to have him around for dinner. It was a pretty close community. He was far beyond any of us intellectually but ...'] *He was no problem to have around; he was a great guy.*

What about his teaching? *Yeah he did ... he really inspired a lot of kids to like English, poetry in particular. I'm sure the kids' poetry in the annual next to his poem was all inspired by him. There's this one girl in there, Jo-ann Hannah, who went on ... she's got her doctorate in English [Not English; DAI 5312A 4486; CWM & RT].[3] She lives in Ontario now. She was one of his prize students. She was a bright girl. She really thought Arthur was just the cat's meow as a teacher and a person.* [McPhedran: 'I would think a lot of those young girls would have crushes on him. He was young. And I think high school girls tend to do that.'] *He was sorta what you might call a cool cat ya know, nothing seemed to ruffle him. He kept his suave, debonair demeanor. And, you know, he always wore a suit and tie to school and was very properly dressed, sort of in English fashion. The old Oxford tie kind of thing.* [McPhedran: 'He always referred to women as birds.'] *But, he was really an intellectual. He could talk to anybody on any level about most any topic. But like I say the poetry and the music were the main things. The Beatles were hot then of course. At the school he had this listening club. It was quite a large club actually. These kids would get together and listen ... He liked all kinds of music: modern and classical. He just liked music. Yet if you had a party or something he wasn't much to get up and dance or whatever. After he'd had a few drinks he might get up and do a dance with somebody or other.*

Did he ever discuss South Africa? Politics? *No. Surprisingly little to me anyway.* [McPhedran: 'I got the feeling he was very very troubled about his African past.'] *Yeah. He gave the impression that he didn't want to talk about it almost. Whether that was a part of his being a private person, I don't know. I got the impression that he was raised by his mother. I gathered that there was no father, that his mother had raised him. Someone at his school saw his intelligence and gave him the push and help to get on.* [McPhedran: 'He was certainly bitter about that, the colour issue from Africa.'] *I somehow got the impression that he was a, I don't know, an activist in South Africa. Anything that he did mention definitely was against apartheid and whatnot. But we had very few conversations about that sort of thing. Not really wanting to talk about it, the conversation changed, that's all. He was certainly a good teacher.* [McPhedran: 'He was very accepted by the teaching community because at that time we had a ... there was lots of socializing after hours and things like that. He was always well treated and included.'] But I imagine this weekend binging – he didn't get falling down stupid drunk – but he drank a lot on weekends. He'd go through quite a bit of rum, go through quite a bit, then reach a level, and ...

Were people aware of him as a poet? *No. He was very humble about it. I knew he wrote poetry when he was here because he told me so, but I've never seen what he did. I knew he was writing poetry but that's about all he said.* Was he published locally? *Not to my knowledge. He was quiet about his own personal life. He never really opened up, you know. He'd talk about anything but he just, he never, what would you say, never bragged about his accomplishments in school or scholarships that he got.*

Did he seem an activist; or, was his time here quiet? *Yes, very quiet.* [McPhedran: 'I never could figure out exactly why he'd come here.'] The newspaper suggests that there was a lot of external recruitment in the school district in the late 1960s. *A number of teachers from Australia particularly, and that's the way he came to be here alright. And I assume when he left he was on to bigger and better things or whatever.* He moved on to Alderwood Collegiate, part of the Etobicoke School District, in Toronto? *I know nothing of that.* [Mrs McPhedran: 'When he left here he left for Toronto.'] *Yes. He just ... I don't know of anyone that he contacted. He wasn't one to send cards.*

How did people know about his death? There's nothing in the newspaper. *I don't know. Someone knew him who knew people in Hope? I really don't know how the word drifted down. I can't even remember who told me that he had died. The story here was that he went with ... booze and alcohol. That did him in. It wasn't like he blew himself away. The story we got was that it was suicide.*

Synopses of critical pieces; please respond if anything rings a bell. 'Deep disappointment in love'? 'Donald Arthur'? 'Olga Reed'? 'Emigrated'? *No, no, no, I don't really know.* 'Atmosphere of mood and preoccupation'? Only four poems – new teacher, probation, the job at hand? *He would only be on probation for the first year. From there on it'd be a continuing appointment if he wished to stay; there was nothing untoward in that respect as far as a job is concerned. He could have had a continuing appointment. It was his own decision to leave.* What kind of communicating he'd been doing with Toronto I have no idea.

Except that at the end he was going from here to Ontario. Then the word came that he had gone back to England. Again, I don't know where that came from. This love affair in the poetry I knew nothing about.

Several of his poems chart a woman's image across the country. *Really?* What about Charles Davidson – his immigration sponsor? *Nope, not to my knowledge. Charlie Davidson was a friend of a number of these new teachers who came over. Old enough to be their grandfather.* [Mrs McPhedran: 'They liked to party there, at his place. That was the connection.'] *They did.*

David Bunn writes that there is a concern with 'consumer insanity'? It is suggested in a letter to Raymond Leitch: 'Ray Jay wrote. I had half a mind to piss off to Europe for a week or two. Too expensive right now – first thing I have to do is go to driving school & buy an *automobile* to outclass your model Galaxy. Could be a Maverick right out of the box ... Must impress those Etobicoke shits other than with my piercing wit & charismatic sensuality' (31/5/69) [McPhedran: 'I don't recall anything; it was so long ago.'] *I don't recall him being like that but I can see where it would come from. Here where people have two cars and whatever the latest toys are, I could see that it would seem to him as consumer insanity. Because he was very simple in his own life. He wasn't very interested in owning things or whatever.* [Mrs McPhedran: 'The mere fact that he was happy living up above that 'Trash and Trade' place was an indication.']

What about issues of class? *No.*

Chapman, among others, writes of Nortje's 'traumatic love affair'. [Mrs McPhedran: 'I don't think that he had any love affairs here, did he?'] *No.* [Mrs McPhedran: 'Was she an older woman? or married?] I'm not sure.* [Mrs McPhedran: 'It looks like Toronto is where you should look.'] *I think he spent his holidays back east, you know, like the Christmas holiday and the summer holiday, back east in Toronto.*

Raymond Leitch notes Nortje's concern over the suicide of a friend in BC; was that Mr Storey? *I don't think they were bosom buddies particularly, any more than he and I were bosom buddies, so to speak. Mac was quite an outdoorsman. Mac had his life and Arthur had his, but I think they were good friends but not great ones. That was a tragic incident all right. Mac blew himself away across the bridge here.* Did he die before or after Nortje left? *Arthur was here.* He was an outdoorsman, canoeing, camping, nothing that Arthur got involved in? *No.*

I read aloud a brief commentary on the effect of apartheid on 'coloureds'. *I could see him being upset. He was more 'Why do I have to bother with all of this dribble. Let's get on with the job.' He was a bright man alright.* [McPhedran: 'He was so young to die.']

Looking at the high-school yearbooks; McPhedran reads the poetry. *He was right up the alley with his interest in the Beatles. Most of us old crocks would criticize the Beatles. Well this guy was right in there. That was part of his popularity to the youth, relating to the youth, having a teacher who was interested in the Beatles.* There's a slightly different picture the first year; his hair is shorter. *He certainly wasn't a long hair, so to speak. Certainly easier to comb with a washcloth or something.* [McPhedran: 'They [the poems] seem to have a very melancholy air.'] *He never struck me as a man of violence, he was very gentle. He used to come over and help with the correspondence. You never had such good English marks.*

What about narcotic use? Several newspaper articles have stories of amphetamine use in this area at that time. *That was something I never ever saw him take drugs ...* [McPhedran: 'I think he did though.'] *I have a hunch he did, but I don't know that because he never took drugs or smoked marijuana, anything, in front of me. So I was surprised with the story we got on his suicide that it was a combination of drugs and alcohol.* Read aloud the account of Nortje's Oxford neighbour. *As near as I know he stayed clean all week. The weekend, that was his free time.* That's fairly standard. Laughter. *Is there any chance that it was accidental?* The coroner's report suggests that possibility. [McPhedran: 'If he asked someone to wake him up in the morning, he obviously wasn't planning to ...'] *The word we had was that Arthur had committed suicide. I wondered at the time, still do actually, if he was in enough of a stupor that he took other pills without realizing it.* There's only one poetic line – 'my wrists can stain the razor' – that suggests suicide.

[McPhedran: '*Conversation at Mathilda's*, British Columbia, 1967, that would be Tilly; she knew Arthur really well.'] *Mathilda Landry, she taught French and Physical Education here.* [McPhedran: 'She left here in 1972. She used to have punch parties, with every kind of booze in the world in it.'] *I think she had everything she had left over in it including tea.* [McPhedran: 'She'll talk your hind leg off, but she'll probably know quite a bit about Arthur.'] *She's back in Cape Breton now. We were back there a few summers ago.*

I appreciate your time and assistance. *No, we wish we could be of more help. Arthur was quiet.*

Toronto, Ontario

Toronto is not the artistic fulcrum of the world. Even so, Nortje could not get published here because the local dilettantes, if you like, thought his style 'dated' and his subject matter not 'relevant' ... He was popping amphetamines and barbituates, absenting himself from his job and being unusually concerned about his health. (Leitch 'Arthur Nortje')

... when the University of Toronto insisted that he complete honours courses there before being allowed into graduate school, [he] decided to return to Oxford. (Barnett, *A vision of order*)

If the funeral arrangements had been made by the local authority it would have meant a pauper's funeral. Mrs Reed made several calls to South Africa and England and ... had received permission to make the funeral arrangements. ... Mrs Reed's instructions were simple, 'Get the best, I will foot the bill.' ... Mrs Reed had her wish, and she paid every account outstanding in his name at Oxford, including the College bills. (Arthur 1973)

While not 'the artistic fulcrum of the world', Toronto would have offered Nortje considerably more opportunities than had Hope. The second largest Canadian city at the time,[4] it was also one of the most ethnically diverse, trailing only Winnipeg in this regard among large Canadian cities (Herberg 46). Very little of this diversity, however, consisted of black or coloured immigrants from Africa. Large-scale immigration from Africa to Canada did not begin until 1972 when Idi Amin expelled 50 000 Asians from Uganda (*Countries of the world* 2002:1294). In the five years prior to 1972, the number of African immigrants to Canada (race was not specified) ranged from 2 800 to 5 200 (between 2 and 2,8 per cent of the Canadian total) and South African immigration to Canada ranged from 599 individuals in 1969 to 1 366 in 1967, the year of Nortje's arrival in Hope (*Historical statistics* A407–416).

Toronto's black population was increasing during Nortje's brief stay there, due almost exclusively to the beginning of large-scale immigration to Canada from the Caribbean. Of the approximately 300 000 Caribbeans who arrived in Canada between 1967 and 1989, two thirds landed in Toronto (Driedger 223–225). A 1970 *US News and World Report* article (quoted in Davis & Krauter 40) estimated the black population of Toronto to be 35 000. Around the same time, Canadian blacks showed signs of political organization, as evinced by the founding in Toronto in 1969 of the National Black Coalition of Canada (Walker 1983:19).

Another measure of the context in which Nortje found himself in Canada is the opinion toward South Africa of the Canadian media, politicians and public. In the 1960s, says Winks (445), '[t]he rapid march of apartheid in South Africa attracted much attention in the Canadian media' and Prime Minister Diefenbaker was instrumental in provoking South Africa's withdrawal from the Commonwealth (447–448). Around the time of the Sharpeville Massacre (1960), the Canadian edition of *Time* published several articles about South Africa, all of which were opposed to the actions of the South African police and military in Sharpeville.[5] A 9 May 1960 *Time* article which notes a rally at Toronto's Massey Hall organized by a 'Committee of Concern for South Africa' and attended by 2 800 people who 'cheered South Africa's explusion from the Commonwealth' and a vote by the 1,25 million-member Canadian Labour Congress at its annual conference to boycott South African goods illustrates that Canada's citizens were also actively opposed to the apartheid regime.

Canadian media coverage of South Africa appears to have tailed off by the time Nortje arrived in Canada. An analysis of the *Canadian Periodical Index* (*CPI*) for the years 1967–1970 reveals a total of just twenty-one English language articles about South Africa published in the approximately seventy English language periodicals indexed by *CPI* at the time. Of these twenty-one articles, twelve address issues of commerce with South Africa, four are travel articles and only three could be considered to address the politics of South Africa.

In 1996 Tyner contacted Raymond Leitch in the hopes of gaining some insight into Nortje's life in Toronto. Although seriously ill at the time, Leitch was gracious enough to grant an interview at his home in Toronto. Leitch, whose friendship with Nortje dated back to 1962 and with whom Nortje taught and lived in Toronto in 1969 and 1970, described himself as 'like a big brother' to Nortje.

Raymond Leitch, Toronto, Ontario, 18 July 1996

What was your relationship with Arthur Nortje? *I got to know Nortje very well ... I met him a long time ago in 1963 or 1964 in Cape Town. He came to visit me with some students from what we called the 'Bush College', the University of the Western Cape. There were some students from Hewat, which was a training college for teachers ... I lived in a part of Cape Town called Athlone, subdivision Belgravia. The boys were, you know, boys, young fellows, young men – loud and we drank quite a bit. But Nortje impressed me because he didn't say anything; he just sat there. And then we started talking about ... [the liberation movement?]. The liberation movement had basically been crushed, or was in retreat. There were people in hiding and so on. So there was a general mood of pessimism in the place. There was nothing much to do apart from drinking and carrying on and of course that's what I did with those young fellows that day. And then a week or so later he wrote me a letter ... he impressed me with his writing, his competence. So we got in touch and that's how it started. I got to know him very well indeed. He became what we call in Cape Town a 'huiskind', basically a house child, you know that's the kind of person who doesn't need to ask permission to come around or announce that he will visit, he could simply visit. And of an afternoon after school I would find him there at which time we got into my jar of wine ... I'd supply a gallon jar ... He would have been 21 or 22. He didn't seem to be much interested in his studies at the time. We would speak about poetry, mostly ... He got a BA and then he went to teacher's college and he spent a practice teaching session stint with me at a high school called Alexander Simpson High School in Athlone. We were a riot together. I was kind of his bigger brother.*

We went on a trip to Port Elizabeth in '64 while he was still in Cape Town. There were four of us: a fellow called Rousseau – Frenchie Rousseau – myself and a guy called [Tape indecipherable] Roland [Rowan?] Allan [?]. We went to Port Elizabeth by train, travelling third class. It was one hell of a bloody ride. I think about that trip and it makes me sad. But I did meet his mother. He spent a long time keeping us from his mother because basically he was ashamed of the conditions under which he lived. She went out of her way one night and she invited us over and she fried some steaks up – it must have cost her a lot of money. But, she said to me that I must look after him. She didn't tell Frenchie and he had known Frenchie since his childhood. So I kind of kept an eye on him and I became kind of his alter-familius. *He always came to me ... He was certainly a very obnoxious fellow. People didn't like him – some people did – you either liked him or you didn't like him. I recall an occasion at Frenchie's ... Frenchie's wife* [Rita] *decided to cook us a meal. We sat down to the meal. He just gobbled his down and said afterwards 'this food tastes like shit ... but I'll have some more.' He was someone you either liked or didn't like. Mrs Reed, who lives here in Toronto, took a great liking to him ... she's still alive. She and her family really took to him; to this day, I don't know why. They found him to be a very engaging fellow ... she met him through me. They liked the son of a gun ...*

Were you in contact with Nortje between the time you knew him in South Africa and when he came to Toronto? *Oh yes. I met him in London in 1966 on my way to Canada. We had a great time ... We wrote to each other. In 1968 he immigrated.* Was that because you had immigrated? *Well, I can't tell you what was going on in his head. It seemed that he was going to Canada for two reasons ... well, one reason I know for definite. First of all there was the business of opportunities for teaching, writing and so on and the other one was that he had a girlfriend on the prairies* [Joan Cornelius] *– I forget where ... That was the one woman he was really in love with.* Did he meet her in SA? *Yes, I met her in SA. It could have been that he went to BC to have access to his girlfriend. He saw her and then he found out that she was either pregnant or she had been pregnant and she was shacked up with her old man. That was a disappointment. She was an unlikely woman, I thought, that he would fall in love with ... she was tallish, tall and small-breasted, not my idea that that would be Arthur's choice at the time ... And then of course he got the job in British Columbia. He stayed with this fellow for a while – I forget the fellow's name. I think he left because this guy was gay.*

Why did he come to Toronto? *I think in part to be with me.* Perhaps to get away from Hope? *Well, he definitely wanted to get away from Hope. I saw the town. Before he came* [to Toronto] *in 1969 to live here, he came on a visit in 1968.*

In your thesis you state that Nortje wrote 65 poems while he was in Hope, one of his most productive periods, but that only six were included in *Dead roots*, which you discuss in your MA thesis. Do you remember how you would characterize the other 59 poems? *I can't tell you offhand. I must look through them again. I made copies and sent them to Olga ... and to a woman in South Africa called Hedy Davis. Olga knows her well. I think I have them somewhere in the garage.*

In your thesis you mention Nortje's *Journals*. Do you still have the *Journals*; or, are they part of the collection at the University of South Africa? *No. Mrs Reed insisted that they be sent to the University of South Africa. I tried to oppose it. I think I might have a copy of it ... I promise to look.*

What was Nortje's state of mind while he was in Toronto and in Canada? *He looked fine and dandy. It was only after he left that my wife told me that he was doing drugs. I didn't know at the time. When he came in 1969 he stayed with* us for quite a while, until he got a job, because it was summer, and then he went to live on Roncesvalles. [My wife] noticed that he was taking drugs because she was working for a drug company so she knew. But on the surface, everything was just hunky-dory. I didn't know he was taking drugs. Did you perceive that he was depressed? Well, he was a strange fellow to penetrate. He presented different faces to different people, quite deliberately so; that's why the Reeds would like him but other people could despise him.

Was he politically active in Canada? No. Not at all. There was a focus on himself which I found discouraging. He'd talk about politics but never very knowledgeably. I mean about politics of South Africa, or any politics for that matter. He was not interested. He writes about Oxford and knocking the stuffing out of some people that had something to do with some organization, [It was JACARI]. There's a sense of almost contempt ... But then, he would write very poetically about ... exiles. He certainly had a great deal of respect for Dennis Brutus – not for Dennis's poetry, by the way, but his politics. Once again, a sense of ambivalence about politics. I think this business about making speeches for money really turned him off. He was obviously committed to the liberation of South Africa.

Was he creatively active in Toronto? He was writing poems ... He went to Oxford in 1970 ... he just left his job part way through the school year. We can tell from the poems that he was cracking up ... He ran into a South African exile and a woman ... and she was pretty disgusted with him. I met him in July or August of 1970 in London and he carried on about Canada in the pubs ... I left early because it annoyed me. He carried on in a positive way? Yes, very positively about Canada, singing its praises. In Toronto, he ran the place down, ran the country down; in London he was singing its praises.

Was he otherwise active in Toronto? No. What about music? He was interested in music. When the Beatles came out we were disappointed in him because we thought he was a jazz man. We thought it was a betrayal.

Do you have any idea of the relationship Nortje had with his colleagues and students at Alderwood? No. I don't know. But it must have been heavy because he left during the school year. I don't know if that had anything to do with the staff as such. Where was Alderwood Collegiate? In Etobicoke.

Do you know Jo-ann Hannah? No. Other than Mrs Reed, are there other contacts in Canada that you know of? That fellow he stayed with in BC [Davidson]. I'd like to read some phrases to you; respond as you see fit. 'Balsam Street'? Balsam Street is where Olga lived. 'The dormant seed of syphilis'? I don't know.

When Nortje lived with you, did you live in this house? No. We lived in an apartment on Lawrence Avenue West. Would you care to read some of the letter? [letter from Nortje to RL, 5/31/69] I'll give you just a flavour of it because if I gave it to you you wouldn't understand it. Reads:[6] 'Now assuming that, mutatis mutandis, the same insidious American ... melting-pot exists in Canada, it would spell out a revealing fact: that a cultural minority of one I, K. Artur Patat, am *fighting a rearguard action of universal significance to the furtherance of Deadinghtuesse [?] in Hope. Attie Superego Africanus versus ta hideous assortment of loggers, miners, misguided Japs, frigid vrouniense [?], junkstore Polacks, pseudo-intellectual hippies, et sedera ek sê vir ha'.'* What he does is he takes Afrikaans and the patois of Cape Town and writes in that style. Stuff like this would be difficult to translate. Based on the letter, he really seemed to want to get out of Hope. *Yeah, I didn't want to say so but he really wanted to be with me. There's a poem that he dedicates to me, it's called 'Continuation'.*

Why were only six of 65 poems Nortje wrote in Hope published in *Dead roots? This guy Dennis Brutus was in too much of a hurry to get them published. The agreement was that Olga Reed and I would search his luggage for the poems, type them up, Brutus would send us copies, we would send him copies of what we had, we'd compare notes and then publish. But this son of a gun wanted to get into print very quickly. He made all kinds of mistakes. He was in too great a hurry, otherwise we could have had the others published. Bit of a prima donna, Brutus. I'll search for the poems and I'll let you have them. I don't know how much success you would have with the Journal because a lot of it is in patois.*

You have to understand, one reason Nortje was not interested in politics: he and I grew up in a totally coloured township and Nortje could not relate with the black South African liberation movement, the ANC, etc. Nortje wanted to be of South Africa, but not in South Africa.

Others

Letters to the Etobicoke School district, the Faculty of Graduate Studies, University of Toronto and Mrs Olga Reed met with little success. The school board confirmed that Nortje had worked for them in 1969. The Faculty of Graduate Studies indicated that records are only available for successful applicants. Olda Reed wrote to say that all records in her possession were 'sent, after Ray Leitch completed his work for his MA degrees in 1975, to Hedy Davis in Pretoria, South Africa ... I had visited her in 1981 and organized the transference of Arthur's papers to a university in South Africa when she had completed her [MA] work ... All I have are his letters to me from Oxford from Sept. 1970 to Dec. ... I do not think that my recollections of a lovely person I knew for only a year would be of much help [to researchers]' (6 August 1996).

Revived leads

In the early Fall of 2001 we received an unexpected letter, unexpected because we assumed all leads had dried up. The letter was from Cliff Mack, of Hamilton, Ontario. He writes:

I was a student of A. K. Nortje at Hope Secondary school in Hope B. C. for 1968–1969, my graduating year and the year previous. Mr. Nortje was my English teacher, and for one year, my home room teacher, so his signature is on my report cards, along with his notes. I was surprised to learn that Nortje took his life not long after I finished school – I learned this many years later when reading a collection of African poets – I was also surprised that he was an important writer. I read his poems very carefully and it took me back over all of those years.

He was younger than the other teachers, and much different. Some of our staff, including the Principal, were war vets, and approached as drill sergeants. Nortje was actually excited about English literature, and he made Shakespeare come alive in our classes. Quite a contrast to the analytical hatchet jobs that we were used to.

Although from S. Africa, Nortje did not discuss politics in class, which I found odd. I assumed that he had been told to keep his mouth shut. He did, however, have private conversations with some of the students – about poetry, and perhaps other questions. Some of the young women were writing poems, and shared them with their teacher – he encouraged them loudly. Erin McConnell was one – she may still live in the Hope area, but with a different name.

Nortje was particular about his name being pronounced correctly. We all started calling him NORT-GEE, and he would patiently correct us, NOR-KEE.

He dressed well. I was surprised to see him walking about town with a jacket and vest and polished loafers. He stood out in a community of loggers and miners, construction workers and petty shop owners. And he was also black.

[I was] told, in casual conversation, that Nortje smoked marijuana with some of the students from the school. This was back in the 1970s, but that conversation stuck in my mind. Perhaps a rumour, but [the individual who spoke to me], at that time, was a small time dealer, so he knew the users pretty well.

In many ways, Nortje was just a teacher, and I was just one of many students. We did not have any special conversations about life or the world. But he was part of something that was happening ... an air of change. The war in Vietnam, the civil rights movement in the U.S., May-June '68 in France, the Soviet invasion of Czechoslovakia, a lot of things were happening, changing. And the music and the drugs.

Nortje was part of this picture. A young black man from South Africa, in our small town. He reminded us of many things, by only his presence.

I would suggest contacting JOANNE [sic] HANNAH.

Thanks to Cliff Mack's assistance, contact was made with Jo-Ann Hannah the following day. She writes:

I did a BA in English Literature and then did a PhD in Psychology – not English.

So many of us were impressed with Mr. Nortje. I still see my other 4 girlfriends who really liked Mr Nortje ...

Mr Nortje seemed so cool to us, but most important we really took English seriously. He did not relate to us on a person[al] level – at least not me[–] but always around English. I still remember him talking about poems and really speaking from his interest in the poetry – not trying to be cool or impress us. And it was not dry or boring. Quite amazing that he could share his interest in literature and not get cynical, being in the classroom with teenagers who had a million interests besides school. He always seemed very patient, never got angry despite the stupid things students did. I think we were better behaved in his class. I have journals that I wrote from the time, I think I even have my class notes!

He gave me a book to read: Dickens['] The Old Curiosity Shop. He said it was very funny, and I also thought it was funny. I was surprised that a teacher would take the time to do that. I went on to read all of Dickens after that.

Conclusion

What remains of Nortje in Canada, then, are some private letters to Olga Reed, the remains of the letters and other material photocopied by Raymond Leitch, the Hope District School Board files, and the memories of a significant number of students and teachers, whom we continue to trace.

This evidence suggests two apparently contradictory forces at work during Nortje's stay in Canada: alienation (Hell's Gate) and engagement (Hope). That Nortje felt alienated is not surprising, given his exile from South Africa; it is manifested both in his poetry and in his behaviour, as reported by those people who knew him during that time. It is arguable that Nortje's alienation, directed against Canada's consumerism, and compounded by the betrayal by the object of his love, began before his arrival in Canada. For in South Africa Nortje was already somewhat of an exile; as a coloured, he sympathised with neither the ruling white minority nor the black activists of the ANC. Or, as Leitch so eloquently stated, Nortje 'wanted to be of South Africa, but not in South Africa' (Tyner 1996.)

Nortje's engagement is less obvious than his alienation. His engagement was not political for, as noted above, he did not identify with the political causes of his homeland. However, interviews with former colleagues and students, notably in Hope, describe a man who was engaged with his work as a teacher and with his students, both in the classroom and in the 'Listeners Club'. Nortje was also creatively active in Canada, having written sixty-five poems during his two years there, a fact that is not noted by most of his critics. On the contrary, many of his critics have portrayed his stay in Canada as a time of creative stagnation. 'Walking' (*AD* 281) illustrates some engagement with local politics, though the phrase 'the politics of sacred' is most likely an editorial slip, as the context enforces a reading of it as 'the politics of Socred'; that is, the Social Credit Party of British Columbia. This misconception is due to the hasty editing of *Dead roots*, which includes only six poems written in Canada. Dirk Klopper's *Anatomy of dark: collected poems of Arthur Nortje* (Unisa Press 2000) fills this gap.

Nortje is a strong poet, whose early death leaves us with a body of work that, because it remains at different levels of revision and polishing, concludes an apprenticeship in his vocation. The unfulfilled potential, banale and clichéaic as it sounds, is a loss. Yet, the greater loss is that of a human being who had come to terms with his life, had returned to Oxford to undertake research in literature, seemed likely to be on the cusp of achieving more than the brief, fleeting moments of happiness that had punctuated his life until that return.

Notes

1   An earlier version of this biographical sketch first appeared in *English in Africa* 26.2 (October 1999):1–54.
2   The table was prepared by Prof Ivan Townshend, University of Lethbridge.
3   Jo-Ann Hannah completed a PhD in Psychology. (e-mail, 4 October 2001).
4   As of the 1971 Census, its population was 712 786, compared to Hope's 3 153 citizens. (*Canada year book* 1376–1377)
5   For example, *Time*, April 25, 1960, p 42: 'if someone could shake the long-held rationale of the Dutch Reformed hierarchy, South Africa's stubborn men might at long last be shaken in their self-righteous faith in *apartheid* itself'.
6   The passage read is an abbreviated version of the letter.

Works cited

Arthur, Donald H. 'Arthur Kenneth Nortje: poet and teacher', *Lonely Against the Light: New Coin Poetry* 9.iii/iv (1973):8–18.

Barman, Jean. 'History of BC'. *The encyclopedia of British Columbia*, ed Daniel Francis. Vancouver: Harbour, 2000: 331–342.

Barnett, Ursula A. *A vision of order: a study of black South African literature in English: 1914–1980.* Cape Town: Longman, 1983:85–89.

'Bennett, William Andrew Cecil'. *The encyclopedia of British Columbia*, ed Daniel Francis. Vancouver: Harbour, 2000:71.

Berthoud, Jacques. 'Poetry and exile: the case of Arthur Nortje', *English in Africa* 11.1 (May 1984):1–14.

Bunn, David. 'Arthur Nortje', *Dictionary of literary biography*. 125:170–77.

Bunn, David. 'Some alien native land: Arthur Nortje, literary history and the body in exile', *World Literature Today* 70.1 (Winter 1996):33–44.

Canada year book. 1972 ed. Ottawa: Statistics Canada, 1972.

Countries of the world and their leaders yearbook. 2002 ed. Ed Jennifer L Jackson. Detroit: Gale, 2001.

Davis, Morris & Joseph F Krauter. *The other Canadians: profiles of six minorities*. Toronto: Methuen, 1971.

Driedger, Leo. *Multi-ethnic Canada: identities and inequalities.* Toronto: Oxford University Press, 1996.

Hannah, Jo-Ann. E-mail to Craig McLuckie and Ross Tyner, 24 September, 2001.

Herberg, Edward N. *Ethnic groups in Canada: adaptations and transitions.* Toronto: Nelson Canada, 1989.

Historical statistics of Canada. 2nd ed. Ed FH Leacy. Ottawa: Statistics Canada, 1983.

The Hope Standard.

Leitch, RG. 'Arthur Nortje: 1942–1970', *Lonely against the light: New coin poetry* 9.iii/iv (1973):1–7.

Mack, Cliff. Letter to Craig McLuckie. 23 September, 2001.

McLuckie, Craig W. Interview with Brian Warner. Hope, BC, July 2, 1996.

McLuckie, Craig W. Telephone interview with Tama Kawase. Hope, BC, 2 July, 1996.

McLuckie, Craig W. Interview with Victor Smith. Hope, BC, 2 July, 1996.

McLuckie, Craig W. Interview with Peter McPhedran. Hope, BC, 3 July, 1996.

Nortje, Arthur. *Anatomy of dark: collected poems of Arthur Nortje,* ed Dirk Klopper. Pretoria: Unisa Press 2000.

Nortje, Arthur. *Dead roots,* eds Dennis Brutus et al. London: Heinemann, 1973.

Nortje, Arthur. The Oxford Journal. Pretoria, University of South Africa.

Nortje, Arthur. Letter to Raymond Leitch. 31 May 1969.

Reed, Olga. Letter to Ross Tyner. 6 August 1996.

Smith, Holly and Jac. Conversation with Craig McLuckie. February 2002.

Tyner, Ross. Interview with Raymond Leitch. Toronto, Ontario, 18 July 1996.

Walker, James W St G. *Racial discrimination in Canada: the black experience.* Ottawa: Canadian Historical Association, 1985.

Winks, Robin W. *The blacks in Canada: A History.* 2nd ed. Montreal: McGill-Queen's University Press, 1997.

Chapter 9: The sense of exile in the poetry of Arthur Nortje

Annie Gagiano

> lack of belonging was the root of
> hurt
> the quick child, he must travel

In the strict sense of what it means to be in exile, Arthur Nortje, who left his mother country to study in Britain and afterwards travelled between the United Kingdom and Canada on a South African passport, could not be said to have experienced this condition, particularly as he was still legally free to return to South Africa at the time of his premature death. Yet the Nortje poems that use the term 'exile' and those that give voice to what can be termed the existential condition of exile are among Nortje's most famous and memorable utterances, and (to date) the majority of essays and commentaries concerned with Nortje's work allude to or use the term 'exile' in their titles.[1] Nortje is ineluctably a *poet of exile*, then.

It will be the argument of this chapter that not only in the looser sense of 'exile' as the condition of one who feels forced away from her or his country of origin and who has nostalgic feelings about it, *but* in the still broader meaning of someone experiencing a crucial 'lack of belonging' (see the epigraph above), Nortje did feel himself to be ostracized, shut out, *exiled* – long before he left South Africa.[2] The quotation used above as the motto to this chapter (*AD* 180) indicates indeed that what propelled the poet's quest was both an urge to escape the psychic damage that he knew was being done to him in the South African setting and the need to find a context suitable to and appreciative of his genius. The cleverly placed adjective 'quick' hence not only suggests the poet's precocious sense of his giftedness, or an adolescent restlessness, but also expresses the recognition of a growth urge (or quickening) that requires a less barren soil than his immediate environment provides. So organic a body is the ten-year harvest of poetry gathered now in the Klopper edition that 'quick' prefigures the recurrent and eventually tragic image of 'roots' that Nortje employs so often, particularly in the later poems.

In the epigraph (*AD* 180), the term features as 'the *root* of hurt' (emphasis added) to suggest that the poet is (like Yeats) 'hurt into' writing, simultaneously indicating that an anguish is bred into him from the very beginnings of his existence. It is not difficult to work out that a South African child born to a poor, unmarried, coloured mother (like Nortje was) who finds out that his abandoning father was Jewish (hence classified white) and a student would from the start have sensed himself irrevocably an outsider of some kind to both of the larger, main South African racial categorizations of the time. 'White' then meant (simultaneously) superiority, privilege, first-rate education – and 'non-white' (as we know) inferiority, indigence and (generally) an inadequate education. Mark Espin writes that 'perceptions of non-identity and self-doubt are vividly illustrated in his work' (Espin 1993:8). Nortje was so aware of the forces that had shaped his destiny that one finds him referring in a brief poem of 1968 to 'the slummed lust yearning for redress / *But with no resolution of desire*' (*AD* 277) to explain his speaker's apparently inexplicable rejection of possible long-term sexual partners in liaisons ensuring prosperity. Both 'beautiful dowager' and 'substantial heiress' are incapable of satisfying the unassuagable 'froze[n]' heart of the speaker. The evidently phallic image of the 'slacked snake' suggests the inevitable, eventual failure of desire or 'yearning' *itself* – in a sense much larger than the sexual, because of the early thwarting of impulse. In a complex metaphor from a late poem (or section) titled 'Exile from the first', Nortje articulates his understanding that 'exile was implanted / in the first pangs of paradise' (*AD* 376).

The point that birth in an 'alien native land' (*AD* 374) prompted thoughts of going into exile in even the adolescent fledgling poet is discernible in the earliest poems in the Klopper collection. It is more important, however, to recognize the extent to which, from the very beginning of his poetic career, this led to Nortje's expressions of the moral and psychic complications of his 'unhomely' state. The poet's recognition of the 'split soul' (*AD* 273) of one who grows up as he did in 'this bizarre country' (*AD* 108), apartheid South Africa, indicates that his condition is less simple than an emotional schizophrenia, since his is a soul whose fissures split in several ways. The *agon* of this condition stayed with Nortje throughout his short life and could be said in one sense to be the only homeland he knew. We see it depicted in the earliest of the *Collected poems*: the young poet's 'ambition' is thwarted (in South Africa, evidently) by 'the corrugated iron partition' representing the class/race barrier, but his aspiration to 'the crystal-perfect chalices' (an image alluding at once to success, fame, and wealth) is apparently called into question in the penultimate line by the 'dead voice' of the heroic anti-apartheid activist and journalist Christopher Gell, to whom the poet (in the title) dedicates this poem (*AD* 2).

The inextricably entangled and guilt-ridden sense of anxiety to which

Nortje gives expression throughout his oeuvre (and it is in this sense, as I see it, that he was a perpetual exile) results – on the evidence of the poetry – from conflicting urges he could never resolve. The reader's sense of Nortje as a fundamentally suffering human being is a recognition of the unforgettable expression Nortje gave to this very South African condition: intertwined feelings of class exile and of racial solidarity, *and* of racial betrayal, pulling the poet in often 'opposite' directions. The index of a complex anguish, it is also a pointer to the source of Nortje's artistic power and depth. He expressed the realization that he 'wrote poems' in order 'to choke down an unutterable cry' (*AD* 269), indicating how the interaction of utterance with what was inexpressible would remain an energy source, a horror, and a war within. The issue of the poet's imagined audience must have remained crucial yet baffling – *for* whom, *to* whom does such an 'exiled' poet write?[3] Few of those who shared the poet's experiences had access to his poetry; we who now read and study Nortje's work can (on the other hand) only enter his state of mind with the passports of what to him was mostly an unimaginable future land.

In the poems (dated 1960 to late 1965; *AD* 2–147) which he wrote before he left South Africa, Nortje touches often – implicitly and also explicitly – on the theme of exile, both in the technically precise and in the broader existential sense of this condition. A number of poems refer to friends or his lover leaving South Africa. The speaker in a particularly interesting and ambitious poem titled 'To a friend departing for Canada' (*AD* 6–10) repeatedly and poignantly requests: 'Remember though that I am one of you, I am one of you' (*AD* 6, echoed on pages 8 and 9). In an even earlier poem he describes how he 'hear[s] ship-horns echo voyages for others' (*AD* 4). A feeling of abandonment and isolation is expressed in a poem from his Bellville period: 'I'm lonely. / Lately escape became the fashion' (*AD* 75). Those 'others who talked and vanished / without ... an echo' (*AD* 89) may well include exiles as well as the detainee explicitly mentioned; he thinks of his lost beloved[4] at this stage as having gone 'somewhere I can never travel' (*AD* 119).

Some of the poet's reasons for going into exile – such as racial stigmatization and humiliation – are also reasons that life in the 'motherland' is experienced like a condition of exile. The 'Mother republic' poem (dated 1960, when South Africa became a republic) bristles with grim images of 'dungeon-mesh' and 'barbed wire spikes' and alludes to the speaker's 'ice-cold anger', imploring more whipping in order to 'merge / with dungeon black' (*AD* 3). The bitterness conveyed (in another poem) by the poet's deliberate employment of the 'official' Afrikaans term 'KLEURLING' for a South African classified 'coloured' like himself (*AD* 77; capitals in the original), is unmistakable. Lines such as 'I travel / a land of bitter efficiency second-class' (*AD* 88); or 'the executives / Nordic in comparison with me' and 'o where is home?' (*AD* 99) explain the deeply shocking statement: 'I feel like evil in this bizarre country' (*AD* 108). Awareness of Khoisan ancestry is expressed as 'below life fossils of my fathers'; their successors are seen as 'footballing students brown with the complexion of guilt' (*AD* 117). The Port Elizabeth setting is depicted as surrealistically filled with 'sombre ruins' and with 'the bizarre / wreckage of raids and deprivations' (*AD* 137), evidence of social and political breakdown.

Nortje's sense of class exclusion is notable: he sees 'fine young whites' in a park and refers to '*their* houses of parliament' (*AD* 112, emphasis added). He knows himself to be 'grimly' clutching 'hope beyond / my means', shut out by 'the barbed wire spikes' (*AD* 3). Futile thoughts of the 'sweet ... island' Britain contrast with the 'blond-bossed kingdom' where the poet can only 'hold / a five-cent passport to Athlone desert: / [he has] not been to London to announce [his] freedom' (80).[5] Sardonically adapting TS Eliot, he hears 'the voice of the world' say 'to [his] coloured education, / Go now, brown man, go ...' (*AD* 87). Around him, 'torpid with suffering [his] people / shop in the baasskap markets / and wend their cattle ways to bus stops' (*AD* 118). Open-eyed about the conflicting urges propelling him, the speaker in 'Song for a passport' acknowledges: 'I gravitate to what is comely, / having tasted contumely / because my crust is black and hard'; seeing the 'bright enticement' to 'leave a land of problems'. This poem ends: 'O ask me all but do not ask allegiance!' (*AD* 140–141).

A deep sense of entrapment and thwartedness is conveyed in many of Nortje's South African poems. The speaker in one poem refers to 'hope's emergence' and to 'blood's fresh chance to change and mingle', obliterated when 'hopefulness is buried in an iceberg / of arctic yesterdays, and blank tomorrows' (*AD* 77). In contrast with those who 'fly away / to Europe or America' the speaker is 'house-bound and law-arrested' (*AD* 86) and the sense of a perpetual stasis ('No change: / we stay strange', *AD* 96) oppresses him. Shortly before leaving, he writes of wanting 'to earn more purpose than this narrow world / affords its children' (*AD* 139). In the poem 'At a demolition site' (dated February 1965) the poet alludes clearly to political oppression and its consequences for the artist:

... Among this rubble
edge uneasy thoughts along
the roadblocked mind in early dark.
Curfew on actions, ban on contact,
the loss of voice or some other fear
which grey dead weather can make so bearable. (*AD* 118)

Another moving poem relates how 'the long silence speaks / of deaths and removals' while 'restrictions, losses / have strangled utterance' (*AD* 127), and the speaker is left with the 'husks of the exile' (*AD* 128).

The fear that the apartheid state's vigilance against almost any form of resistance or questioning might harm him shows up in several early Nortje poems – in the speaker's sense of 'danger' (*AD* 11) from the 'jackboot's bite and bone-crush, / slash-flesh, fear- and frightful rod' (*AD* 12) of the oppressor.

He asks his departing beloved to explain 'the anatomy of fear' (*AD* 87) to those outside, who do not know how, in South Africa, 'darkness comes and goes, / assuming shapes of terror' (*AD* 113).

Anticipation of an Armageddon-like racial conflagration in South Africa, something he at times keenly anticipated ('I welcome all violence / for peace and prosperity's sake', *AD* 12), on other occasions is shown to arouse apprehension: 'A red, an alarming sunset sails / hard down on the sea of us, all of us; / hard labour to carry its cargo of nails / hell- heaven- or homeward. Who knows?' (*AD* 7). 'Whose prayer,' the speaker asks, 'will hold back the blind vicious war?' (*AD* 87). Clearly there were times when Nortje saw himself as an outsider to the black majority: 'Struggles are for multitudes. / They cast you out unsound' (*AD* 15), he wrote in 1962.

Even before he left South Africa, however, the poet had begun to sense something of the emotional and moral dilemmas besetting his position and the roles he might choose to adopt. In 'For Gerald going to England' he had written: 'Are there no ways or means / of silencing our much unminded moans / other than leaving the land it is duty to defend?' (*AD* 11), anticipating the 1965 statement: 'my people / you beg the rain of mercy: / travels can make me forget it' (*AD* 113). There seems at least a touch of self-justification in the speaker's statements that his 'friends had approved' his departure (*AD* 146), offset by his vision of those less privileged whom he is leaving behind (*AD* 147). Earlier, even to 'board a brown train' seems an '[escape]' (*AD* 46). An especially complex poem is called 'The exiles silenced' (*AD* 22). In a subtle train of thought, Nortje seems here to weigh up the validity of the claim that only an act of political violence will resolve the psychic, political and even 'artistic' dilemmas caused by the South African situation. 'About action all we know revolves / around the easy friability of words: / or alternatively despair composes life into the suicidal statement of a gun', reads the paradox-fraught opening stanza. Clearly the reference to words as 'friab[le]' suggests their weakness; yet it is through this unreliable medium that the call to 'action' comes, or through 'despair' – whether in suicidal political action, or in actual self-murder, is debatable. Nevertheless such a 'despair[ing]' act may be the only way of achieving 'compos[ure]', 'soldering the crack between anger and fear' into a final wholeness of being and outdoing the compositions or words that only reveal the fractured self. Political 'fury' may remain merely 'mute' by being expressed in words *instead* of in action, if the latter method is the only effective way of "getting heard". Written when Nortje was merely twenty, this brilliant, complex poem clearly anticipates many of his most famous later compositions. The sardonic image of 'exile' as the 'spill[ing]' of 'milk' over 'wounds' acknowledges its ineffectuality in healing and its self-indulgent, 'unheard' crying (over spilt milk, instead of blood?).

In the poems written during his first sojourn in Britain (from November 1965 to July 1967, *AD* 150–246) Nortje expresses full awareness of his inclination to cynical betrayal of his South Africanness (as a moral-political cause) through sensuous indulgence: 'my devil is the bastard of desires: / outlaughing remembrances, he spits on the shards' (*AD* 168). The poet evidently enjoyed the upward social mobility made possible by his transfer to the Oxford University environment, where he noticed how 'gentlemen drift in from squash or dining' (*AD* 150), and enjoyed the communal ease of British life (*AD* 155). He could feel the 'searing [South African] years' now soothed by 'softer rain' (*AD* 151) in the 'sheltering island' (*AD* 152). His speaker's declaration: 'I have fled with my wounds the colossal crises' (*AD* 153) registers a sense of betrayal of duty and a moral failure ('fled'), as much as it does an urgent need for recovery from 'wounds' – *and* an awareness of the overwhelming, intractable nature of the South African 'crisis'.

Even in 'acquired England' (*AD* 160), though, 'nightmares' could haunt the exile. Here too Nortje began to lay claim to the history or ancestry of the all but exterminated Khoisan ('and the blond invaders coming on horseback / along the empty valleys when the drums / went silent'), for these nightmares were now a heritage to be contrasted with the bland privileges of a Bohemian British existence (*AD* 160–162). Instead of 'outlaughing remembrances' (*AD* 168), as described in an earlier poem, the poet could now refer to himself as a 'memory merchant', one 'hog[ging his] emotions' (*AD* 163). Yet the images of sterility and growth failure now begin to be associated with the poet's distance from his motherland: enforced 'wander[ing]' occurs 'among the ruins and the crushed roots', where he feels 'dead sequences burn in the nerves' (*AD* 164). As he had so often done, Nortje at this period too associated his loss in love with a sense of the political severance brought by exile (*AD* 166; 168).

The poem 'In exile' of 1966 vividly articulates the psychic 'hunger' Nortje began now to experience with particular intensity – an agony of longing that in the poem leads the speaker to the self-chiding reminder of the brutal fact that 'wrong pigment has no scope' in South Africa at this time, and that to avoid the deceptions of nostalgia, he must 'clot the blue channel of memory'. Yet *without* fond memories 'the soul decays in exile' (*AD* 171). In the deservedly well-known poem 'Cosmos in London' (*AD* 175–176) the poet adapts the ANC rallying cry (*mayibuye iAfrika!*) to express his own yearning: 'O come back Africa!'. And yet the poem as a whole suggests the psychic danger that nostalgia holds for the exile, for 'tears may now / extinguish even the embers under the ash' and 'memory disturbs the order of the song'. The exile who recalls too fondly his land of origin and its 'forgotten', imprisoned leaders is like a person 'who escapes / a lover's quarrel' and 'will never rest his roots'.

For all the friendly acceptance that seems to have been his general experience of life in Britain, Nortje in some poems expresses a sense of cultural and social rejection of what he felt to be his un-British inclination to 'give tongue to truth' – the pronoun in earlier lines from the same poem is telling: 'outspokenness they consider lacks / insight, identity, coolness of the heart' (*AD* 180). These 'British' standards were evidently as much a social and political as an artistic issue for Nortje. In among the poems for Sylvia Plath and his satirical ventriloquising of American views is the beautiful and empathetic poem imagining or recalling a political prisoner's 'Letter from Pretoria Central Prison' (*AD* 185–186). Nortje's warm 'London impressions' (*AD* 188–189) precede his 'September poem' expressing 'lonel[iness]', 'vague unease' and the feeling of being 'disembodied as a cloud'. Here he acknowledges that the 'past does not cling, but spreads and settles / like colour in the water, heart's diffusion' (*AD* 190). Even in 'cocoons of warmth' (*AD* 191 – elsewhere identified as 'the refugee's privilege' – *AD* 193), and even in a poem titled 'At rest from the grim place' (193), the poet's haunted sense of severance is evinced in his question: 'Why is there no more news?' (*AD* 194).

The strange poem 'Autopsy' (*AD* 194–197) is one in which Nortje explicitly concerns himself with those (like Dennis Brutus) forced out of their countries into political exile, compared to whom he refers to himself as 'too nominal an exile / to mount such intensities of song'. But although Nortje endows them with the stature of 'dark princes', his imagery (and the general tone of lamentation of his poem) views them also as 'burnt ... offer[ings]', and their cause as a defeated one. He seems simultaneously to maintain an ironic distance from their political idealism, and to empathise with their tragic position, considering them 'to their earth unreturnable'.

'Assessment' (October 1966) registers again Nortje's sense of a fractured self, phantasmagorically split between a 'survivor' who is a 'wraith', and 'this other half' (*AD* 199). In January 1967 he writes the harrowing poem called 'The near-mad' (*AD* 207–208). In it, his obsessive, poignant use of the notion of his own uprootedness re-emerges: 'anchors have snapped and roots are severed' reads one line, and the next refers to 'terribly shrivelled ... tendrils of feeling', while the following poem refers to 'want ... mauling the roots' and to 'the dead- / lock of the heart' (*AD* 208–209). Similar images in a poem written shortly afterwards are of 'the heart's worn cogs, the mind's snapped links'. 'Night ferry', written soon after, asks 'What purpose / has the traveller now, whose connection is cut' (*AD* 217)? Nortje's seemingly perpetual, haunting feelings of guilt and betrayal emerge in what appears to be a reference to his South African background: 'Obscene are the unborn children, insane are the destitute mothers, / I do think, who have known them, disowned them' (*AD* 218). At the end of his highly appreciative poem about a trip to Ireland, Nortje refers to 'the long-lost / Cabo de Esperancia'[6] and he ends the poem by saying 'there is something missing / always, that I hope to find again' (*AD* 223).

In 'My mother was a woman' Nortje's speaker declares that 'there are those who hope, like me, not to arrive' (*AD* 229), and that 'From Cabo de Tormentoso I was hounded / the salt in my flesh clouded my bones with pain' (*AD* 230); yet the very next poem ('Apology from London') has a speaker stating: 'We must all return and break more stone // south over the sea to where the diseased wind / rages in the dockyard of the soul' (*AD* 231). These images and sentiments point forward to the final poem of the first British period, Nortje's 'Waiting' (*AD* 243–244) with the famous opening lines: 'The isolation of exile is a gutted / warehouse at the back of pleasure streets'. This beautiful, deeply melancholic poem moves from the gritty realism of the seedy dockside scenery of the opening (the 'underside' of the glamourizing misconceptions that seduce prospective exiles) to the surreal images of a mind in decay, whose very creations (poems) testify to its crumbling condition. Again Nortje refers to transplanted 'roots' that are now ironically 'withering' (*AD* 244), since it was to escape the 'fire' causing that very effect that the 'voyager' moved to 'another continent'. The haunting image of the Robben Island prisoners ('the breakers of stone') recurs here, as does the cry 'Come back, come back mayibuye' – simultaneously summoning the speaker to return to the cause, and invoking the dawn of liberation. In the middle stanza the poet 'transfers' the image of his personal suffering to those hemmed in by the apartheid state's machinery: 'loneliness' is now *their* condition, yet the magnitude of their 'strangled throat of multi-humanity' (implying a huge silencing) still links them with the exiled poet's 'suffer[ing] the radiation burns of silence' and with his 'solitude that mutilates', leaving its 'ash' to prove *his* 'withering', burnt-out condition.

From 1967 to 1970 (*AD* 248–364) Nortje lived in Canada, working as a schoolteacher. The first poem from this period is titled 'Immigrant', oscillating from the nonchalant declaration 'I am an acceptable soldier of fortune' (*AD* 248) to the imagined (self-?) chiding demand:

Where are the mineworkers, the compound Africans,
your Zulu ancestors, where are
the root-eating, bead-charmed Bushmen, the Hottentot sufferers?
Where are the governors and sailors of the
Dutch East India Company, where are
Eva and the women who laboured in the castle?
You are required as an explanation. (*AD* 249)

The whole gamut of South African peoples and history is evoked in these lines as the baggage of accountability that the supposedly free-spirited 'soldier of fortune' is nevertheless burdened with. The 'posture of acquired nonchalance' of 'exiles' like himself (referred to in the next poem) makes him cheerfully hopeful that a 'leaf' may yet sprout from the 'roots' (*AD* 251). Some months later the lines 'Quiet night, no stars, because of curtain, / was not a problem, it was never there / for who belongs nowhere, is to nothing / deeply attached without nonetheless laughter' (*AD* 259) begin to show the dreary feeling of *malaise* which Nortje's poems written in Canada express with increasing intensity.[7] In 'Draft History' he evokes the 'road to exile', but the speaker who 'emerge[s]' from the South African 'emergency' is 'free and lonely in the bubble sky' rather than 'happy'(*AD* 260–261).

The poem 'View from the village' (presumably Hope, BC) lapses from describing the prosperous Canadian scene into a nightmarish evocation of the wounded South African landscape (262–264), and in the next month Nortje prefaces the poem 'Blank sanity' with a Dostoevsky quotation referring to 'a gloomy sensation of agonising, infinite isolation and alienation' (*AD* 266). The speaker in this poem sees his own face as 'foreign' and full of 'horror' while 'outside the world is white', suggesting at once its racial otherness, its climatic strangeness (to an African expatriate), and its alien blankness. He is 'black-humoured' in a 'world looking white' (*AD* 267). The poem '25' (evidently referring to Nortje's birthday) concludes despairingly: 'The power failed, / the power failed. / Your career has come full circle' (269). A title such as 'Dangerous silences' (*AD* 275) gives further indication of the psychic fears the poet suffers from. The lines (from the poem 'Fragment') that read 'nostalgia burns the limbs that wander / along a pavement of laundromats and poolrooms' (*AD* 277) succinctly express Nortje's alienation from what he depicts as the bourgeois comforts of Canadian life. Ironically, here where none of the 'barbed wire spikes' of apartheid rules exclude him, he evidently finds it impossible to develop a sense of belonging. A phrase like 'the white oblivion of escape' (*AD* 283) in one poem contrasts with a reference to 'the black memories' (*AD* 285) in another, indicating that in Canada Nortje experienced exile in an increasingly racialised manner. In one poem the speaker proclaims that 'the white wounds will not heal' (*AD* 288) and in another he declares: 'I am black ... / transplanted like an export seed', feeling evidently ill at ease in 'the coca-cola cities'. In this latter poem, too, he refers disparagingly to himself as a 'voyeur' in contrast with 'those who must return' to 'the boss camps and the slave plantations' (*AD* 289).

The image 'welfare of the glaciers' in the latter poem is recalled in a subsequent reference to 'an ice paralysis' (*AD* 294). In the poem with the revealingly disconsolate title 'A further season in a mountain town' the speaker declares that 'big river / is not my country at all', but acknowledges that 'Art maybe has / failed the natives'[8] since (with a pun on 'guilt'?) 'on his gilt eyes settle / the bitterness ashes and nullity / of mechanical tree scenes' (*AD* 296). Many poems of this period refer to Nortje's evidently increasing psychic desperation ('twenty four hours a day dying' (*AD* 299)). An image such as 'the black crow / looks for seed' evinces the soul starvation Nortje experienced as an African in North America, despite the superficial comforts of his 'successfully' middle-class life. His 'Poem in Canada' (*AD* 303–304) ends with a stanza stating: 'son of the albatross, the native thus / weeps, which has / nothing to do with new business / or these majesties of mountains, quiet woods: / but the gold boss who whips / the black bull in full view / of the sun' – clearly South African references. Like a 'needle' he cannot help 'encompassing / those often exiled / black soil lovers'. The next poem, 'Looking', drably acknowledges, however (in the voice of Nortje's speaker), that 'the deep soldier fades in me: / look at / the dried-up singers, exiles, those departed / from yesterday cities' (*AD* 304). It seems as if the sardonic reference later in this poem to Nortje's own conception by a white father is a self-blaming attempt to account for the deep guilt he felt at his seeming betrayal of the cause of black liberation in Southern Africa: 'wasn't / Zimbabwe or the miracle we come from / discovered by the blond giant? / My father served that sailor / tilling in the black soil' (*AD* 305), the speaker states. A poem about Toronto refers to 'the monstrous landscape of

133

apartment towers / parking lots and pizza drive-ins' and states that 'exile makes no sense / and whatever past there was is amputated' (*AD* 308). Elsewhere the line occurs: 'you do not live in a country any more' (*AD* 310).

Terms like 'nostalgia' or 'longing' are inadequate to describe the deep sorrow evinced particularly in the poems written during the last two years of Nortje's writing life; his writing of this period conveys something more like the work of mourning. The word 'native' which he so often uses to refer to himself – ironically or mockingly, as in the title 'The alter native' (*AD* 312) – begins to carry an increasingly tragic weight. Many poems refer to his insomnia: 'night eyes that won't close' and that are both 'lost' and 'ridiculous / riddled with the pale dream' (*AD* 313) – and also to his evidently increasing alcohol and drug dependency: 'alcoholic dawns / reveal skies livid', for 'here / memory is implausible' (*AD* 314). A Christmas dinner, eaten 'solitaire', prompts thoughts of the Hobson's choice faced by exiles like Nortje: 'deportment / from limbo homelands where the souls erode / to the white north where they die: choose which / transportation it is to be' (from 'White Xmas', (*AD* 315)). Where he now lives, 'the heart's estate withers away', the speaker says (316). A poem like 'Spiders' uses the image of eerie 'alien web-threads' that entrap the speaker and indicate the anxieties (both morally and narcotically induced) that beset Nortje at this time. A poem titled 'Quiet desperation' (*AD* 336–337) acknowledges: 'My mind hurts with consistent / intake of chemicals.'

In March 1970 Nortje paid a visit to England, evidently a relief 'after abortive America' (*AD* 339). Admitting to a sense of 'nostalgia' (*AD* 228), he resumes the posture of 'a cool drunk, Afro-Saxon bred', and says of London that 'despite the irony, she, city, / suckled my exile' (*AD* 339) – the poem is titled 'Return to the city of the heart'. It is at this time that Nortje, slightly melodramatically and unusually self-pityingly (for him) creates the image of himself as 'having stood / lonely against the light / with my dark hands full of melodies' (*AD* 340).

Some of Nortje's best-known and most moving poems were written during the latter part of his period in Canada, when he stayed in Toronto. His anguished meditation on his own fraught life and its possible meaning and destiny, 'Dogsbody half-breed' (*AD* 344–345), stems from this period. It is (as a poem) a recognizable expression of a sense of exile only because, although written in Toronto, it is exclusively concerned with the history, and the future, of South Africa – and with the speaker's possible role in that past and future. Nortje reverts to the South African preoccupation with supposed racial purities in the speaker's wry reference to his 'mixed-blood' origins; the overtly contemptuous title of the poem is recalled in the reference to the South African racially determined class hierarchy (which ranks the speaker a mere 'factotum' as against 'the master'). In the longer second part of section II (*AD* 345) Nortje enlarges the sense of a personally split self to include the entire South African population, in a remark pertaining particularly to its ruling class: 'divided from yourself'. Seen against the many expressions of a racial fury, hatred, or resentment in Nortje's oeuvre, this poem is remarkable for the way it addresses the racial divide in a tone of lamentation ('glittering with tears') – while noting the hypocrisy of the white ruling class and the sufferings of the oppressed. The 'hybrid' speaker, a denigrated 'dogsbody', nevertheless identifies the role of 'mixed-blood' South Africans as that of a 'buffer', presumably preventing the ultimately destructive clash of races. This melancholy recognition of unheroic 'usefulness' contrasts with the (for Nortje) quite resolute dedication (in the next poem) to a liberatory purpose: 'out of ... the luck of birth' the speaker imagines 'work[ing]' against 'resistance', but propelled by 'strength of seed and courage of decision' (*AD* 346).

Within the same month, though, Nortje reverts (in a poem such as 'Leftovers') to the more characteristic stance of drab despair. The 'dreams' mentioned here have a 'stench' and are now associated with 'phobias / obsessions / guilts' which make the speaker's 'waking life / a paranoidal nightmare'. He imagines his mind being wrecked by the 'merciless pendulum' of these terrible emotions (*AD* 348). So Nortje's poems from this period convey the anguishing oscillation of idealistic political purpose with a despairing sense of his own betrayal of that cause. In the latter state he needs to 'buy off [his] inquisitors', and 'hold back a scream of terror in the ghost-infested midnight' (*AD* 349). Touchingly, the next poem refers to 'my love / my now distant land' (*AD* 351), evincing the speaker's enduring commitment to, as much as his sense of severance from, South Africa. This preoccupation of Nortje's with his motherland is maintained in 'Poem: South African' (*AD* 352–353). Beginning on a note of 'nostalgia', as so often in his poems Nortje offsets that longing with the cold political realism of 'shattered faces dark with terror' and 'scarred landscapes', and of many others (those forced into exile?) who 'crowd the ports' (presumably in South Africa). As in 'Dogsbody half-breed', however, and more clearly discernible here, the speaker (as if impelled to this, despite all the evidence to the contrary) imagines a future of racial reconciliation ('at last / get us all together'). He notes 'the man with the whip who beats [his] emaciated words back', yet offers himself (perhaps in his 'mixed-blood' origins, or in his affiliation to both an African and a European heritage?) 'as evidence' of the possibility of such a reconciliation, however dangerous and arduous (indicated in 'the man ... who beats' and in 'stumble to ... the hill') such perhaps Christ-like idealism may be.

The mood of the latter, very moving poem seems not to have been sustained. Those that follow speak of moods 'when the heart sits like a rock in the throat' (*AD* 353) and of 'memories swirl[ing]' while 'gallstones of fear jab at [the speaker's] shredded feelings', his 'brain ... reek[ing] with guilt' (*AD* 358–359). The most memorable poem of this period, written not long before Nortje left Canada, is 'Native's letter', a poem in which Nortje's experience and vision of exile is the central theme. Nortje's unmistakable declaration of love for and commitment to his 'homeland' – evinced in the speaker's reference to 'my dear land' and his plea to be 'remember[ed]' as one continuing in his own way to strive for his people in the 'hard cities' of exile – is one of Nortje's most enduring legacies to his country of origin. Recognizing as it does the complex of conflicting aspirations of any exile from an oppressed society, Nortje seems nevertheless, in this poem at least, to have seen a way out of the terrible guilt and fear that beset exiles like himself. In the role of witness to and interpreter of oppression, Nortje (here) sees an alternative – but significant, and legitimate – way of opposing 'the guns of supremacy'. Because the poem in its poignancy testifies to how hard-won and exceptional this rare self-exculpation was (compared to the generally guilt-plagued utterances of the poet), its singular occurrence among Nortje's far more numerous statements of self-blame would in itself ensure its special place in his oeuvre.

The last months of Nortje's life were spent in England, to which he returned in 1970 for further study at Oxford. The poems of this period (*AD* 366–401) range from some initially mostly cheerful considerations of the poet's 'lyrical' sense of 'revivals' brought about by his return to Britain (*AD* 367) to the recognition of some unidentified 'grey / fear [that] persists' (*AD* 366). A poem such as 'What is mundane' (*AD* 370) still evinces ambition in the artist, and here an insouciant attitude towards British cultural standards combines with the speaker's awareness of the decadence of his lifestyle. In 'Love of perversity' one finds the mockingly self-deprecating boast: 'now I loaf among the well-to-do / and not among the louts and down-and-outers, tramps' (*AD* 371). That the second of the lines quoted above may be a reference to Nortje's South African past is confirmed in the shallow sense of class and race 'upward mobility' expressed in 'Natural sinner': 'invisible has become I hope the stamp of birth, of blackness, criminality' (*AD* 372). But the probably deeper, inextricable psychic entanglement of Nortje with South Africa and its socio-political, racially coded crises of oppression re-emerges explicitly in the series 'Questions and Answers' (*AD* 373–377). The by now familiar dilemma, the 'incurable malaise' of a 'colourful' person (*AD* 373) who has 'white trash / coursing through [his] blood / ... inalienable' (*AD* 376), and of one who senses that he is needed at the 'forefront' yet dreads the 'bloody ... reprisals' (*AD* 377), erupts irrepressibly in the poetry of this period. The impasse is particularly well expressed in some lines from 'I who wear' (*AD* 377–379), finely employing intertextual references to the titles of Kafka's works to convey the poet's sense of the intractable nature of the South African racial-political situation and of his own 'impossible' role in it:

> Though now I partake at a distance of the trials,
> muzzlings, deprivations,
> I too walk on the thin edge, a figure in Kafka,
> and do not for a moment forget the towered castles
> or relinquish the title deeds of birth[.] (*AD* 378)

The tender phrase 'my dear country' (*AD* 379), an unmistakable expression of commitment, helps to explain the anger expressed in the next poem ('My country is not' *AD* 380), against both 'suburban', condescending Europeans and South African icons like the singer Miriam Makeba and the surgeon Chris Barnard. Even in a poem (*AD* 383–385) concerned very topically with international relations around the Suez blockade and the Israeli-Palestinian tensions of the time, Nortje brings in specifically South African references. He refers (in another poem) to himself as a 'prodigal', but seems to foresee his 'redemption' (*AD* 388). The curtailed, parenthetic quotation '(Breathes there a man?)'[9] (*AD* 390) is a further indication of a need Nortje seems to have experienced at this time to affirm his (South African) patriotism.

More powerful, and more convincingly expressed, is the poet's tragic sense of an irreversible severance from his native country and from the cause of South African liberation: in 'Dead roots' (*AD* 391–392) the image of curtailed growth and a process of withering recurs. Ostracized as 'hotnot'[10] in his motherland, the speaker is now ineffectually 'dispersed' to life in 'this temporary isle' (Britain), whereas his paternal 'white blood' is that of a 'disparaged jew'. In this poem Nortje's reverent sense of the political prisoners on Robben Island is felt to have dimmed in 'memory' to the image of 'ancestral / totems that inhabit dreams'. Deeply moving and especially melancholic is the speaker's sense that the revolutionary fire has died out even among the heroes of the struggle ('They are dead igneous'), their defeat registered in the humiliating and meaningless task of 'breaking rock' (the image doubling to suggest that they, too, are 'crumbling'), while he himself is felt to be in the position of the army scout who has 'lost / sight' of the beacon 'fire' of the cause, signifying the dying down of hope and inspiration in the 'dispersed' speaker.

The images of this powerful lyric are picked up in the next poem ('From the way I live now'), in which the speaker declares himself 'no longer the watchman', 'but merely a mouthpiece', nevertheless wryly hinting of inner guilt by noticing the way he imagines himself perceived – as 'radical manqué' perhaps guilty of just a touch of 'cowardice' (*AD* 392). The speaker condemns 'the way [he lives] now' as basely 'accepting smiles and favours for my buried ones', and he ends the poem with the plea that those still toiling 'under the broiling sun' of oppression should '*convict* [him] for [his] once burning ideals' (*AD* 393, emphasis added to indicate the punning reference to those imprisoned in South Africa for their political aspirations). 'Exit visa' (*AD* 395) is a minor poem, but it too implies a somewhat cavalier, nonchalant quality in the speaker's re-evocation of his departure from his homeland – again something of a self-indictment. The third but last poem of the collection testifies pitiably to a self felt to be ruined and empty: 'Supports collapse. Self falls back on its vaults.' The speaker is conscious of 'inalienable blemishes'. Horrifyingly, he is likened to a 'harried rat in a sparked cage that's foodless' (*AD* 398).

Although the question of how exactly Nortje's death came about may never be finally resolved, 'All hungers pass away' (*AD* 398–399), the poem popularly assumed to have been the poet's last one,[11] testifies explicitly to so drastic a failure of vitality that it is no melodramatic distortion to describe the condition as a death of the soul. Clearly this poem too indicates the extent to which the speaker's state of suffering is tied up with his sense of himself as an exile of a particular kind, one guilt-ridden by a sense of betrayal for which the comforts and 'pleasures' of life in Britain ('the sherry circuit, arms of some bland girl') could never compensate. Nortje in the deepest impulses of his art was always a South African poet, in fact incapable in his writing of denying his passionate concern with the fate of his people.

In this poem, the haunting lines 'Drakensberg lies swathed in gloom. / Starvation stalks the farms of the Transvaal' indicate how much larger than any merely personal unhappiness the despair was that most likely contributed crucially to the poet's death.[12] The impulse to fulfil his genius and to earn the accolades to which this might entitle him (recalling 'crystal-perfect chalices' of the first poem in the Klopper collection (*AD* 2)), brought Nortje to 'a land where rhythm fails' and 'famous viands [taste] like ash'. At the heart of the poem lie the images of the 'gloom' and 'starvation' suffered by the compatriots the poet had left behind, in the face of which no personal achievements in Britain could destroy what seems to have been a sense of both artistic and moral-political failure: 'the wasted years'. The adjective in that poignant phrase maintains (punningly) the sense of a starved, 'shrunken corpulence' – it seems, because the true sources of spiritual feeding and psychic health, the connection with the motherland, were cut. In the midst of wealth and plenty the privileged exile adopts (in the image of the final stanza) 'the dark posture' of isolation and starvation and abandonment, enacting and empathising with the deprivation suffered by his people.

Notes

1 See the Bibliography for the titles of essays by Berthoud; Bunn; Chapman; Jacobs; Lefevere and Klopper.

2 In his interesting essay on Nortje, whic "chart[s] the changing function of political agency in Nortje's word ... [as] usually embodied in references to the South African landscape" (34), Bunn writes (of Nortje's early poetry): "Robbed of an audience, the poet speaks *against* a landscape he cannot inhabit, a landscape representative of a new national symbolic scattered with flags flying the banner of the triumphant [South African] Republic" (Bunn 1996:36). See also my own entry in volume 225 of the *Dictionary of literary biography*.

3 In "Exile, the tyranny of place and the literary compromise", Es'kia Mphahlele writes of "intellectual and spiritual alienation" as a "dimension of exile". He emphasizes that at this time "most black South African writers living in exile [were] banned for their native readership", indeed were "like disembodied voices that echo from hill to hill" (1979:42, 41).

4 Berthoud suggests that "Nortje may have learnt from Dennis Brutus ... to treat patriotic and personal love in terms of each other" (Berthoud 1984:5).

5 "Athlone desert" is a bitter political metaphor: Athlone is a Cape Town suburb (fairly new at this time) set aside for separate "coloured" occupation. For prose expression of Nortje's resentment at the racial isolation of "coloured" students, see the two essays "Down at Bush" (Nortje 1964).

6 This is a version of the name early Portuguese explorers gave to the Cape, here slightly shortened by Nortje to mean "Cape of Hope". In the next paragraph of my chapter another such name, "Cabo de Tormentoso" (meaning "Cape of Storms") is cited from another of Nortje's poems, written soon after.

7 McLuckie and Tyner in their article object to what they describe as "an unjustified negative account of Nortje's time in Canada" in Bunn's article (3) for suggesting that there was no happiness during Nortje's time there. Although the poems from the Canadian period in the Klopper collection do reflect much unhappiness, it might be added that Nortje's entire oeuvre (in whatever setting he wrote) tends overwhelmingly to express anguish and melancholia.

8 It needs to be understood that Nortje invariably employs the term 'native/s' to refer to South African indigenes and in using the expression he alludes to the very specific *racialized* meaning of the way this word was used at the time to refer (more euphemistically than some other, more overtly insulting terms, but still condescendingly and humiliatingly) to all 'non-white' (but particularly to black) South Africans. No doubt Nortje was especially aware of the galling irony that most of those *native to* the country (South Africa) were being denied the rights of citizenship.

9 [Eds. The phrase is from Canto VI, i of Sir Walter Scott's *The lay of the last minstrel* (1805).]

10 This wounding, denigratory label was derived from the colonial term "hottentot" (for the Khoikhoi people), and applied to "coloured" South Africans by racist whites.

11 My reading of the last poem Nortje is known to have written, "Wayward ego", differs quite radically from the 'optimistic' interpretation offered by Hedy Davis (Davis 1981:24). The final two stanzas of this poem confirm Nortje's sense of the let-down of exile: the speaker remains the outsider "lean[ing] against black railings", but even a probably British *insider* at whom the speaker stares from outside a window is depicted as "old" and "sad", passively watching the "sponsored glossolalia" of television rather than saying, or creating, anything new or worthwhile (*AD* 401).

12 Hedy Davis (to whom all Nortje readers owe much for her crucial efforts in collecting and preserving his work) has been criticized (see Bunn 1996:43) for her theories concerning the causes of his death. In the earliest of four relevant commentaries she wrote that "Nortje's passport was about to expire, and he would have been deported to South Africa as he had been unable to obtain British citizenship" (Davis1979:6). In the second, she refers to "the stand taken by Nortje in October 1970 [as] that of the poet, no longer prepared to compromise his talent for a polemical cause [evidently, she means the exiled anti-apartheid movement] with which he could not sympathise" (Davis 1980:31). In a 1981 article she writes: "[Dennis] Brutus states that Nortje, in a fit of despair deliberately committed suicide ... as his passport had expired and he was threatened with deportation to South Africa", adding in a later paragraph the apparently then established information that "from Nortje's personal documents several facts emerge [which] refute [the above] allegations. Nortje's South African passport had been renewed in 1968 and his visa to visit the United Kingdom was valid until July 1971. His original application for British citizenship gave him until 20 December 1970 to make his final application, which would have been granted, for he

had fulfilled all the required conditions. Furthermore he left an estate of close on £2 000 and was not in financial straits" (Davis 1981:19). In the fourth commentary, her (unpublished) MA thesis, she wrote the following: "Nortje's defiant stand at Leeds three weeks earlier would undoubtedly have harmed the credibility of the anti-apartheid movement, and it seems highly probable that he did make an attempt to dissociate himself once and for all from the movement. It does not seem likely that the organization would release a person who they felt had a part to play in the struggle" (Davis 1983). It is to the latter statement particularly that Bunn (correctly) objects as resting on "some vague sort of conspiracy theory" (Bunn 1996:43 – footnote 13).

Works cited

Berthoud, Jacques. 'Poetry and exile: the case of Arthur Nortje', *English in Africa* 11.1 (1984):1–14.

Bunn, David. ' "Some alien native land": Arthur Nortje, literary history, and the body in exile', *World Literature Today* 70.1 (1996):33–44.

Chapman, M J F. 'Arthur Nortje: poet of exile', *English in Africa* 6.1 (1979):60–71.

Davis, Hedy. 'Arthur Nortje: the wayward ego', *The Bloody Horse* 3 (1981):14–24.

Davis, Hedy. 'The poetry of Arthur Nortje: towards a new appraisal', *Unisa English Studies* 18.2 (1980):26–32.

Davis, Hedy. 'Arthur Nortje: a forgotten South African poet', *Reality* 11.4 (1979):5–6.

Davis, Hedy. The poetry of Arthur Nortje: a critical introduction. MA dissertation (unpublished). Pretoria: Unisa, 1983.

Espin, Mark. 'A book that changed me: *Dead roots* by Arthur Nortje', *The Southern African Review of Books* 5.3 (1993):8.

Gagiano, Annie. 'Arthur Nortje 1942–1970' in *Dictionary of literary biography volume 225: South African writers,* Ed Paul A Scanlon. Detroit, London (etc): The Gale Group, 2000.

Jacobs, J U. "In a free state: the exile in South African poetry", in *Momentum: on recent South African writing*. Eds MJ Daymond, JU Jacobs, Margaret Lenta. Pietermaritzburg: University of Natal Press, 1984.

Klopper, Dirk. 'Politics of the self: exile, identity and difference in the poetry of Arthur Nortje', *English Academy Review* 10 (1993):26–35.

Lefevere, Andre. 'Arthur Nortje's poetry of exile', *Restant: Tijdschrift voor Recente Semiotische Teorievorming en de Analyse van Teksten* 8.2 (1980):39–45.

McLuckie, Craig W & Tyner, Ross. "The raw and the cooked': Arthur Kenneth Nortje, Canada, and a comprehensive bibliography', *English in Africa* 26.2 (1999):1–54.

Mphahlele, Es'kia. 'Exile, the tyranny of place and the literary compromise', *Unisa English Studies* 17.1 (1979):37–44.

Nortje, Arthur. *Anatomy of dark: collected poems of,* Ed Dirk Klopper. Pretoria: Unisa Press 2000.

Nortje, Arthur. 'Down at Bush (1: The Students). An inside view by a student of the Cape's "Coloured' University College", *The New African* (11 July 1964):134–135.

Nortje, Arthur. 'Down at Bush (2:The Staff). Concluding the views of a student at the University College of the Western Cape', *The New African* (March 1965):19–22.

Appendix A: Chronology of South African political and cultural history

1876

- Solomon Thsekisho Plaatje is born.

1884 & 1885

- European countries meet in Berlin to lay down rules for the new competition for lands in South Africa.

1899–1902

- Anglo-Boer War.

1900

- An agreement is signed that gives British citizens a privileged position in the British colony of Uganda.
- 90 per cent of Africa is divided into colonies.

1908

- Mahatma Gandhi and others are imprisoned in South Africa for refusing to register under the Asia Registration Act (aka the Black Act).
- Gandhi is released after serving three weeks of a 2–3 month sentence.

1912

- South African Native National Congress founded.

1913

- The Native Lands Act prohibits land ownership by Africans and creates 'Native reserves'.

1914

- First South African Native National Congress Delegation to England: 1914–1917, including Sol T Plaatje.

1919

- Peter Abrahams leaves South Africa for Britain.

1930

- Sol T Plaatje's *Mhudi* is published.

1931

- South Africa gains independence from Great Britain after the passage of the Statute of Westminster by the British Parliament in December 1931 and its acceptance by South Africa in June 1934.

1934

- South Africa accepts Statute of Westminster in June 1934.

1942

- Arthur Kenneth Nortje is born in Oudtshoorn, South Africa, the second illegitimate son of Cecilia Nortje – a 'coloured' woman – and a Jewish father.

1946

- The South African Government (under Field Marshal J C Smuts) enacts the Asiatic Land Tenure and Indian Representation Bill; Gandhi issues a statement of protest and sends Smuts a letter asking him to reconsider.

1948

- 26 May 1948: The conservative Afrikaner-dominated National Party wins parliamentary elections and gains control of the South African government. The party, under new premier Dr Daniel F Malan, begins taking steps toward implementing apartheid, the national policy of racial separation.
- Alan Paton's *Cry, the beloved country* is published.

1950

- The Group Areas Act is introduced, 13 June 1950. It segregates communities and relegates the black population to a minor percentage of the nation's land.
- 7 July 1950: Population Registrations Act is enacted. It requires all South Africans to register their race with the government.

1951

- Legislation is passed to change the Constitution and to remove coloured people of the Cape from the voters' roll. Large-scale protest meetings are held.

1952

- Nelson Mandela and Oliver Tambo open the first black legal firm in South Africa.
- Enactment of pass laws. The laws require blacks to carry passbooks so that the government can regulate their travel through the country.
- In September SACPO (South African Coloured People's Organisation) (later Coloured People's Congress) is formed.

1953

- Separate Amenities Act is enacted, establishing separate public facilities for whites and nonwhites.

1954

- Peter Abrahams' seminal autobiography of life in South Africa, for a 'coloured', *Tell freedom: men of Africa*, is published by Faber & Faber, London.

1955

- The African National Congress and other opposition groups including SACPO adopt the Freedom Charter, calling for equal political rights for all races.

1956

- Nelson Mandela and 155 others are charged with high treason and Mandela is found not guilty.

1959

- Parliament passes new laws extending racial segregation by creating separate bantustans, or homelands, for South Africa's major black groups.

1960

- Black protests against apartheid reach a peak following police killing of 69 people during the Sharpeville Massacre.
- The remaining African and coloured representation in parliament is terminated.
- African political organisations are banned.

1962

- Nelson Mandela is arrested.
- Nortje achieves top three standing in the Mbari Poetry Prize.

1963

- Nortje receives his BA from Bellville Coloured College (BA 1963), now the University of the Western Cape.
- Nortje meets Joan Cornelius.
- Andre Brink's *Caesar* wins the Eugene Marais Prize.
-

1964

- Nortje teaches at South End High School (1964–1965), Port Elizabeth.
- Joan Cornelius emigrates to Canada.
- Nelson Mandela is convicted of sabotage and trying to overthrow the government. He is sentenced to life in prison.

1965

- Rhodesian prime minister Ian Smith announces his country's Unilateral Declaration of Independence. Only whites are represented in the new government.

- Nortje leaves South Africa.
- Dennis Brutus is arrested, shot while 'escaping' and imprisoned.

1967

- Brutus is exiled to England.
- Nortje receives a BA from Oxford University. Emigrates to Canada. He teaches at Hope Secondary School, Hope, British Columbia (1967–1969).

1969

- Nortje moves to Toronto.
- He is employed by the Etobicoke Board of Education, Ontario, Canada, from September 1969 to June 1970.
- He attempts to gain entry to the University of Toronto as a postgraduate student.

1970

- Nortje begins postgraduate studies at Jesus College, Oxford.
- He dies; in spite of the presence of amphetamines and alcohol, the coroner leaves 'an open verdict' on the cause of his death.

1973

- New Coin Poetry publishes *Lonely against the light* posthumously; it is the first volume of Nortje's poetry.
- Heinemann publish *Dead roots* in its prestigious African Writers series.
- The Athol Fugard play *Sizwe Banzi is Dead* is banned before it is about to begin for a coloured audience. Apartheid regulations prevent Africans from performing for such an audience without a permit.
- Alan Paton's *Apartheid and the archbishop* wins the CNA Literary Award.

1974

- Because of apartheid South Africa is expelled from the United Nations.
- Nadine Gordimer's *The conservationist* is co-winner of the Booker Prize and winner of the CNA Literary Award.
- The South African government bans Andre Brink's Afrikaans novel *Kennis van die aand* ('*Looking on darkness*').

1976

- At least 575 people are killed in Soweto.

1977

- The leader of the Soweto protests, Steve Biko, is killed in police custody.
- J M Coetzee wins the CNA Literary Award for *In the heart of the country*.

1979

- Nadine Gordimer's *Burger's daughter* wins the CNA Literary Award.

1980

- Zimbabwe gains independence.
- J M Coetzee wins the CNA Literary Award for *Waiting for the barbarians*.

1981

- Nadine Gordimer's *July's people* wins the CNA Literary Award.

1983

- The government allows farmers to re-arm, to protect themselves from dissidents.
- J M Coetzee's *The life and times of Michael K* wins the Booker Prize.

1984

- Archbishop Desmond Tutu wins Nobel Peace Prize.
- J M Coetzee wins the CNA Literary Award for *The life and times of Michael K.*

1986

- Wole Soyinka is the first African to win the Nobel Prize for Literature.

1990

- The state of emergency is not renewed.
- F W De Klerk lifts the ban outlawing the African National Congress.
- 11 February: De Klerk frees Mandela from prison.
- Nadine Gordimer's *My son's story* wins the CNA Literary Award.

1991

- 9 January 1991: black students enter previously all-white public schools.
- 5 June 1991: The Lands Acts of 1913 and 1936 and the Group Areas Act of 1950 are repealed.
- 18 June 1991: The Population Registration Act of 1950 is repealed.
- 10 July 1991: President George Bush lifts most US economic sanctions against South Africa.
- 4 September 1991: De Klerk outlines his government's proposals for a new constitution that will provide suffrage to the black majority for the first time.
- Nelson Mandela becomes president of the African National Congress.
- International Olympics Committee lifts a 21-year ban barring South African athletes from Olympic Games.
- Nadine Gordimer is the first South African to win the Nobel Prize for Literature.

1992

- 17 March 1992: South African whites, voting in record numbers, overwhelmingly endorse De Klerk's reform policies in a referendum on whether to negotiate an end to white minority rule through talks with the black majority.

1993

- Nelson Mandela and F W De Klerk win Nobel Peace Prize.
- October: UN lifts most remaining economic sanctions against South Africa.
- 18–23 November: Twenty-one of South Africa's black and white political parties approve a majority-rule constitution that provides fundamental rights to blacks.

The document calls for the election of a coalition government that would remain in office for five years after the elections, and for the dissolution of the country's ten black self-governing homelands.

- The US repeals remaining sanctions against South Africa.

1994

- 2 May 1994: Mandela declares an ANC victory, and De Klerk offers his cooperation in the post-election government. The new parliament is set to meet the following week, and Mandela is sworn in as president on 10 May.

1995

- The Commission for the Restitution of Land Rights and the Truth and Reconciliation Commission are inaugurated.

1998

- Solomon Plaatje is posthumously awarded an honorary doctorate in literature from the University of North-West (Mafeking, South Africa).

1999

- J M Coetzee's *Disgrace* wins the Booker Prize.

2000

- The authoritative *The collected poems of Arthur Kenneth Nortje*, edited by Dirk Klopper (Pretoria: Unisa Press) is published.
- J M Coetzee's *Disgrace* wins the Commonwealth Writers Prize.

Appendix B: Bibliography

Introduction[1]

The following annotated bibliography is an attempt to place all print and electronic sources by and about Kenneth Arthur Nortje before the scholar of African literature, culture and politics. In this endeavour, we are appreciative of the assistance of librarians at Okanagan University College, as well as the Africa Book Publishing Collective, the pioneering work in Africana bibliography undertaken by Bernth Lindfors, particularly his *Black African literature in English, 1987–1991* (London: Hans Zell Publishers, 1995), the *MLA Bibliographies*, the *ALA Bulletin* bibliographic updates, and all of those interested in Nortje who responded to our call for information through the *ALA Bulletin* and on the internet.

The aim is for comprehensiveness and accessibility, so that new, fresh, and invigorating perspectives on the issues that concerned Nortje may be produced.

Poetry (Journals)

Adelphi New Series 2 (August 1962).
Adelphi New Series 3 (October 1962).
Adelphi New Series 4 (November 1962).
Adelphi New Series 6 (January 1963).
'Five Poems', *Black Orpheus* 12 (1963):24–26.
Purple Renoster 6 (1966):23–24.
Anglo-Welsh Review (Summer 1966):124.
African Arts/Arts D'Afrique. (Palo Alto) 1.4 (1968).
Strumpet 5 (12 February 1971). (Oxford students' magazine).
'Poems of travail', *Sechaba* 5.xii/6.i (1971):36–7.
The Literary Review 15.1 (1971):82–3.
Gloucester Green 1 (1971).

Poetry One (Summer 1971).
The Greenfield Review (New York) 8.1&2 (1979):5–17.

Poetry (books)

Anatomy of dark: the collected poems of Kenneth Arthur Nortje. Edited by Dirk Klopper. South Africa: Unisa Press 2000.
Dead roots. AWS 141. London: Heinemann, 1973.
Lonely against the light. Eds. Guy Butler and R. Harnett. New Coin Poetry Special Issue. 9.3 & 4 (September 1973).

Anthologized Work

African Literature Today; 10: Retrospect and Prospect. Ed Eldred Durosimi Jones. London: Heinemann, 1979:231–2.
An Anthology of African and Caribbean Writing in English. Ed. John J. Figueroa. London: Heinemann Educational Books in Assoc with the Open University, 1982:181, 202.
Apartheid: A Collection of Writings on South African Racism by South Africans. Ed Alex La Guma. New York: International Publishers, 1971:41–3.
Arthur Nortje and Other Poets. Ed Peter Horne. Athlone, South Africa: COSAW, 1988.
Bluesprint: Black British Columbian Literature and Orature. Ed Wayde Compton. Vancouver: Arsenal Pulp Press, 2002:147–152.
The Broadview Anthology of Poetry. Eds Amanda Goldrick-Jones and Herbert Rosengarten. Broadview Press, 1993.
Broken Strings: The Politics of Poetry in South Africa. Eds Stephen Finn and Rosemary Gray. Cape Town: Maskew Miller Longman, 1992:81–84.
Explorings: A Collection of Poems for the Young People of Southern Africa. Ed Robin Malan. Cape Town: David Philip, 1988:102.
From South Africa: New Writing, Photographs, and Art. Eds David Bunn, Jane Taylor, Reginald Gibbons, Sterling Plumpp. Evanston, Ill: Northwestern University Press, 1987:382–386.
The Heinemann Book of African Poetry in English. Ed Adewale Maja-Pearce. London: Heinemann, 1990:71–83.
Literatures of Asia, Africa and Latin-America. Eds Willis and Tony Barnstone. New York: Prentice-Hall, 1999.
A New Book of African Verse. Eds John Reed and Clive Wake. London: Heinemann, 1984:53–57.
A New Book of South African Verse in English. Eds Guy Butler and Chris Mann. Cape Town: Oxford University Press, 1979:240–44.
A New University Anthology of English Poetry. Eds M C Andersen, S G Kossick, and E Pereira. Cape Town: np, nd.
The Paperback Book of South African English Poetry. Ed Michael Chapman. Craighall: AD Donker, 1986:135–136.

The Penguin Book of Modern African Poetry. Eds Gerald Moore and Ulli Beier. Harmondsworth: Penguin, 1984:274–275.

The Penguin Book of Southern African Verse in English. Ed Stephen Gray. Harmondsworth: Penguin, 1989:227–231.

Poems of Black Africa. Ed Wole Soyinka. London: Heinemann; New York: Hill and Wang, 1975:28, 63, 106, 185, 187, 261, 262.

Poets to the people: South African freedom poems. Ed Barry Feinberg. Introd Hugh MacDiarmid. London: Allen & Unwin, 1974. London: Heinemann, 1980:148–54.

Ranters, ravers and rhymers: poems by black and Asian poets. Ed Farrukh Dhondy. London: William Collins Sons, 1990:136–7.

The return of the Amasi bird: Black South African poetry 1891–1981. Eds Tim Couzens and Essop Patel. Johannesburg: Ravan Press, 1982:182–3, 187, 275, 281–2, 284.

Seasons come to pass: a poetry anthology for Southern African students. Eds Es'kia Mphahlele and Helen Moffett. Cape Town: OUP, 1994:228.

Seven South African Poets: poems of exile collected and selected by Cosmo Pieterse. London: Heinemann, 1971:101–126.

Shades of Adamastor: Africa and the Portugese connection, an anthology of poetry. Ed M van Wyk Smith. Grahamstown: Institute for the Study of English in Africa, and National English Literary Museum, 1988:204–205.

Somehow we survive: an anthology of South African writing. Ed Sterling Plumpp. New York: Thunder's Mouth Press, 1982:18–19, 22–23, 24, 49–50, 95, 117, 118, 119, 120.

South Africa in Poetry. Ed J Van Wyk. Pinetown: Owen Burgess, 1988:464, 502, 503.

Ten South African Poets. Ed Adam Schwartzman. Manchester: Carcarnet, 1999.

Twenty-five years of South African poetry. Grahamstown: Rhodes University, 1989:65, 120, 120–121, 152, 165.

Voices of the land: an anthology of South African poems. Eds Marcia Leveson and Jonathan Paton. Craighall: AD Donker, 1985:36–7.

When my brothers come home: poems from central and Southern Africa. Ed Frank Mkalawile Chipasula. Middleton, Connecticut: Wesleyan University Press, 1985:202–7.

Non-poetic work

Quarry 80–82.

'Down at Bush (1: The Students)', *New African* 3 (July 1964):134–35.

'Down at Bush (2: The Faculty)', *New African* 4 (March 1965):19–22.

Letter to Raymond Leitch. 31 May 1969.

Secondary sources

Adey, David, Ridley Beeton, Michael Chapman and Ernest Pereira, eds *Companion to South African English literature.* Craighall, South Africa: AD Donker, 1986:146b–147b.

Alvarez-Pereyre, Jacques. 'Arthur Nortje', in his *The Poetry of Commitment in South Africa*. Trans Clive Wake. London: Heinemann, 1984:153–169.

Anon. 'In Memoriam. A Nortje, 23/8/91', *Taalgenoot* 61.3 (March 1992):30.

Anon. 'Off the shelf', *The Satr* (S.A.), 15 December 1971.

Anon. *New Nation*, 02 October 1992[?].

Anon. *D'espoir.* Hope, B.C.: Hope Secondary School, 1968.

Anon. *D'espoir.* Hope, B.C.: Hope Secondary School, 1969.

Anon. 'School enrolment showing increase', *The Hope Standard* (Wednesday, 13 September 1967):1, 8.

Anon. '500 expected to attend fall classes at Hope Secondary', *The Hope Standard* (Wednesday, 28 August 1968): 1.

Anon. '22 Fraser Canyon teachers resign', *The Hope Standard* (Wednesday, 11 June 1969):1.

Anon. *The Hope Standard* (Wednesday 18 June 1969):10.

Arthur, Donald H. 'Arthur Kenneth Nortje: poet and teacher', *Lonely Against the Light: New Coin Poetry* 9.iii/iv (1973):8–18.

Barnett, Ursula A. *A Vision of order: a study of black South African literature in English: 1914–1980*. Cape Town: Longman, 1983:85–89.

Berthoud, Jacques. 'Poetry and exile: the case of Arthur Nortje', *English in Africa* 11.1 (May 1984):1–14.

Brutus, Dennis. 'Protest against apartheid: Alan Paton, Nadine Gordimer, Athol Fugard, Alfred Hutchinson and Arthur Nortje', in *Protest and conflict in African literature*. Eds Cosmos Pieterse and Donald Munro. London: Heinemann; New York: Africana, 1969:93–100.

Brutus, Dennis. 'In memoriam: Arthur Nortje', *Research in African Literatures* 2 (1971):26–7.

Brutus, Dennis. 'Poetry of suffering: the black experience', *Ba Shiru* (Madison, WI) 4.2 (1973):1–10.

Brutus, Dennis. 'Two poems by Nortje with a note', *African Literature Today* 10 (1979):231–2.

Brutus, Dennis. 'Nortje at the Bod', *Echoes of the sunbird: an anthology of contemporary African poetry*. Ed Don Burness. Ohio University Press, 1993:53.

Bunn, David. 'Oxford Journal', *Somehow we survive: an anthology of South African writing*. Ed Sterling Plumpp. New York: Thunder's Mouth Press, 1982:116.

Bunn, David. 'Arthur Nortje', *Dictionary of literary biography* vol 125:170–177.

Bunn, David. 'Some alien native land: Arthur Nortje, literary history and the body in exile', *World Literature Today* 70.1 (Winter 1996):33–44.

Chapman, M J F. 'Arthur Nortje: poet of exile', *English in Africa* 6.1 (1979):60–71.

Chapman, M J F. 'Biographical sketches and notes', *The paperbook of South African English poetry*. Johannesburg: AD Donker, 1986:309.

Chapman, M J F. *Modern South African English poetry: a consideration of representative poets (1960–1982)*. DLitt et Phil, University of South Africa.

Chapman, M J F. '5: Poets and anti-poets', in his *South African poetry: a modern perspective*. Johannesburg: AD Donker, 1984:243–253.

Chapman, M J F. Colin Gardner and Es'kia Mphahlele, eds. *Perspectives on South African literature.* Johannesburg: AD Donker, 1992:54–5, 354.

Choice 12.4 (June 1975):544.

Clarke, George Elliott. 'A primer of African-Canadian literature', *Books in Canada* 25.2 (March 1996):7–9.

Colman, David. 'For D B: after reading Nortje', *Vent* 1.2:8.

Cornwell, Gareth, comp *South African English poets.* Grahamstown: Cape Provincial Library Service on behalf of the National Library Museum, 1985.

Dameron, Charles. 'Arthur Nortje: craftsman for his muse', in *Aspects of South African literature.* Ed Christopher Heywood. London: Heinemann; New York: Africana, 1976:155–62.

Davis, Hedy. 'Arthur Nortje: the wayward ego', *Bloody Horse* (Johannesburg) 3 (January/February 1981):14–24.

Davis, Hedy. 'The poetry of Arthur Nortje: towards a new appraisal', *Unisa English Studies* (Pretoria) 18.2 (1980):26–32.

Davis, Hedy. 'Arthur Nortje: a forgotten South African poet', *Reality* (Pietermaritzburg) 11.4 (1979):5–6.

Davis, Hedy. 'Extracts from unpublished letters', *Quarry '80–'82: New South African Writing.* Ed Walter Saunders. Cape Town: AD Donker, 1983:159–66.

Davis, Hedy. 'The poetry of Arthur Nortje: a critical introduction'. MA Pretoria, Unisa, 1983.

Espin, Mark. 'A book that changed me', *Southern African Review of Books* (May/June 1993).

Espin, Mark. 'Elegy: for Arthur Nortje, 1942–1970', *Upstream* 6.1 (1988):32.

Finn, Stephen M. 'Transcolonial metapoetry in South Africa', *Span: Journal of South Pacific Association for Commonwealth Literature and Language Studies* 36 (1993). (http://kali.murdoch.edu.au/~cntinuum/listserv/SPAN/36/Finn.html)

Forstreuter, Burkhard. 'Nachwort' in *Gedichte.* Trans. Karl Heinz Berger et al. Ed Burkhard Forstreuter. Berlin: Volk und Welt, 1975:141–150.

Gagiano, A H. 'Arthur Nortje', *Dictionary of literary biography, volume 225: South African writers.* A Bruccoli Clark Layman Book. Ed Paul Scanlon. Detroit: The Gale Group, 2000:322–327.

Gray, Stephen. 'A new talent emerges and is lost', *The Star* (SA), 18 January 1974.

Hannah, Jo-Ann. E-mail to Craig McLuckie and Ross Tyner, 24 September 2001.

Haresnape, Geoffrey. 'Literature and revolution: some samples of South African English poetry as a discourse leading to revolution'. Unpublished paper presented at the Third International Festival of Poetry (Jerusalem) 1996.

Haresnape, Geoffrey. 'Oxford University visit: in memory of Arthur Nortje', *Upstream* 3.1 (1985):15–16.

Herdeck, Donald E. *African authors: a companion to Black African writing: Volume I:1300–1973.* Washington, DC: Black Orpheus Press, 1973:295–296.

Jacobs, J U. 'In a free state: the exile in South African poetry', in *Momentum on Recent South African Writing.* Pietermaritzburg: University of Natal Press, 1984:243–259.

Klopper, Dirk. 'Arthur Kenneth Nortje: South African Poet' in *Encyclopedia of post-colonial literatures in English*, Volume 2. Eds Eugene Benson and L W Conolly. London: Routledge, 1994:1105.

Klopper, Dirk. 'Politics of the self: exile, identity and difference in the poetry of Arthur Nortje', *English Academy Review* 10 (December 1993):26–35.

Knipp, Thomas. 'English language poetry' in *a history of twentieth century African literatures*. Ed Oyekan Owomoyela. Lincoln: University of Nebraska Press, 1993:105–137.

Lefevere, Andre. 'Arthur Nortje's poetry of exile', *Restant: Tijdschrift voor recente semiotische Teorievorming en de Analyse van Teksten,* (Antwerp) 8.2 (Spring 1980):39–45.

Leitch, RG. 'Arthur Nortje: 1942–1970', *Lonely Against the Light: New Coin Poetry* 9.iii/iv (1973):1–7.

Leitch, R G. 'A critical analysis of the poetry of Arthur Kenneth Nortje'. MA thesis, University of Toronto, 1975.

Leitch, R G. 'Nortje: poet at work', *African Literature Today* 10 (1979):224–230.

Mack, Cliff. Letter to Craig McLuckie. 23 September 2001.

McLuckie, Craig. ' "Breathes there a man?": A note on allusion in "Prison mirror of the self" ', *Notes on Contemporary Literature* (2002):5–7.

McLuckie, Craig. Interview with Brian Warner. Hope, BC, 2 July 1996.

McLuckie, Craig. Telephone Interview with Tama Kawase. Hope, BC, 2 July 1996.

McLuckie, Craig. Interview withVictor Smith. Hope, BC, July 2, 1996.

McLuckie, Craig. Interview with Mr and Mrs Peter McPhedran. Hope, BC, 3 July 1996.

McLuckie, Craig and Ross Tyner. " 'The raw and the cooked': Kenneth Arthur Nortje, Canada and a comprehensive bibliography", *English in Africa* 26.2 (October 1999):1–54.

McLuckie, Craig and Ross Tyner. 'Arthur Nortje', LitEncyc.com

Nel, Jo. 'Words of despair: review of *Anatomy of dark: collected poems of Arthur Kenneth Nortje.' Daily Mail and Guardian* (Johannesburg), 4 December 2001.

Nkondo, G M 'Arthur Nortje's microscopic eye and literal imagination', *ACLALS Bulletin* (Mysore) 6.1 (November 1982):89–99.

Nkondo, Gessler Moses. 'Arthur Nortje's double self', *Africana Journal* 12.2 (1981):105–121.

'NORTJE, Arthur' *The Oxford companion to twentieth-century poetry in English*. Ian Hamilton. Oxford University Press, 1996. Oxford Reference Online. Oxford University Press. 16 MAY 2002.
<http://www.oxfordreference.com/views/ENTRY.html?subview=
Main&entry=t58.000865>

Ola, Virginia U. 'Language and protest in the poetry of Arthur Nortje', *NJALA* 7 (1985):72–81.

Owomoyela, Oyekan. *A history of twentieth century African literatures*. Lincoln: University of Nebraska Press, 1993:131–132.

Peacock, Dennis. *(Other) Voices*. 1996.

Pordzik, Ralph. ' "No longer need I shout freedom in the house": Arthur Nortje, the English poetical tradition and the breakdown of communication in South African English poetry', *English Studies in Africa* 41.2:35–53.

Potter, Jill (ed). *Poetry II*. London: np, 1971.

Ravenscroft, Arthur. 'English speaking South African literature' in *English Speaking South Africa today: Proceedings of the National Conference July 1976*. Ed Andre de Villiers. Cape Town: Oxford University Press, 1976:328.

Ravenscroft, Arthur. 'Arthur Nortje' in *A guide to twentieth century literature in English*. London: Methuen, 1983:200–201.

Reed, Olga. Letter to Ross Tyner. 6 August 1996.

Rive, Richard. 'Arthur Nortje: poet', *Lonely Against the Light: New Coin Poetry* 9.iii/iv (1973):19–21.

Rive, Richard. 'Four South Africans abroad', *Contrast* (Cape Town) 10.3 (1976):49–57.

Rive, Richard. *Writing black*. Cape Town: David Philip, 1981.

Rive, Richard. *Selected Writings*. Johannesburg: AD Donker, 1977:107.

Rive, Richard. 'Writing or fighting: the dilemma of the black South African writer', *Staffrider* 8.1 (1989):48–54.

Roscoe, Adrian. *Uhuru's fire: African literature east to south*. Cambridge University Press, 1977:152.

Shava, Piniel Viriri. *A people's voice: Black South African writing in the twentieth century*. London: Zed, 1989:45.

Seymour-Smith, M. 'South African Literature' in *Guide to modern world literature*. London: Macmillan, 1973 (rev 1985):1174.

Smith, M van W. *Grounds of contest: a survey of South African English literature*. Cape Town: Juta, 1990:116.

Smith, Rowland. 'Autobiography in black and white: South African views of the past', *Commonwealth: Essays and Studies* 7.2 (1985):72–82.

Solomons, Abu. 'Arthur Nortje: forging links between poetry and society (Canada, 1967–1970)', *AKAL* 1.2 (1989):10–20.

Solomons, Abu. 'Engagement, alienation and self-discovery in the poetry of Arthur Nortje'. MA Thesis. University of the Western Cape, November 1986.

Standard encyclopaedia of Southern Africa, Vol. 12, Supplement and index. np. Nassou, 1976:70b.

Tyner, Ross. Interview with Raymond Leitch. Toronto, Ontario, July 18, 1996.

Wake, Clive. 'Poetry of the last five years' in *Soweto Poetry*. Ed Michael Chapman. Johannesburg: McGraw-Hill, 1982:213–218.

Watts, Jane. *Black writers from South Africa: towards a discourse of liberation*. London: Macmillan, 1989:217.

Williams, SH Colenbrander and C Owen, comps. *A bibliography on Kenneth Arthur Nortje (1942–1970)*. Pretoria: Subject Reference Department, University of South Africa Sanlam Library, 1980.

Wooley, H and S Williams. *A bibliography of Kenneth Arthur Nortje: 1942–1970*. Pretoria: Unisa Sanlam Library, 1979.

Zell, Hans M, Carol Bundy, and Virginia Coulon, eds. *A new reader's guide to African literature. 2nd ed.* London: Heinemann; New York: Africana, 1983.
A bibliography of criticism of South African literature in English.

Nortje collections

Melville J Herskovits Library of African Studies, Northwestern University, Evanston, Ill.

The National English Literary Museum, Grahamstown, South Africa

Correspondence at NELM

The following summaries are derived from the NELM abstracts of the correspondence held there. Items are listed in chronological order.

- Sutherland, John S. Letter to Guy Butler. 7 January 1971, NELM. (One letter re the death of Nortje.)
- Mphahlele, Ezekiel. Letter to Donald Arthur, Oxford. 3 June 1971. (Re the death of Nortje, with a note added by Arthur.)
- Butler, Guy. Letters to Mrs Olga Reed. 1971–72, NELM. (Two letters re the life and work of Nortje.)
- Butler, Guy. Correspondence with Donald H Arthur. 1971–73, NELM. (18 letters re Nortje and the circumstances of his death.)
- Butler, Guy. Correspondence with Ruth Harnett (Heinemann). 1972–3, NELM. (Seven letters concerning publishing Nortje's poetry in *Dead roots* and *Lonely Against the light*.
- Leitch, Raymond. Correspondence with Guy Butler and Ruth Harnett. No dates, NELM. (16 letters and one postcard.)
- Butler, Guy. Correspondence with the Administration of Coloured Affairs. 19 January–12 April 1972, NELM. (Three letters re the unused portion of a grant given to Nortje.)
- Rive, Richard. Correspondence with Guy Butler. 1972, NELM. (Brief request about knowledge of Nortje in Oxford.)
- Jones, R. Letters to Ruth Harnett. 9 May 1973, NELM. (Re the legal consequences of publishing two of Nortje's poems.)
- Alvarez-Peyrere, Jacques. Letter(s) to Guy Butler. 1974, NELM. (Requests copy of *Lonely Against the Light.*)
- MacKenzie, Wally. Letters to Guy Butler. 1974, NELM. (Butler's response seeks help 'in an effort to get Nortje's poetry better known'.)
- Brutus, Dennis. Letter(s) to Guy Butler. 1974, NELM. (Brutus seeks material on Nortje. Butler notes that there have been few reviews of N's work. Brutus claims that N's poetry will be published in an anthology, *you'd better believe it*, and *Black images* (Toronto) will devote an issue to Nortje. Also acknowledge that *The Greenfield Review* published a Nortje poem under Brutus' name. Questions who is in receipt of Nortje's royalty payments.)

- Butler, Guy. Letter to Robert Greig, 1974. NELM. (Discusses Nortje's two collections of poetry.)
- Ravenscroft, Arthur. Letter to Guy Butler. 1976, NELM. (Ravenscroft describes Brutus and Ravenscroft's editing of Nortje's poetry for *Dead roots*.)
- Mphahlele, Ezekiel. Letter to Guy Butler. 1987, NELM. (Mention of Nortje's work.)

Other documents at NELM

- Coroner's inquisition into the death of Kenneth Arthur Nortje. 1970. (Contains the coroner's verdict; post mortem report; transcription of evidence at the inquest; Grant of letters of Administration to D H Arthur.)
- Brutus, Dennis. File Containing Poems by Nortje, Correspondence about Nortje's poetry, and articles on Nortje's poetry, nd. (Mainly photocopies.)
- McLuckie, Craig W. Audiotape interviews from Hope, BC.
- Nortje, Arthur Kenneth. Arthur Nortje poetry MS, nd. (Poor quality photocopies with holograph annotations by Dennis Brutus.)
- Nortje, Arthur Kenneth. Lonely against the light: poems by Arthur Nortje. 1973. (Photocopy of the *New Coin* poetry volume; 'holograph notes by Brutus regarding the inclusion of poems by Nortje in certain anthologies'.)
- Povey, John. 'The heart's country.' 1975. (Ms of paper given at the Symposium on Contemporary South African Literature, 1975. University of Texas at Austin.)
- Rive, Richard. 'Arthur Nortje: poet.' 1973. (*New Coin* 9, 3 & 4 (September 1973).

The University of South Africa

A H Gagiano (2000) notes that the University of South Africa, Pretoria, 'acquired copyright to Nortje's literary estate in 1989'.

A M S van der Walt has compiled a document, 'Inventory of the Arthur Nortje manuscripts collected by Hedy Davis' (1990). This manuscript breaks the material down as follows:

1 Journals
    1.1 Notepad A
    1.2 Notepad B
    1.3 School Diary
    1.4 The Oxford Journal
    1.5 The Little Exercise Books
2 Poem manuscripts
    2.1 J Davidson ms
    2.2 Olga Reed ms
    2.3 C M Rousseau ms
    2.4 Dr A E A Roman
    2.5 Other poem manuscripts
        2.5.1 Athol Fugard ms

Index

Notes on contributors

Amanda Bloomfield: Pursuing a career in cultural journalism.

Annie Gagiano: Lecturer, University of Stellenbosch. *Achebe, Head, Marechera: On power and change in Africa* (2000).

Kelly Hewson: Professor, Mount Royal College. Articles and book chapters on J M Coetzee, Nadine Gordimer and Salman Rushdie.

Dirk Klopper: Rand Afrikaans University. Editor. *Anatomy of dark: collected poems of Arthur Nortje* (2000).

Graig McLuckie: Associate professor in English, Okanagan University College. Co-editor of *Ken Saro-Wiwa: writer and political activist* (1999).

Aubrey McPhail: Lecturer, Mount Royal College. co-editor of *Ken Saro-Wiwa: writer and political activist.*

Sarah Nuttall: Lecturer, University of Stellenbosch. Co-editor of *The making of memory in South Africa* (1998).

Tanure Ojaide: Professor, African-American and African Studies, at the University of North Carolina, Charlotte. *The new African poetry: an anthology* (2000). Recipient of the Commonwealth Poetry Prize and the All-Africa Christopher Okigbo Prize.

Kwadwo Osei-Nyame Jnr: Lecturer in African Literature at the School of Oriental and African Studies, London. 'Pan-Africanist ideology and the African historical novel of self-discovery: the examples of Kobina Sekyi and J E Casely Hayford,' *Journal of African Cultural Studies* 12.2 (December 1999).

Ross Tyner: Librarian, Okanagan University College; Publications include: 'Arthur Kenneth Nortje' in *Major African writers of the twentieth century* (forthcoming).

Richard Volk: Pursuing a career in academia and the theatre.